SCARCELY ENGLISH

Also by Simon Heffer

Moral Desperado: A Life of Thomas Carlyle

Power and Place: The Political Consequences of King Edward VII

Like the Roman: The Life of Enoch Powell

Nor Shall My Sword: The Reinvention of England

Vaughan Williams

A Short History of Power

Strictly English: The Correct Way to Write . . . and Why It Matters

High Minds: The Victorians and the Birth of Modern Britain

Simply English: An A to Z of Avoidable Errors

The Age of Decadence: Britain 1880 to 1914

Staring at God: Britain in the Great War

Sing As We Go: Britain Between the Wars

As editor

Henry 'Chips' Channon: The Diaries (Vol. 1) 1918–38

Henry 'Chips' Channon: The Diaries (Vol. 2) 1938–43

Henry 'Chips' Channon: The Diaries (Vol. 3) 1943–57

SCARCELY ENGLISH

An A–Z of Assaults on Our Language

Simon Heffer

HUTCHINSON
HEINEMANN

1 3 5 7 9 10 8 6 4 2

Hutchinson Heinemann
20 Vauxhall Bridge Road
London SW1V 2SA

Hutchinson Heinemann is part of the Penguin Random House group of companies whose addresses can be found at global.penguinrandomhouse.com

Copyright © Simon Heffer 2024

Simon Heffer has asserted his right to be identified as the author of this Work in accordance with the Copyright, Designs and Patents Act 1988.

First published by Hutchinson Heinemann in 2024

www.penguin.co.uk

A CIP catalogue record for this book is available from the British Library.

ISBN: 9781529152791

Typeset in 12/14pt Bembo Book MT Pro by Jouve (UK), Milton Keynes

Printed and bound in Great Britain by Clays Ltd, Elcograf S.p.A.

The authorised representative in the EEA is Penguin Random House Ireland, Morrison Chambers, 32 Nassau Street, Dublin D02 YH68

www.greenpenguin.co.uk

Penguin Random House is committed to a sustainable future for our business, our readers and our planet. This book is made from Forest Stewardship Council® certified paper.

To the Burgharts of Greenstead

Contents

Introduction
ix

Author's Note
xxxi

SCARCELY ENGLISH
1

Appendix of Grammatical Terms
209

Acknowledgements
235

Introduction

In *Middlemarch*, young Ben Garth, a child whose serious and intelligent mother is educating him at home, rebels against having his English corrected. He protests to her: 'I hate grammar. What's the use of it?'

Mrs Garth is in no doubt. 'To teach you to speak and write correctly, so that you can be understood,' George Eliot has her say 'with severe precision'. Today, Mrs Garth might feel forced to qualify her statement somewhat. The purpose of speaking and writing correctly is not just in order to be understood – we have become used to understanding (while not condoning) all sorts of abominations in the misuse of the English language, of which this book contains a wide selection of examples – but so that those with whom one speaks, or who read what one has written, should treat the speaker or writer as an intelligent and thoughtful person as opposed to an ignorant one.

It is not unique to the British, or indeed to Anglophones, that we make assumptions about others the moment they open their mouths. If we hear people mangle their grammar or use the wrong word, the consequent assumption may well be that they are stupid, which is not a badge anyone especially wants to wear. Not that long ago, in the last part of the twentieth century, a remark such as that would have passed without comment, its being classed as what was, and perhaps by some still is, regarded as 'a statement of the bleeding obvious'. Now, when apparently everything to do with our social state and condition is regarded as potentially aggressively political, it is treated in some quarters with outrage. Possibly the gravest offence in our current society is to cause offence; and a reason why the guardians of our modern ethics find it so appalling that some of us should seek to improve the state of the English language is that it so often entails correcting another's ignorance. Since we are all ignorant of something, and most of us are mature enough to admit that, this strikes me and others like me as being something of an extreme position.

The English language belongs to everyone who purports to speak it. Anyone critiquing it needs to bear in mind that the English, and indeed the inhabitants of the United Kingdom, are not the only people who speak it, even if they largely invented it (or perhaps it is more accurate to say, developed it). Ever since the Ancient Britons and various Picts, Gaels, Celts and other indigenous peoples were speaking in their own tongues, there have been impositions on that base by Angles, Saxons, Jutes and Normans. Then, there were wholesale thefts from German dialects, borrowings from French in various iterations, acquisitions from Latin, Greek, Persian, a number of Indian and African languages. More recently, English has been expanded by some of the cultures that took the language overseas in the first place – notably by the Americans, whose effect on changing the way the English language is spoken in the British Isles is increasingly prevalent and, for those of us who like the distinctions of British English, depressing and corrosive because it is almost always unnecessary.

At a time before the early nineteenth century, when literacy was far from universal and the absence of national newspapers, the railway or broadcasting prevented any degree of standardisation of English in Britain and Ireland, most people spoke in regional dialects that had words and grammatical forms that were peculiar to each. Back in the Middle Ages, once the Norman ruling class had been marginalised and after the advent of the printing press, a small, educated class spoke and read a common language – the language of Chaucer – and it became the language used by those at Court, in what passed for the government, in the Church and in the ancient schools and universities. Slowly, literacy spread, and with it social mobility, engagement in politics and political discourse, and the wider deployment of a written language. The period leading up to and during the Civil Wars exemplified this movement, and Milton, in his prose works and political writings, was perhaps foremost among its practitioners. However, it would be centuries before something called 'standard English' would be properly developed. That would take widespread literacy (which did not come until the nineteenth century), easy access to and comprehension of the printed word whether in broadsheets, newspapers, pamphlets or books, and a standardisation of spelling and vocabulary that was only really settled by the publication of the *Oxford English Dictionary*. Work on this authoritative guide to the English language – in relation to which it immediately acquired an effectively biblical status – began in 1857. It was not, in its first edition, completed until 1928. A sign of how rapidly new words, or new meanings for old words, entered the vocabulary was shown by the fact that the first supplement to the dictionary came out only five years after its publication, in 1933; and further supplements appeared, then a second edition, and then a third, which is now so vast and so frequently in need of updating that it is wholly electronic and, so the Oxford University Press says, unlikely ever to be printed.

With language changing so quickly and comprehensively, one might ask why on earth one should bother sticking to old rules, when new rules seem to impose themselves all the time? Perhaps a short answer is that grammar, which has evolved to a point where it helps make language comprehensible and free from ambiguity, now varies from the standard only when mangled by someone who has failed to learn its rules – rules that, in the interests of effective and reliable communication, remain important. As for the 'rules' concerning the meanings of individual words – the definitions in the standard dictionary – these may be altered for one of two reasons. The first is that the word comes to be applied to something other than has hitherto been the case: for example, a *wallet* was long a small leather or canvas case in which people, mostly men, kept their money and documents essential to them when on the move; now it is also a file on a smartphone in which one can keep electronic documents such as tickets and passes. Such an extension of the original meaning is entirely legitimate. The second is that someone simply does not know the correct meaning of a word – as in the phrase 'he's giving me a lot of aggravation'. That reason for change is not remotely legitimate.

Standard British English, of the sort I defend in this book, and defended in its two predecessors, *Strictly English* (2011) and *Simply English* (2014), seems now to have assumed the status of a dialect – or rather a lingua franca, which the dictionary (and, for the avoidance of doubt, when I refer to 'the dictionary' throughout this book, I mean the *OED*) defines as 'any language that is used by speakers of different languages as a common medium of communication; a common language'. It is the form of English that the proprietors and editors of most printed matter in the British Isles choose their publications to be written in – certainly its national newspapers – and which major broadcasting organisations use to communicate with their audiences. It is also readily understood by English speakers from other cultures where their own version of English prevails, such as in America, or Australia, or India. This would seem to place it at the top of a hierarchy of versions of English (whether one accepts such a concept or not, reality dictates that such a thing exists), thereby underlining the importance of mastering its subtleties for those whose careers, or the smoothness of whose lives, may depend on fluency in it. That those editors make this choice is because it remains the standard educated dialect, and it respects the intelligence of an audience of readers and listeners. Some years ago I revised the style book for *The Daily Telegraph* in what turned out to be a mostly successful effort to provide the newspaper's readers with journalism written in a form of English with which they were familiar. Any deviation from that standard was met with ferocious complaint, and rightly so. Whether the 'experts' who decry such a disciplined approach to our language like it or not, millions of people who speak and read British English have a definite view of how their language should be maintained. Those who seek their custom as readers know better than to try to challenge that. I know too that businesses or public bodies whose employees communicate with their customers or clients in poor English earn the disdain and even contempt of those who feel they are written or spoken to in a sloppy fashion. Insulting people's intelligence is never an especially satisfactory method of keeping them happy.

When I published the previous two books on the language various teachers of linguistics howled at me in reviews for refusing to accept that language changes. Had they read either book properly they would have deduced that I had done nothing of the sort. For reasons to which I have already alluded, I am not remotely against change in the language, nor do I deny that it happens: I should have to be exceptionally obtuse to take any other view. Such change has happened since the Dark Ages and will continue to do so. What I maintained was that there is an idea of a standard English, which covers the operation of particular rules of grammar and the meanings of words, and forms a consensus around that idea. If one wishes to be understood by, and indeed to understand, as many people as possible, and to give the impression that one has an informed and intelligent grasp of the language, then it is as well to master these things. An example of the importance of this is the distinction between **disinterested and uninterested**, which many people seem to think no longer exists. It does exist and it is usually vital to get it right, even if there will be some who are blissfully unaware there is a distinction. A judge who claims to be *disinterested* in the outcome of the case he is trying is ideal; one who is *uninterested* could prove a disaster to justice.

Many people wish standard English to remain the principal form of communication in the British Isles – not necessarily in colloquial speech, which has always had an air of casualness and informality – but certainly in formal documents, letters, or in newspaper articles and broadcasters' scripts. People wish this form of English to survive because they consider it has authority, and that it has authority because it is clear and unambiguous: no one who reads it or hears it, if what they read or hear has been written or spoken correctly, should be in any doubt about its meaning. Equally, that is why people whose business is communication use it. Those who choose not to do so may find themselves at a disadvantage.

It is not least because such a disadvantage is unnecessary that I have written this book, which reflects largely on new problems with the language in the last fifteen years or so since I started to write my first tract on this subject, *Strictly English*, or problems that have remained tiresomely persistent and, therefore, persistently confusing or irritating. As already noted, new items, experiences, processes and so on often

INTRODUCTION | xv

require a new word, or an old word 're-purposed': look, for example, at the evolution of the meaning of the noun *sympathy* over the last four centuries, which the dictionary outlines. What I do object to, in an era when a standard dictionary of the highest degree of scholarship exists, is when words are used wrongly out of ignorance, and so-called experts decree that that is a perfectly acceptable usage – and, furthermore, imply it is evidence of a high form of bigotry to condemn such a thing. It does not help that the dictionary occasionally recognises the existence of completely wrong usages of words; wrong because in his or her ignorance the speaker has confused one word with another (*see, for example*, the entry on **flaunt and flout**), and not because some new concept or item has come into being that borrows an existing word to describe itself (of which there have been many in recent years, some of them – and I have already given one example, but there are countless others – connected with the latest instalment of the technological revolution: such as *tweet*, *platform*, *streaming* and *application*). That is an example of the great fear among some more radical academics, in this respect, of branding anyone as ignorant in his or her use of language; for some of them all usages, however bizarre (and however corrupted the grammar in which such usages are couched), are to be deemed legitimate in the free-for-all world of the evolving language. I do not share that fear, and I do not share it precisely because I do not wish innocent people, often victims of an inadequate education system, to be damaged by such patronising indulgence.

To an extent this book reviews progress – or rather the lack of it – in keeping English on the straight and narrow in the last decade or so, using some specific examples I collected from the printed and broadcast media in the couple of years immediately after the worst of the Covid-19 pandemic that began in the early months of 2020. I still shudder at the memory of a BBC reporter, in the late 2000s, discussing foul play in a football match and describing one of the participants as having 'flaunted' the rules. For a moment I pictured the footballer running round the pitch waving a rule book at his comrades, opponents, the officials and the crowd. It is regrettable that the dictionary now concedes that *flaunt* has been known to be used in place of *flout*. It might as well say that *fart* is an acceptable substitute for anyone devoid of the brainpower needed to use the word *fort*.

When it comes to grammar, there is a logic behind it that, as it has developed over the centuries, has helped eliminate ambiguity from the language. The violations of grammar since I wrote my previous two books appear mainly to concern the elimination of prepositions, a habit we have imported from America, and of which many examples are cited in the A to Z that follows. Because we appear to live in a fractious and unhappy world, one of the most frequent examples is the removal of the prepositions associated with the verb to **protest**. One used to protest in favour of something, or against something, or about something: now one simply protests something, and to hell with the preposition or prepositional phrase. Another example is the verb to **debate** which, I mention in the text, can cause confusion when its preposition is abandoned. One would normally say 'I debated against John' or 'I debated with John'. If one simply says 'I debated John', then the listener is left with the impression that John was the subject under discussion.

This brings us back to young Garth. Children are not to be blamed for struggling to understand why one day their livelihoods, or in extreme cases even their lives, may come to depend on precision in language, and be grateful for the freedom from confusion or misunderstanding that correct grammar generally provides. It is astonishing how many ambitious immigrants to Britain grasp this, whereas those who have lived here for generations fail to do so. Articulacy and precision in speech and writing are, history more often than not relates, central to such success, as many who originally spoke English as a second language will readily testify. It is notable, too, that many of the experts who rejoice in the 'anything goes' school of British English speak and write correct English themselves; and the periodicals and newspapers they tend to read do so too.

Crossing the Atlantic

Long before colonialism was formally dead and buried the English, or British, had lost control of their language. As English-speaking people were exported, transported or simply migrated to distant parts of the globe, the language they took with them began to develop of its own accord and not in accord with the English spoken in the British Isles after their departure from the native shore. In some regards the language they took with them remained more conservative than that continuing to develop in the mother country: that the Americans still say **gotten**, and are careful in their use of the subjunctive mood in a way that hardly anyone in the British Isles now is, reflects this, and not some degree of perversity on the part of the descendants of those emigrants. In that respect, Americans speak and write English just as our common forebears did four hundred years ago. But as American life, society and culture have diverged from British life in those four centuries, so have various words, idioms and grammatical constructions. Such a process was inevitable; and the Americans have a perfect right to develop their version of English in whatever way their culture dictates. And, equally inevitably, there have developed different dialects and standards within the American version: the relatively rarefied diction of magazines such as the *New Yorker*, or newspapers such as the *Washington Post*, does not match with the American English one hears in films or television programmes, or reads on certain popular American websites.

However, just as America has colonised much of the world with McDonald's, Starbucks and Coca-Cola, so it is colonising much of the English-speaking world (and not just the British Isles) with its version of our common language. Given the sheer size (a population five times that of the United Kingdom) and the domination of the Anglophone world in the digital age this should be no source of surprise. This has been the most prevalent current in British English in the last fifteen years or so, and it is a direct result of the ubiquity of American entertainment in cinemas, on television and (via the internet) on computer screens. Indeed, the velocity of change and what seems like the almost daily awareness of new, intrusive idioms or expressions in our supposedly shared language is directly attributable to digital media, and the way in which American media of that sort dominates the Anglosphere.

Culturally, therefore, America has a huge influence on the English-speaking world, and nowhere more than in the very place from which the English language originated. In this book I point out the most common occurrences of American English in the language spoken here, and argue that there is no reason not to maintain the distinction between the two versions of the tongue. The alternative is to allow the American variant and its idioms to swamp British English, and to do away with the historical distinctiveness that has long suggested that the British Isles has a culture, or perhaps more correctly a series of cultures, of its own. Perhaps within another decade or two the American cultural force will have proved irresistible, and my and others' attempts to try to prevent it will have failed. For the moment, given the unanswerable point that we are separate cultures, I see no reason not to carry on fighting. After all, we do not yet drive on the right side of the road, and we are not in the habit of eating grits.

Yet it will be argued that the language belongs to all of us who use it, and we users can do pretty much as we like with it. If an overwhelming mass of speakers of British English decide to use the American variant of the language, then that is their privilege. In that sense language is a democracy, and if most people choose to speak it in a certain way then others will be forced to follow. Something similar happened in twelfth- and thirteenth-century England: the Norman conquerors and their immediate descendants spoke and conducted official business in French. However, within a hundred years the predominantly Anglo-Saxon argot of the conquered majority was not only thriving in the land, it was part of the linguistic armoury of the governing class too. Within another hundred years everyone was speaking Anglo-Saxon English, with a few French words infiltrating their way into it as required.

Perhaps something similar is under way now: if a generation or two of younger people find it pleasing and natural to speak American English in metropolitan and provincial Britain, then those who choose not to do so will before long find themselves stranded in the manner of the men and women of Norman blood who eight hundred years ago ran up the white flag and resigned themselves to speaking in the tongue of the supposedly conquered people. That they did was, politically, an act of reverse conquest. Perhaps that is what American culture is doing to us now; and every time unwitting descendants of the Anglo-Saxons, or those who have integrated into their language and way of life, talk of a **train station**, or ask for a **raise**, or even about **standing in line**, they contribute to that new act of conquest.

There are also what Ralph Waldo Emerson might have called 'American traits' – habits our cousins in the United States have in handling our common language as it continues to develop, and whose germs, thanks to the influence of digital media, we catch all too easily. One of these – a habit admittedly known here throughout the evolution of the language – is of turning nouns into verbs. For example: the noun *table* has existed since the era of Old English, before the Conquest, but the verb – *to table* a document for discussion – dates from the fifteenth century. Nouns used to be made into verbs because no satisfactory verb existed. The difficulty now is that nouns are made into verbs where a perfectly serviceable verb or verbal phrase exists: and the world of sport is a serial offender. Someone who is placed in a race – in other words, comes first, second or third – is no longer 'placed', but is said to have **podiumed** or **medalled**. Perhaps when I have finished writing this I can be said to have 'booked'. For the moment such silly coinages have the status of slang; it may be in twenty or thirty years' time that no noun is considered to be unverbable [*sic*]. Another American trait of which we must be careful is with the use of the word *like* to indicate reported speech: 'So I'm, like, what are you doing? And he's, like, I'm reading a book.' This only exists in British English in demotic speech or slang but in America it intrudes into reputable printed matter, and will do so here before too long.

However, if it is true that the language belongs to all who use it, then people who wish to speak American in England have an absolute right to do so, whatever the damage caused to an otherwise sound linguistic structure, and to the joys of cultural distinctiveness. We are brought up, quite rightly, to respect the cultures of others; what a pity we choose, in terms of our language and the peculiarities of British English, not to respect our own. It is very much the same as allowing one to destroy or misuse any item of which one claims ownership – a person can drive a car in a way that is dangerous purely to him- or herself, or can drink a supply of alcohol until falling over, or can be careless with clothes to the point where they are soiled or torn; so, some feel, can the English language be kicked around, manipulated and damaged and no one should have the right to criticise such a practice.

Many people still share Mrs Garth's view: those fierce diatribes that some newspapers receive when they use what their readers consider to be 'bad' English, remains testimony to that, as do the letters' columns of the better newspapers in which readers protest about the incomprehensibility of much bureaucratic English, or the dismal impression created by the letters and emails correspondents receive from businesses or corporations of which they are clients. Few things create a bad impression among serious people so effectively as bad English, however much the 'experts' might regret this narrow-mindedness.

Politics and the English Language

Such people, who study language professionally, ridicule these supposedly bourgeois attitudes, which conflict with their ideas about the development of language. This is an indication of how effectively language (like so many studies in the humanities) has become politicised and made into a weapon in the culture wars, and in several regards. Relevant here is the assertion that to condemn someone for writing or speaking English badly exhibits some degree of prejudice, and therefore becomes a form of hate crime. Prejudice, however, entails judging some people on grounds other than those of hard evidence, and use of bad English in many people's views provides precisely that evidence. Thus does the use of British English provide another means of dividing a society that is already suffering rather too badly from other attempts to polarise groups of people against each other. An 'anything goes' view about the use of language – try it on any reasonably educated French citizen about his or her own tongue and see what reply you get – opens that language up to corruption; but it also undermines it as a form of effective communication (and effective communication, as Mrs Garth would tell you, is all about being understood, and understood unambiguously).

As I have indicated, politics (and with it, sad to say, a marked contraction in what we used to understand as free speech) has inserted itself nakedly into the English language even in the last fifteen or so years. Many of you will know that I have borrowed the title of this section from a famous essay that George Orwell published in *Horizon* in April 1946, an essay that began with the observation: 'Most people who bother with the matter at all would admit that the English language is in a bad way, but it is generally assumed that we cannot by conscious action do anything about it.' He said the decline in the language had political and economic causes; something he stated having already referred to the arguments that 'Our civilisation is decadent and our language . . . must inevitably share in the general collapse.'

He continued that 'any struggle against the abuse of language is a sentimental archaism'; but argued, nonetheless, for a certain standard in English. He accepted that, in the English language, there was such a concept as decline, something that would simply not be entertained by many supposed experts these days; what Orwell called 'decline' they would consider simply to be change, or evolution. He warned his readers that the malign effects of certain writers were not solely to blame, but that in terms of the influence on deterioration each of them had, 'an effect can become a cause, reinforcing the original cause and producing the same effect in an intensified form, and so on indefinitely'. He compared the problem with that of a man who drinks heavily because he thinks himself a failure, but then fails all the more because he drinks. Applied to the English language, he said: 'It becomes ugly and inaccurate because our thoughts are foolish, but the slovenliness of our language makes it easier for us to have foolish thoughts.' Readers may think I bang on in the entries that follow about the importance of thinking before saying or writing anything. However, the link between precise thinking about the use of language before expressing oneself and the achievement of precision and freedom from ambiguity seems self-evident. Orwell's point not least is what influences me in emphasising the importance of this. If we can't convey meaning exactly as we intend, we have failed in our ability to communicate; and as such, our use of language becomes largely futile.

Quoting some passages of ugly and imprecise English, Orwell complained that a 'mixture of vagueness and sheer incompetence is the most marked characteristic of modern English prose', and he identified the main repository of such inadequate thought and expression as political writing. He felt that in political polemic, or speeches, there was too much abstraction, and that the writing consisted 'more and more of phrases tacked together like the sections of a prefabricated hen-house'. Orwell was driving at the deliberate obfuscation of writing with a political message: it was part of the confidence trick, it was there to confuse. Also, it was there to impose the values of the writer, without question, on those of the reader. He said such writing consisted of 'dying metaphors'; of clumsy and verbose phrases used instead of simple verbs (such as 'make contact with' instead of just 'meet') or instead of simple conjunctions; of sentences ending with 'resounding commonplaces'; of 'pretentious diction' that was 'used to dignify the sordid processes of international politics'; of 'meaningless words', which he defined as 'in the sense that they not only do not point to any discoverable object, but are hardly even expected to do so by the reader'. He deplored the use of the passive voice, because it detached the agent from the action, and of a preference for classical words over 'Saxon' ones.

These all contributed to the 'swindles and perversions' he found inherent in much political writing, writing he believed was intended principally to deceive those who read it. He set out various rules, of which perhaps the two most significant were that the writer should ask him- or herself 'What am I trying to say?' and, having said it, to ask further 'Could I put it more shortly?' And he emphasised again that if one could not be bothered there were always 'ready-made phrases' available, which simply indicated that the writer or speaker had delegated his or her thinking to someone else. Expressing his feelings at witnessing some political oratory or reading some political prose, Orwell said that 'one often has a curious feeling that one is not watching a live human being but some kind of dummy . . . A speaker who uses that kind of phraseology has gone some distance toward turning himself into a machine.' In 1946, in political discourse, Orwell felt there was nothing new to say: and the use of flannel to say it, the 'vagueness' he lambasts again and again, is, he feels, all part of the euphemism essential to make political concepts palatable to most of the electorate.

Since he wrote this, almost eighty years ago, the relationship between politics and the English language has become even more complicated, though the fundamental problems he identified – about executing the confidence trick of which so much politics consists – remain unchanged. The rise of identity politics has had its impact on the way some people speak and write, and this has seeped more widely into the language, thanks to the broadcast media in particular obeying new and specially manufactured linguistic conventions in order to avoid offending any self-declared minority. Whether we like it or not, this has an effect on the way some people feel they have to speak or write English. In my entry on **pronouns** I discuss the effect that ideas about gender – ideas held by a small minority and considered irrelevant or just bizarre by many outside that group – have had on English.

According to data published by the National Library of Medicine on an official website of the United States government, 'the true prevalence of intersex' – people who by their phenotypes are 'not classifiable as either male or female' – amounts to 0.018 per cent of the population; in other words, 99.982 per cent of human beings are born either male or female (https://pubmed.ncbi.nlm.nih.gov/12476264/). I am not for a moment disputing that, once they achieve the age of reason, some of those people may wish to exercise their human right to think differently about their gender; some of them may even wish to have a series of surgical procedures that change or 're-assign' their gender from male to female, or vice versa. Others may wish to consider themselves as embracing both genders, or no gender at all: I cite in my entry on **pronouns** the opinion of a learned woman who asserts what she calls the 'fantasy' of gender. It is her right to do that; but it is also the right of others to disagree with her, and I suspect I am not alone in doing so.

Because this question has become so highly politicised it has, in Orwellian fashion, proceeded to have an effect on our language. Before this debate arose, the pronouns *they* and *their* were used informally in constructions where one would correctly, in formal writing, say 'he or she' (as opposed to 'he and she') or 'his or her' (as opposed to 'his and her'): for example, someone might be asked 'Would you prefer John or Mary to give you their opinion first?' The correct grammar of that sentence would be 'Would you prefer John or Mary to give you his or her opinion first?' but no one would say and virtually no one would write such a sentence because of its prolixity. Now, this plural pronoun has been adopted not by those who wish to talk about both genders in a construction where singular pronouns would technically be required, but by those who have identified themselves as having elements of both genders. Some singular human beings now insist on using, and having others use, the pronouns *they* and *them* in referring to themselves, despite these pronouns in such usage having long been considered ungrammatical or illogical. Indeed, some people now instruct others at the end of formal letters or emails how they wish to be addressed, with the instructional '(Pronouns: they/them)' by their signatures. This can indeed sometimes be helpful, or deemed redundant when one receives a letter signed by John Smith with the instruction '(Pronouns: he/him)' next to it.

As with so much in life, this must remain a matter of personal taste: although it has always been good manners to address people in the way they wish to be addressed, it will grate with some to hear a person who appears to be a man or a woman being described as 'they'; others will find it preposterous and, if so, good manners require that they keep such a view to themselves [*sic*]. Either such a usage will become accepted, and in ten years' time no one will think anything of it, or it won't, and there will be a reversion to using the pronoun we think a person requires, until or unless we are told otherwise. It will depend on how desperate the desire to avoid causing offence becomes, and how influential or otherwise the minority who wish to alter the language is; it may not form part of the experience of large sections of society. It is deeply regrettable that throughout the ages minorities have come in useful to a certain section of society for a form of verbal target practice; human nature has often caused this to be the case and it has been reflected in the evolution of derogatory language, much of which no decent person would use today.

As society changes, so too do the minorities who are at the forefront of its consciousness; and language changes accordingly, and will do if the present minority interest in identity passes. This book seeks to avoid politics wherever possible, and is aimed at those who simply wish to compensate for the dismal standards of our education system in the last thirty or forty years, and to use their inherent intelligence to master the written and spoken language to a degree they had hitherto feared was unlikely.

I had a conversation with a fellow journalist, employed by a different newspaper, pointing out that his publication had confused **the firing line** with **the line of fire**. I was told without his missing a beat that everybody confused these terms these days and that I should simply accept it. Well, I don't, and neither should any publication that wishes to be regarded as serious. The people who feel they must defend such ignorance are then saddled with the need to be consistent, and thus have to defend every other absurdity that is perpetrated. Such people, I have noticed, tend not to make such mistakes themselves, which makes their attitude all the more deeply patronising.

Accentuate the positive

Irrelevant to an idea of correct English is the use, in speech, of an accent. Even in a small country such as the United Kingdom, not to mention in the rest of the Anglosphere, there is a multitude of these. One can speak English correctly in any accent: the idea of received pronunciation, the clipped and formal style of speaking English that was associated with the cream of society, and which countless others sought to emulate in some measure in order to create an impression of salubriousness, is far from de rigueur now, and even in its heyday was a minority pursuit. Lord Reith, a refined Scotsman who sounded like one, insisted on it when he ran the BBC from 1922 to 1938, and it thus became embedded in the national consciousness as some sort of spoken standard. It is said that no BBC employee was allowed to broadcast in a regional accent until, under the strictures of wartime, Wilfred Pickles, a popular North Country actor, read the news on the Home Service in a broad Halifax accent. It was said that Pickles's West Riding cadences were unleashed on the public in order to make it harder for Nazis to imitate an authorised broadcast. Any bloody fool, or traitor, could make a stab at RP – as William Joyce, alias Lord Haw-Haw, proved. I have been unable to trace whether Joyce (born in America to a family of Anglo-Irish emigrants, but brought up mainly in Ireland and England, where he attended a minor public school) ever attempted to pass himself off as a Yorkshireman: I doubt it.

Accents are often associated with dialects, and as I have mentioned earlier these often have their special local words and even grammatical constructions. So long as speakers of, or writers in, dialect understand that most people from outside their region may not understand some of the words they use, and that grammatical variants will not be considered standard English, no harm is done in using these forms, whose use of local words has a cultural and historical richness and (literally) says much about the nature of the region. However, they are not suitable for documents designed for mass communication, nor for formal speech such as broadcasting, because comprehension of what is said in them must by definition be restricted. That is where standard English as a lingua franca comes in so useful.

Dialects are outside the scope of this book, given its purpose to profess that there is such a concept as Standard British English and great value in mastering it. It also seeks to highlight what the most recent trends contrary to that standard are; and to weigh up whether they have improved or damaged it. I fear most of the developments since my last two books on the English language have done the latter: and usually because they are entirely unnecessary when it comes to reducing the danger of ambiguity or confusion (in the case of alterations to grammar or syntax) or because they concern the minting of words or phrases that are simply otiose, because existing words or phrases deal with the matter adequately. I know some will disagree; and others will always choose to use contemporary slang because they feel comfortable with it. Such slang is seldom enduring, however: phrases from a century ago (think of Billy Bunter's 'I say, you fellows, draw it mild!' or Bertie Wooster's 'what ho!' and 'bally') sound archaic or even ridiculous now, as doubtless our slang will in the 2120s. But if this little book helps some of those disobliged by the British education system to improve their communication skills, to progress in their careers or even to become advanced writers themselves, then I should be happy. Our language is a supreme instrument but, as with many of those used to make music, it can acquire a bad reputation by being played badly. Those who inflict its sound on others should take sufficient care to ensure they have reached a decent standard of proficiency in it first.

We have not yet reached (and are not anywhere near reaching) the stage at which the most respected British publications or the most highly regarded works of non-fiction are written in anything other than what this book seeks, incrementally, to define as Standard British English: fiction, with its various voices, is a different matter, though even the novel and the short story continue to obey certain conventions. As an admirer of our language I take these important acts of continuation as signs of grace; one hopes the writing of our era will be as comprehensible to readers in two or three hundred years' time as the novels of Jane Austen or the polemics of Milton remain to us. If that is to be so we need to reassure ourselves that there is nothing to fear in guarding an idea of Standard British English, just as we respect the right of Americans, Indians, Australians, Africans and all others who speak and write a version of English to maintain theirs. The idea of the English language flourishes by such distinctions, whereas a conformity produced by digesting the latest, often illogical and unintelligible, fashions can only dilute the strength of the existing standard, and rob it of its distinctiveness and richness. A conscious act of preservation where Standard British English is concerned is not to be treated lightly or frivolously, but as an act of cultural necessity.

Author's Note

Any reference to 'the dictionary' is to the *Oxford English Dictionary* in its most recent edition, which is to be found online and is subject to continuing revision.

A

Academic speak It remains astonishing, given how clever those who hold academic posts are supposed to be, that relatively few can be let loose on the English language without mangling it and rendering an attempt at communication with it almost pointless. Those who have been through the university system will be used to phrases peculiar to these people such as *positing* this and that, *control groups*, *disciplines*, *protocols* and *core*. But in recent years the language has become yet more abstruse, to the point that it becomes nearly incomprehensible even to relatively intelligent outsiders. As with **corporate speak**, the exclusivity of the argot is designed to keep outsiders out, and to show off to insiders that the user is one of them.

Here is a world-class masterpiece from *Counterpoints*, Vol. 422 (published in 2012):

> The material domain of discriminatory social practices is constituted by the cultural politics of an exclusionary agenda tending toward the disequalization of subjectivities, difference from the accepted 'norm' being accorded a pejorative connotation vis-à-vis highly arbitrary criteria of judgment that are based on the problematic categories of race, ethnicity, class, gender, or sexuality. This conscious disenfranchisement of alternate subjectivities is therefore a societal production of the meaning of representation, which

measures difference in relation to cultural ordinances of aspect, conceived as a narrowly defined and fixedly qualitative measure of personal or group 'characteristics'. Moreover, the question of difference elides with how the dominant ideology defines selfhood. And the transversal function of an amassing of diverse ideologies under the overarching structure of a single 'controlling culture' has been a key factor for theories of subjectivity attempting to explain the social interpellation of the individual into 'subject' (Althusser, 1971).

Scarcely English is aimed at intelligent people who wish to improve their written and spoken English. Sadly, some people are such hopeless cases that they must be destined to remain beyond its reach. See also **oracy** *and* **oriented**.

Accede In the preparations for the Coronation in 2023 there were occasional references to King Charles's having 'acceded' the Throne. There had certainly been an accession, which the *Oxford English Dictionary* in this context defines as 'the attainment or acquisition of an office or position of rank or power, *esp.* that of monarch'. Shortly after Queen Elizabeth II's death an Accession Council was held at the proclamation of the new monarch. However, the idiomatically correct verb is either *ascend* or *succeed*, and *accede* seems an odd mixture of the two, minted in confusion. The verb *accede*, according to the dictionary, has as its principal meaning 'to agree' or 'to consent to'. In Britain a new monarch either **ascends** the Throne (no preposition required) or succeeds to it. *Accede* is not idiomatic usage, and on the rare occasions it has been used (the dictionary supplies nine quotations since 1737) it is usually in the form *acceded to*. Unless you wish to indicate agreement, as in 'he acceded to her request', avoid this usage.

Accusatives, misused   On the MailOnline website, on 16 November 2022, readers learnt that 'Queen Rania of Jordan stuns in pleated purple gown as her and King Abdullah II host state dinner . . .' This was a relatively rare, and mistaken, usage of an accusative pronoun ('her') instead of the nominative 'she'. (It might also be noted that the verb *to stun* is a transitive (*see Appendix*: **verbs**), that is, one that requires an object: someone, or something, or some people have to be stunned to make complete sense of the verb. Otherwise, one is left asking, as in this case: 'Stuns what? Or whom?') The far more common inarticulacy is the use of nominative for the accusative – 'he gave a present to John and I', which should be 'to John and me'. This mistake is increasingly ubiquitous, despite the fact that few who utter it would ever, were John not involved, say that 'he gave a present to I'. Perhaps the late Queen, always correctly referring to 'my husband and I', unwittingly misled generations into thinking that the 'proper' usage in all contexts was 'I' rather than 'me'. In demotic speech, we almost all use the grammatically wrong pronoun daily – few can handle the stageiness of saying 'it is I' when nature has taught them to say, far more simply, 'it's me'. But it says something particular about education and articulacy to the English ear when it hears someone say that 'him and me were [more typically, "was"] down the pub last night'. It is all the more shocking that a poem in the *Spectator* (which should know better) in February 2023 should have included the line: 'In chilly rooms where either you or me will linger.' Doubtless a plea of artistic licence can be admitted in mitigation. *See also* **to be, who and whom** *and Appendix*: **nominatives**.

Actor and **actress**   Just as the terms *authoress*, *poetess* and *sculptress* appear to have gone on the endangered – or extinct – list in the last fifty years or so, *actress* may soon join them.

Women who work in film, television or on the stage often make a point of referring to themselves as 'actors', a term traditionally associated solely with men. It is the prerogative of the woman concerned to refer to herself as she pleases. Others will note, however, that most awards ceremonies for this profession still include a 'best actress' category – from the Academy Awards downwards – and until they all stop doing it, the rest of us may feel free to use the phrase as we wish.

Adjectives, hyperbolic Adjectives generally need to be handled with care, and part of choosing carefully is to ensure the adjective is sensible and will not convince your reader or listener that you are a twerp. Sadly, twerpitude [*sic*] is all too easily achieved by the use of an adjective whose meaning is excessive, or sometimes by simply using one wrongly – such as if one were to describe a tall person as 'high', which would prompt a quite different interpretation to do with his or her social position. *See* **epic**, where I outline the dangers of reducing a powerful word to near-meaninglessness by using it wildly in the wrong context. But the same applies to absurd usages (very prevalent in journalism about popular culture, where a sense of perspective seems a definite handicap) such as 'galactic' ('the rock band were a galactic sensation'), and its big brother 'intergalactic', which has become slang for something the speaker finds too wonderful for words, 'gigantic' ('gigantic empty Debenhams store in Wigan to become "Britain's biggest charity shop"', said the *Manc* in August 2023, even though the building was simply part of a shopping arcade and not one covering the whole of Lancashire), 'great' (used ubiquitously about people who usually are not – we used to hear about someone called 'the great Jimmy Savile' – though it should be stressed that not all the ungreat who are wrongly or excessively accorded the adjective are sex offenders), and similarly 'huge', 'massive', 'monumental' ('Statistics spell out Burnley's monumental task against Man City', said *Talksport*) and 'vast'. In most cases *big, considerable, formidable,* even boring old *large* or something similar would have conveyed the reality more accurately.

Adjectives, incomparable   Sometimes one needs to apply a little logic when making adjectives into comparatives (as in *big* and *bigger*) or superlatives, which can be used only when three or more things are being considered (*big* and *biggest*). But what about a word such as **full**? Think of a glass that is full: how could it be any fuller? One might argue that a glass that has three-quarters of a pint in it is *fuller* than one with only half a pint. In fact, the former is nearer to being full; the latter may be considered less full, but in fact it is further from being full than the other. The same applies to *empty*. And certain other adjectives offer even less excuse for being used as comparatives or superlatives – consider *absolute*, or *total*, or (unless one is seeking to be comical) *dead* or *alive*. Such adjectives when applied to nouns mean something that either is, or is not: there are no gradations.

Administrate and **administer**   A man interviewed on the BBC on 4 January 2023 said he had been wrongly accused of 'administrating a toxic substance'. He had in fact been wrongly accused of *administering* a toxic substance. To *administrate* something is to run it or cause it to function. To *administer* something is to give it to someone – whether a toxic substance, or some medicine, a punishment or even some charity or alms. If someone really were administrating a toxic substance he or she would be running or organising it, which is unlikely.

Adulting   The dictionary recognises this word as having originated in America, as have so many that have elbowed their way into British English in recent decades. In 1909, which appears to be the time of its birth, it was used to mean 'maturing'; but its second citation by the dictionary, from seventy years later, uses the word slightly differently to suggest someone behaving as an adult or simply being an adult. The two more recent examples cited are both from that sublime repository of high literary usage, Twitter (now known as 'X'), which gives the measure of the milieu in which such a form of English would be considered acceptable. It is a prime example of the widespread confident assurance with which any English noun can be turned into a verb: or as Twitter or 'X' users would doubtless say, can be 'verbed'. A recent example from the media appeared on the Toronto *Globe and Mail* website in October 2023, in the headline: 'Adulting with roommates: solo living is a luxury in today's rental market'. *See also* **nouns used as verbs**, **medalled**, **netted** *and* **podiumed**.

Adverse and **averse**   The former is an adjective and means difficult, negative, damaging or hostile. It is most often heard in phrases such as 'adverse weather conditions' or the 'adverse effects' of smoking, overeating or excess alcohol. *Averse* is an adjective that indicates a dislike of or an opposition to something, as in 'I am averse to eating curry' or 'she was averse to his reasoning'. They are not synonyms, though one does hear people say that they are 'adverse' to doing something. A frequent coinage is of a noun with 'averse' to indicate something someone does not like doing or something harmful – as in 'work-averse' or 'rain-averse'. A writer for the *Sheridan Press*, a Wyoming newspaper, reviewing a Hallowe'en film in October 2023, described it as suitable for the 'scare-adverse', illustrating his failure to grasp the difference between the two words.

Affect and **effect** On 23 December 2022 MailOnline told its readers how badly someone had been 'effected' by something. This use of the verb was nonsense, and would remain so unless the article went on to inform us how the man had been brought into existence: which it did not. To be *effected* is to be caused to happen or for something to be brought about; an explosion might be effected by dynamite, or a burglar might effect entry into a house by breaking a window. To *affect*, in the verb's most common usage, means to have an effect on a person or a thing: as in 'his drinking affected his work terribly' or 'his health was badly affected by the climate' or 'the damp seriously affected the house's value' – all these things so affected have bad effects. *Affect* as a verb is also used to indicate a degree of pretension ('she affected a disdain for the lower classes') or a certain flamboyance of habit ('he affected red braces and matching socks') or, for example, speech ('he affected a cockney accent'). Such things may indeed have an effect, even if it is only to bore those who witness them.

Aggravate This much-maligned verb serves the very useful purpose of expressing the idea of making something worse – 'her cold was aggravated by her having stood in the rain for two hours' – but it has been adopted in slang and coarse speech to mean something perhaps logically related, but nonetheless inelegant. 'You're giving me aggravation' or, 'you're aggravating me' may indeed mean someone is making the speaker feel worse than he was already, but it would be better to say 'you're upsetting me'. The dictionary cites the use of the verb *to aggravate* meaning 'to provoke, embitter or annoy' as dating back to 1598, but none of its recent examples could be said to be from anything other than demotic English, and it brands this usage 'colloquial and slang' – so not recommended for formal writing or speech. Indeed, in the citations for the noun *aggravation* the dictionary quotes a passage from the *Police Review* of 1984 that claims the usage to mean 'harassment' or 'trouble' originated in the London underworld, and especially in inter-gang warfare, in the 1950s; as did its infant child, 'aggro'. It is definitely not an expression for a vicarage tea party, even in the present Church of England.

Aitch This letter of the alphabet is increasingly mispronounced as 'haitch', in the manner of the cockney caricature that has people dropping the 'h' where it should exist and inserting it where it should not; and therefore saying things such as 'I 'ave 'urt my helbow.' It is spelt *aitch*, from which it can be seen that there is no silent 'h' at the start of the word in the manner of *hour* or *honour*, but rather no 'h' at all. *See also* **historian**.

Alienated with On television in February 2022, as tensions grew between Russia and Ukraine, a television news reporter was heard to remark how within the former Soviet Union certain minorities had grown to feel 'alienated with' the Russians. They were, of course, feeling *alienated from* them. One can also feel *alienated by* something or someone: 'she felt alienated by his hostility towards her', which would mean she was alienated from the man concerned. When someone is *alienated from* something it means he or she is placed apart from a distinct entity, be it a group, a culture or an individual; when one is *alienated by* someone or something it describes the act of being forced into a state of apartness or solitude.

All right This is the now largely forgotten form in which writers of British English spell the term that, under American influence, has now almost universally become 'alright'. Something similar has happened to **under way**, which is now deemed to be 'underway'; and both should be avoided by people who wish to be correct in style.

Alternative   There can only ever be two alternatives, in the strict etymological sense of the word; though the dictionary points out that although the correct meaning is 'of two things', usage has made it now 'frequently of more than two things'. It remains preferable both in strict stylistic and logical terms to use *options*, for example, to express that the range of possibilities is wider than two: so rather than 'three alternatives' there should be 'three options' or 'three possibilities'. Indeed, there can be as many options or possibilities as one likes. It is not unknown for highly educated people to make this mistake, and some have been making it for a long time. 'The third alternative is to attempt to combine the advantages of both the former', wrote John Strachey on page 129 of his 1932 book *The Coming Struggle for Power*, proving that this difficulty is not recent. It was not the only mistaken facet of a book that confidently predicted a Marxist solution to Britain's problems, even if it required the violent coercion of an unwilling populace to bring it about. In 1936 J. M. Keynes used 'the third alternative' in the preface to his *General Theory*. He was, it seems, being consciously satirical or ironic.

Although   This conjunction is sometimes interchangeable with **though**, and some people regard it as superior, with *though* being a coarse abbreviation of it. That may be going too far. One can say, with equal respectability, 'I went up to London, although I had a filthy cold' or 'I went up to London, though I had a filthy cold'. One advantage of using *though* in that sentence is that one can, if one wishes to court pity, accentuate it by saying 'even though I had a filthy cold'. 'Even although' is not only unidiomatic, it is illogical and incorrect

English. Whereas *though* is often used adverbially as a synonym for *however* ('she took rather a fancy to him – he hardly noticed her, though'), *although* is never so used. It would be correct, in that last example, to say 'she took rather a fancy to him – although he hardly noticed her' where the usage is synonymous not with *however* but with *even though*.

Amazeballs   This silly word has been for reasons, one supposes, of completeness admitted to the *Oxford English Dictionary*, which dates it back to 2008 and attributes its existence mainly to usages in social media, and talks of its being used for 'expressing enthusiastic approval' – something which *excellent*, *terrific*, *superb* or even *amazing* did for decades or centuries. Slang catches on fast, but slang is all it is: not a word to use in a job application, unless one is sure the recipient of the approach has a very advanced sense of humour, or one is hoping to work in a therapeutic context with teenagers.

Americanisms   If any single force has dominated the influences on the English language since I wrote *Strictly English* and *Simply English* it is the apparently unstoppable torrent of Americanisms pouring into British English. One used to blame this on the vast power of Hollywood and the penetration of British culture by American television; and before either films or television, by American pulp fiction and comic books that were easily available in Britain from the late nineteenth century. Now it is the effect of the universality of the internet and social media, and the fact that so many of its phenomena are generated from the United States. As I noted in my two earlier books, one of the great beauties of American English, which we have chosen almost entirely to lose, is the use of the **subjunctive** mood (*see Appendix*) – 'I order he be removed from the court' is just one commonplace use of it, whereas a British judge would be more likely to use an auxiliary verb and order that 'he should be removed'. Sadly, this excellent habit shows no signs of catching on here, unlike several other more recent developments. The American habit of dispensing with prepositions after the use of certain verbs *is* catching on here with alarming speed: *see, for example,* **appeal** *and* **protest**. And other phrases of American origin are now suffocating their British English predecessors, not least because of the influence of film and television: *see, for example,* **stand, take the**; **stand in line** *and* **train station**. While the word *pled*, as the past participle of the verb to **plead**, has started to float up the creeks and inlets of British English, as has the past participle **gotten** (archaic usage in Britain, but long since drummed out of standard English in a way that, illogically, *forgotten* has not been), we are yet to accept *dove* (rhymes with 'Gove' and 'Hove', not 'love' and 'shove') as the past participle of **dive**. By far the most offensive, because the most puerile, development, dealt with under **reported speech**, is the fatuous use of the word **like** to replace 'I said', 'he said', 'she said' and so on. However the Americans, as a sign of grace, are scrupulous at maintaining the nuances in language offered by the preservation of the subjunctive mood. *See also* **back in the day, call out, double down, good and well, named for, on the weekend, restaurateur, snuck** *and* **start over**.

Among This word is to be used as an adverb when a position or sense of commonality affecting three or more people, objects or places is being described. It is illogical to say that Mary stood **between** her friends if there are more than two friends. She may well have stood between two of them, but if there were more than two then she in fact stood *among* them. Similarly, one would share sweets *between* two children but *among* three or more of them; or one would say that a love of Beethoven was common *between*, or *to*, a couple of people, but common *among*, or *to*, a larger group of them. *Amongst* as an alternative remains acceptable, though has an increasingly antique flavour.

Anticipate   This verb, which means to do something in advance or to prepare for something, has become even more promiscuously used to mean 'expect' than it was when I last wrote about it more than a decade ago. Its correct use is seen in a phrase such as 'he anticipated his peerage by having some new business cards printed', its incorrect one in 'she anticipated passing her exams', when the meaning is that 'she expected to pass her exams'. The dictionary suggests the verb was minted by Sir Thomas More in 1533, at a time when words of classical etymology were pouring into the language (this one is from the Latin verb *anticipare*); his martyrdom continues every time somebody uses it wrongly, which according to the dictionary some have been doing for the best part of three hundred years. When the problem started to reach epidemic proportions in the mid-twentieth century the old joke was coined that 'to anticipate marriage is not the same as to expect it', and I make no apology for repeating it. Although it is possible to argue that everyone knows it tends these days to mean 'expect', that dilutes and detracts from the usefulness of its proper meaning; and to use the verb correctly will also create a highly favourable impression among the beleaguered minority of readers who know exactly what it should mean, but who so seldom see it deployed in that way.

Any   A well-worn example of the complexities of this little word is the difference between 'Have you any idea?' and 'Have you any ideas?' The former is a rebuke framed in a rhetorical question, as in 'Have you any idea how much misery you have caused?' The latter is a polite invitation, as in 'Have you any ideas about how we might solve the recruitment problem?' In both cases it is used as an adjective, but in the former it is also being deployed as a challenge or an insult, which can and often is compounded by the suffix *at all* – as in 'Have you any notion at all of what this is going to cost us?' *Any* can also act as an adverb, such as in 'you won't be any the wiser by reading that' or 'you won't walk any faster in those shoes'. *Any* as a pronoun refers back to a noun, as in 'he asked me whether we had some cheese, but I told him we hadn't any'. In a question, *any* can be singular or plural, depending both on stylistic preference and on the expected response. One can say 'Does any of you want to come?' either if you are thinking of the answers of individuals or if you expect only one person will come; or you can ask 'Do any of you want to come?' if you are expecting a multitude to agree to the invitation, or are simply speaking colloquially. My own preference in writing is to stay in the singular, hence I would write 'he will ask tomorrow whether any of them wishes to volunteer', but it would not be wrong to write 'whether any of them wish to volunteer'. Compounds of *any* used as pronouns are always singular – 'Does anybody care?' or 'anyone is entitled to come', or 'anywhere is better than this', or 'Is there anything that could be done?' Be clear too about the difference between *anyway*, meaning 'in any case' – 'never mind the weather, I'm going to go swimming anyway' – and *any way*, which means 'by any means' – 'Is there any way that we can persuade her to change her mind?'

Any time soon This is a particular bête noire of the guardians of linguistic rectitude at the Queen's English Society, who sensibly point out that this cliché simply means 'yet', 'soon' or 'quickly' in a negative statement: such as in 'he won't be coming back from the pub any time soon' or 'I won't be seeing her any time soon' or 'it won't happen any time soon'. Like all **clichés** it suggests laziness or a lack of wit on the part of the speaker, who is clearly not thinking precisely about what he or she is saying, but rather talking on autopilot.

Apostrophe, misuse of The use of **it's** when one ought to be writing **its** is perhaps the most ubiquitous and depressing misuse of the apostrophe. It also remains sadly common to see signs such as 'sweet's and ice's': the plurals *sweets* and *ices* require no apostrophe. 'The shopkeeper's mistake' does. Using an apostrophe to indicate a plural is always wrong. When indicating a plural noun's possession of something, the apostrophe appears *after* the plural – 'the boys' night out', or 'the girls' friends'. This does not apply when using a plural noun whose form does not require an -s to be added – so it is 'the women's room', 'the children's playground', 'the gentlemen's club'. One sometimes sees written a noun that ends in -s in any case that has an apostrophe following it but no possessive 's', as if it were a plural. This is always wrong. It is not 'Gladys' hairdo' or 'the Countess' tiara', but 'Gladys's' and 'the Countess's'. The straightforward rule is that if you pronounce it, you write it. *See also* **their, there and they're** *and* **your and you're**.

Apostrophe, redundant *See* **double genitive**.

Appeal In America, one appeals a conviction. In Britain, one appeals *against* a conviction. However, one appeals *to* someone's better nature, or *for* clemency. *See also* **prepositions, missing**; **approve**; **debate**; **disapprove**; *and* **protest**.

Appropriate and **inappropriate** Here we move into politics, and into weasel words. Earlier generations, when confronted with an action, or some speech, that they found deeply offensive said so: if they didn't say it was 'deeply offensive' they might have said it was 'rude', 'disgraceful', 'shocking', 'ugly', 'disgusting' or 'wicked' because it violated society's idea of common decency and proper civilised behaviour. If, by contrast, they approved of something they praised it. Now, something decreed disagreeable – and it is important to note that opinions may vary on whether an action is disagreeable or not – is described as 'inappropriate'. To take something all right-thinking people should agree upon: there was a time when an adult making sexual advances to a minor would have been described as 'depraved', 'perverted' or 'downright criminal'. Now such advances are described as 'inappropriate'. This reflects partly the long-held obsession with **euphemism**, such as in people no longer dying, but 'passing away'. But *appropriate* and *inappropriate* have also become staples of the group-speak of the censorious or puritanical wing of society, and all in that group know what is meant by them. Thus it is now usually 'inappropriate' for a man to make a comment about the appearance of a female colleague, whereas once it would instead have been regarded as *unprofessional*, *tasteless*, *embarrassing*, *offensive* or *rude* – although inevitably in certain circumstances, depending on context, it might have been taken as a compliment.

In August 2023 the *Mirror* reported that a mother felt she had to remove her ten-year-old daughter from the cinema where they gone to watch the film *Barbie* because of the 'inappropriate language': what she meant was 'bad' or possibly 'unsuitable' language. The *Sun*, the same month, reported how a talent show on television had featured an act including three naked men. 'Weird and disgusting' was how one viewer described it, which seems reasonable; but inevitably another branded it 'inappropriate'. It used to be the case that *inappropriate* was the term applied to the act of turning up at a black-tie dinner wearing jeans and a donkey jacket, or giving a deaf man a radio for Christmas, but now it has become the key expression of disapproval in the language. In doing so, it has obscured the genuine range of critical terms in the English language, made it less precise and created an equality of unpleasantness that will do a disservice to offences, perceived or otherwise, at either extreme. To refer, as some people would, to both predatory sexual behaviour and an off-colour joke about a Scotsman as 'inappropriate' demonstrates a new limitation being imposed on a language where none need exist.

Approve and **disapprove**   A character in a television drama said of another 'I disapprove his drinking'. Inserting the preposition *of* would make this a correct use of the **gerund** (*see Appendix*) – 'I disapprove of his drinking' – or one could correctly but less elegantly say 'I disapprove of him drinking'. The television character, in a British programme, was speaking fluent American in this instance, as an increasing number of people, especially those armed with words by modern scriptwriters, now do. By contrast, the formal act of approval, as in 'The department approved the new design', requires no preposition; it is the moral sense of the verb that does require one: 'I approve of his going to church.' To say 'I approve his going to church' means you are giving him permission to do so, not judging him favourably for doing so. Similarly, one should say 'I disapprove of his sympathy for that criminal' and so on. However, the dropping of this preposition is now widely prevalent in British English, and should be resisted precisely to avoid such ambiguities as I have outlined above. *See also* **prepositions, missing**.

Arise and **rise**   During the 4th Test Match between England and Australia in 2023, one of the BBC commentators said the whole crowd was 'arising' when Harry Brook scored his half-century. *Arise* in the sense of a person's physical movement is essentially archaic: it is what, in tales of old, monarchs said to men once they had knighted them, and has occasionally featured in poetic diction – though the dictionary cites nothing after Milton (1667) and Keats (1820), the former using it to denote getting up after a fall (in this case, The Fall), the latter as an injunction to get out of bed. Tennyson, in 1859, used it to describe getting out of the grave, and Yeats used it in 1888 in 'The Lake Isle of Innisfree' – 'I will arise and go now' – but it has strictly regulated uses outside poetry. The verb *to arise* has a current idiomatic usage meaning 'to occur', or 'to come up': no committee meeting is complete without an agenda item entitled 'matters arising', and one often hears that 'the issue arose because of . . .'. But the cricket crowd *rose* to applaud a batsman or bowler, rather than *arose*, which in the modern idiom suggests it had suddenly occurred: similarly the sun rises, prices rise, people rise from bed or from an armchair, and tall buildings rise into the sky. People might, in contemporary usage, *arise* as part of a revolution or uprising. *See also* **awake and wake** *and* **raise and rise**.

Arriving into For reasons that escape me the announcers on the train I regularly catch to London have for the last couple of years told passengers, as we approach our destination, that 'we are now arriving *into* London Liverpool Street'. This is quite serious prepositional abuse: it should be 'we are now arriving *at* London Liverpool Street'. Were one charitable, one would seek to understand why this mistake was made: the notion of the train coming in from outdoors into the engine shed of the terminus, perhaps. But it is the wrong idiom. *See also* **prepositions, wrong**.

As a matter of fact Absurdly, this phrase is quite often used when what follows is not a matter of fact at all, for instance, 'as a matter of fact, you're revolting', when the person may well seem perfectly unrevolting to others. In this context it is, as so often, used for the purposes of blind assertion, and quite possibly because the speaker, in seeking to wound or be unpleasant, also knows that what he or she is saying is not 'a matter of fact' at all, but merely wishes to convey an ignorant insult. In other contexts, as with **at the end of the day, broadly speaking, it goes without saying, to be fair, to be honest** and **when all's said and done**, it is almost always an entirely meaningless phrase, a verbal tic used without conscious thought as a form of punctuation in speech. It has no place in formal writing. *See also* **interesting**.

Ascend   Depending on the context in which this verb is used, it either requires, or does not require, to be followed by a preposition. It is correct to say that 'the plane ascended to 35,000 feet', but incorrect to say that 'the King ascended to the Throne'. The idiomatic usage is that 'the King ascended the Throne'. *See also* **accede**.

Ask   There are frequent examples of **nouns used as verbs**, but becoming more apparent are verbs used as nouns. One of the more familiar in recent years – and to the sophisticated ear it has the appearance of slang – is *ask*, as in 'it was rather a big ask that he should have been allowed to bring his wife and children too'. A number of other nouns, all of them well-established, would have done just as well – *request*, possibly *favour*, even more possibly *imposition* or *presumption*, all of which convey the real significance of the action far more precisely. *See also* **overwhelm**.

Assure, ensure and **insure**   If I *assure* you that a house is not haunted, I am making a firm and authoritative statement that it is not; if I *assure* you that I shall repay money you have lent me, then it is a guarantee or a promise that I shall; *assure* has the effect of making a solemn undertaking. The verb *to ensure* means to make certain that something is done, either as a third party or for oneself – 'I want to ensure you get there safely' or 'she ensured she had her handbag with her'. To *insure* something is to enter into a commercial transaction that ensures [*sic*] the retention of the value of a property, item or life in the event of loss or damage: though *life insurance* is sometimes termed *life assurance*, presumably for the guarantee it gives to the dependants of the insured in the event of his or her death and the loss of the deceased's income. The noun *insurance* can also be used figuratively – 'he put on a heavy overcoat as an insurance against the cold'.

At the end of the day An exception to the uselessness of this phrase would be to observe that 'the sun sets at the end of the day', which is a statement of fact. Otherwise, avoid. *See also* **as a matter of fact, broadly speaking, it goes without saying, to be fair, to be honest** *and* **when all's said and done.**

At this moment in time This is a verbose and silly way of saying 'now'. It is also a **cliché** of the worst sort, and to be avoided in any form of communication that one wishes to be taken seriously, for it suggests a complete lack of the ability to think about what one is saying.

-athon and **-thon** Thanks to the widespread understanding of the word *marathon*, and its use to describe any event of long duration (which the dictionary dates back to 1908), both of a physical nature (such as walking marathons, swimming marathons and dancing marathons) and a mental one (reading marathons or viewing marathons), the public was prepared for the development that simply took an activity and planted the suffix *-athon* or *-thon* on to it. Therefore we have had 'swimathons', 'rideathons', 'telethons' and 'readathons'; and as the stunt lends itself to comedy, also 'boreathons', 'yawnathons' and 'snoozeathons'. It hardly shows originality of mind to pursue this course, however amusing it might seem at the time. *See also* **-cation, -gate, -ification, -nomics** *and* **-shame** for other iterations of the unoriginal mind.

Audience When King Charles III **ascended** the Throne, and various dignitaries went to pay their respects to him, it was often noted in the media that they had had an audience 'with' him. They had not: they had had an audience *of* him. His Majesty had received them *in audience*. The usage dates back to a time when those who came to the monarch did so to have him hear what they had to say to him: he was their audience, and logically, therefore, they had an audience *of* him. The monarch, as the man who was hearing them – their audience – was *with* them. The correct forms appear still in the Court Circular: on 17 May 2023, for example, it announced: 'The Rt Hon Penelope Mordaunt MP had an audience of His Majesty before the Council', and the following day: 'Her Excellency Mrs. Carmen Maria Gallardo Hernández was received in audience by The King today and presented the Letters of Recall of her predecessor and her own Letters of Credence as Ambassador from the Republic of El Salvador to the Court of St. James's.'

Autarchy and **autarky** These homophones are such rarefied words these days that few will have the opportunity to use them, let alone confuse them. *Autarchy* is from the Greek αὐταρχία, which means 'a despotism', as in 'Putin runs an autarchy'. *Autarky* is from the Greek word αὐτάρκεια, meaning 'self-sufficiency'; so if a country is an autarky in respect of its food supplies it can feed itself without imports. According to the dictionary both words were hardly used for centuries yet reached a peak of popularity in the mid-twentieth century.

Authored One often sees interviews with writers in which one is told that he or she has 'authored' a book. It is a matter of taste whether this is more or less offensive to good style than **penned**, when it is simpler and more straightforward to observe that the author *wrote* or has *written* the book. The problem is plainly caused by the use of the noun *writer* and a stylistic desire to avoid echoing it in the verb. An example of this usage is given in the dictionary as dating from 1597, but no further citation is shown until 1911; and most subsequent examples are from America. It sounds odd and looks even odder, and is best avoided by serious speakers and writers – and authors. *See also* **nouns used as verbs**.

Averse *See* **adverse and averse**.

Awake and **wake** The former tends to be intransitive and the latter transitive (*see Appendix*: **verbs**), but these usages have been flexible for, it seems, centuries. Therefore, 'I awoke at seven o'clock' (though one hears just as frequently 'I woke at seven o'clock') but 'I woke the children at seven o'clock' (though one hears sometimes 'I awoke the children at seven o'clock').

B

Back in the day This is an **Americanism** that in recent years people have seemed unable to resist, even though to the uninitiated it sounds as if those who use this expression are talking of an event that happened a few hours earlier. In fact, it is used to refer to something that happened some time ago. If one is in the United States and wishes to pass off oneself as having gone native, then doubtless it is a useful phrase to master; otherwise, it might sound less affected and impostor-ish to say 'long ago', 'years ago', 'once' (or even the harmless 'once upon a time', sanctioned by custom and practice) or simply 'in the past'.

Bacteria Like **data** and **media**, *bacteria* is a plural noun (the singular is *bacterium*). So when in August 2023 Sky News reported that 'asylum seekers spent four days on barge after Legionella bacteria was discovered' it should have said 'were discovered'.

Bandwidth This is now a part of **corporate speak**, and is used to signify time and effort, usually in a negative sense – 'John doesn't have the bandwidth to take on that contract', for example. It may also be a synonym for intelligence or ability – 'she's the only one with the bandwidth to solve the problem'. Use of such a term is a remarkably effective way to alienate a reader or listener.

Bare and **bear**   As verbs these homophones have very different meanings. To *bare* something is to expose it, as in 'he bared his teeth' or 'she bared her midriff'. To *bear* something is to carry it, as in 'the cross we have to bear' or (to use the past tense), 'he bore the task lightly'. Someone at Sky News was manifestly unaware of these important distinctions, quoting a Labour Party spokesman as he or she did on the service's website on 8 October 2023: 'Our card bares our pledge to our voters – that Labour will always put the country first.'

Barmy and **balmy**   These two homophones mean remarkably different things. The former, according to the dictionary, dates from 1535, when being unpleasantly rude was not illegal, and meant 'having a mental illness or a mild intellectual disability': the dictionary sanctimoniously tells us that this usage 'is now considered offensive', but then it is hardly ever used in this literal sense. One hears 'barmy' every day to refer to something the speaker considers foolish, damaging, counter to reason, or indicative of most actions taken by the government or the bureaucracy; and indeed there is an organised band of supporters of the England cricket team who refer to themselves as 'the Barmy Army' without, it appears, undue self-loathing. *Balmy*, by contrast, means something that has the attributes of balm – which is easing, warm and possibly even soothing, and is often applied to the weather. That, I think, was what MailOnline was referring to when it wrote that it had been 'a barmy Bank Holiday weekend'; it was not alluding to some of the activities that had taken place.

Baroque   The alleged comedian Russell Brand perplexed much of the nation, when accused of a series of sexual misdemeanours and offences in September 2023, in describing the allegations against him as being contained in 'a litany of astonishing, rather baroque attacks'. Some did not know what the latter adjective meant; others did, and wondered why on earth Mr Brand was using it. It is usually applied to the culture of the period from the early seventeenth to the mid-eighteenth century, following on from (and for a time overlapping with) the Renaissance: Bernini, Juvarra, Wren, Vanbrugh and Hawksmoor are considered baroque architects; J. S. Bach, Purcell, Telemann, Handel and Rameau are among the leading baroque composers, as is the sublimely named Fux, presumably one of Mr Brand's favourites. The word *baroque* is thought to be of French origin, meaning an irregular pearl, and was purloined from jewellers. The dictionary concedes that it can mean 'florid' or 'grotesque', but grotesque in a physical and not in an abstract form. Perhaps Mr Brand was using it as such an abstract. He is not the first to do so: other speakers and writers have used it to mean 'weird', 'strange', 'fanciful', 'bizarre' or 'wild'. Language develops; the dictionary is filled with examples of words whose usage has, with various degrees of nuance, changed over the centuries. Individual writers must judge whether the change imposed on this once quite precise adjective is sensible, or absurd; and if choosing to use it in an ultra-abstract fashion they must convince themselves that they would not, unlike Mr Brand, attract snorts of laughter and ridicule in deploying this word in what he would doubtless call a baroque fashion. If left to these devices, the word would rapidly become meaningless. Something similar is also happening with **rococo**, which perhaps awaits mobilisation in one of Mr Brand's future outpourings.

Basically Except in rare circumstances, when speaking or writing specifically about the fundamental elements or constituents of something – as in 'watermelon is basically water', which is true, as water indeed makes up 90 per cent of one – this is a fatuous and pointless word, used as a filler or a verbal tic. It is often used to start a sentence – 'Basically, I can't come to the pub this evening' – and can inevitably be eliminated. To some it has become unavoidable in speech, but writers should think very carefully before deploying it except for comic effect.

Bathing   This participle derives from two verbs – *to bathe* and *to bath* – and has two pronunciations, even though both are spelt identically. One pronunciation is for the transitive form, the other for the intransitive form – though as I shall show it does have a transitive use as well. *Bathing* – the first syllable rhymes with 'lathe' and has been very rarely spotted incorrectly spelt as 'batheing' – is what one does in a bath, a river, the sea or a swimming pool or by otherwise immersing oneself in water. It means to take a bath, or to have a swim, and now has a somewhat period flavour associated with high-society writers of the mid-twentieth century. It also has a transitive meaning, as in to bathe a wound. *Bathing*, in which the first syllable rhymes with 'path', is what one does when giving a bath to another, usually a small child, as in: 'I was bathing the baby when the telephone rang.'

Batter   This is a verb that describes an action vile men execute on women, or vile adults execute on babies and children. As a noun it is also a glutinous liquid in which staff in fish-and-chip shops dip fish before frying it. However, it has now been decreed by those who run cricket that the term should be used in men's cricket as well as in women's to refer to the player formerly known as a batsman. This fashionable but ugly and contrived use of gender neutrality has been shunned by traditional cricket lovers, and so it should be. It may well be useful as an abbreviation to describe a batswoman; but for men there was nothing wrong with the term *batsman*, as many people with minds of their own in the cricket world realise.

Begs the question The systematic misuse of this phrase remains promiscuous. One hears it used almost daily in news interviews to mean that something invites a further question, for example – Interviewer: 'But how do you defend the massive printing of money during the pandemic?' Interviewee: 'Well, that begs the question of how we would have paid for it without printing money.' No, it does not. I still cannot beat H. W. Fowler's definition in his *Modern English Usage* of what the phrase really means, which is 'the fallacy of founding a conclusion on a basis that as much needs to be proved as the conclusion itself'. Here is a new example: if one were to say 'speaking French is a superb idea because it increases your attraction to the opposite sex', that statement begs the question of whether the assertion about increasing sexual attraction on which the conclusion is based is actually true. It expressly does not mean that it raises another, separate question – and *raising*, rather than 'begging', the question is the correct way of expressing that thought.

Behaviours When the Gray Report and the Second Report of the Privileges Committee of the House of Commons into allegations of degenerate and illegal conduct in 10 Downing Street during the Covid-19 pandemic under the rule of Boris Johnson were published, both cited 'behaviours' that were deemed improper. So, sadly, was this usage. *Behaviour* is an abstract noun that neither needs nor should have a plural; and neither should it ever be used in a phrase such as 'a behaviour', a grotesque back-formation from the bizarre plural noun. If the reports had wished to indicate that there were different types of behaviour at issue, then they should have said precisely that, before listing them. It is a term becoming popular in **corporate speak**, for the usual reason of demonstrating that the user is part of the elite that speaks that non-language. It is perhaps also a sign of how our public life has been taken over by sociology or psychology graduates and those wishing to pass themselves off as such. *See* **learnings**; **plurals, bogus**; *and* **corporate speak**.

Bequeath This is a verb that strongly resists being nominalised (or, as the perpetrators of such an atrocity would doubtless say, 'nouned'). Yet in describing a large amount of money missing from Scottish National Party funds, MailOnline on 1 May 2023 said that the party 'received some large bequeaths in recent years'. What the long-established noun *bequest* had done to merit this peculiar repudiation is unclear.

Best For decades, and possibly centuries, it had been common to end an informal letter, especially to close friends or associates, with the phrase 'best wishes'. Sometime earlier in the twenty-first century time either became so scarce, or the effort of writing so strenuous, that it became routinely shortened to 'best'. The desire to appear brisk seems to have been fostered by the climate of the internet, and the email, where this abrupt and frankly uncharming phrase appears to proliferate. Best what? Man? End? Offer? In an age when we are the worse off for a decline in civility, rescuing the word *wishes* from its early grave might be worth the effort.

Bestow Although some writers have failed to realise it, this verb requires the complement of that endangered species, a preposition. Noting an accolade given to Sir Elton John, MailOnline mentioned that 'the French President was snapped [*sic*] arm in arm with the legendary 76-year-old artist – who he bestowed France's Legion of Honour award . . .' This dog's breakfast of an expression is grotesque even by the contemporary standards of the internet's instant journalism. It lacks not only the preposition *upon*, but also the accusative pronoun: it should have read 'upon whom he bestowed'. *See* **prepositions, missing**.

Between   Something or someone or somewhere can only be between two things, people or places. If three or more are included then the adverb required is **among**. Therefore 'the dog stood between John and Mary' but it 'stood among several children'; 'John had to sit between his brother and sister' but 'he sat among the congregation'. Also, 'Cambridge is between Huntingdon and Newmarket' but 'is among a number of towns along the A14'.

Birthing people   I thought this term was a parody when I heard a maternity paramedic use it on BBC Radio 4 in March 2024, but I was wrong. *The Daily Telegraph* had already reported: 'NHS trust criticised after advertising maternity role to help "birthing people".' For those who feel they have to acknowledge that men can give birth, and not just women, 'birthing people' is now apparently the approved term for all those who bring forth children. If you are one of those 99.999 per cent of people who believe, with some justification, that children are produced by women, the term 'mother' will suffice.

Bon vivant   This is what the French correctly (according to the tenets of their language's grammar) call someone who enjoys the good life, and whom the English too often incorrectly term a *'bon viveur'*. See also **gourmand and gourmet**.

Bored of   One is never *bored of* something: one is *bored with* it (usually if it is an activity) or *by* it (more usually if it is a person, engaging in prolific acts of boredom-inducing behaviour). So one might say 'I am bored with football' or 'Mary was bored by John', though the prepositions may be alternated. But it is highly inelegant to write 'I am bored *of* football' or 'Mary was bored *of* John'; and the BBC website demonstrated this in September 2023 with the coarse headline 'Bored of beef?' *See also* **prepositions, wrong**.

Born and **borne** The former participle describes the coming into existence of a human being, an animal or even a product or an idea: 'I was born over sixty years ago', for example, or 'our puppies were born last Saturday', or, as a metaphor, 'in 1959 the Mini was born'. The active verb is *to bear* – 'she hoped to bear children' or 'she bore five children in their first decade of marriage'. *Borne* is the past participle of the verb *to bear* when used in contexts other than that of giving birth, meaning simply to carry, as in 'my business has borne the brunt of the recession', or 'events have borne out the truth of your assertion'. It is perhaps more familiar in the passive voice: a translation from Ovid has it that 'the burden which is well borne becomes light'; or there is Gore Vidal's 'I have always been a conservative cross, borne sadly by liberal friends'. Sadly, a card in a popular *Lord of the Rings* game is entitled 'born aloft', which may have an unfortunate effect on the impressionable. *See also* **bare and bear**.

Both The positioning of this word requires care if one is to avoid ambiguity or downright mis-statement. 'We should like to see you both for lunch' raises the question what else we might like to see them for: 'both for lunch and for dinner' perhaps? It would be far clearer to say 'we should like to see both of you for lunch', which admits of no other meaning. Similarly, asking two people 'could you both come to lunch' leaves the readers or interlocutors waiting to discover what other pleasure might await them. Again, asking 'could both of you come' is far clearer. *See also* **only**.

Brilliant This is an adjective that, like **interesting**, is often a confidence trick, especially when used in any form of publicity. Newspapers often plaster on the front pages a trailer for a 'brilliant' article inside (which it rarely is), written by a 'brilliant' journalist (usually a matter of debate) that combine to make the paper 'brilliant'. The word has a legitimate metaphorical usage – in being deployed to describe Einstein, or someone of that sort. MailOnline loves the word: 'Woman, 26, details her brilliant "mom [*sic*] hack" for Christmas shopping', it announced in November 2023; but even the elevated *Times*, in the same month, wrote that 'the doctor who does my Botox has created a brilliant cleanser'. In the sports pages the word has become so ubiquitous – anyone scoring a goal or a century is automatically 'brilliant' – that it appears to have lost any meaning whatsoever. Instead of using this word, writers or speakers should search for another that helps convey why something might be considered 'brilliant'. The word does have its legitimate usages, as in 'the sun at noon was almost blindingly brilliant' or 'the jewel shone brilliantly'. *See also* **word inflation**.

Bring to the table   It would be charming if this were to do with feeding people, but it is another perplexing example of **corporate speak**, and refers to what corporate speak would also term an individual's 'skill-set'. So when considering whether to hire (or, indeed, fire) an employee, some swaggering boss will demand: 'What does she bring to the table?' Asking what talents she possesses that the firm could valuably use seems to be too easy.

Broadly speaking   Almost always an entirely pointless phrase, used as a filler while the speaker or writer is thinking of something intelligent to say. It is to be avoided in serious writing. *See also* **as a matter of fact, at the end of the day, it goes without saying, to be fair, to be honest** *and* **when all's said and done**.

C

Call out   This phrase is used to indicate what someone did when in distress, or in the context of calling out a doctor to attend an emergency, or what the man conducting a bingo session does with his numbers. However, it is also now an **Americanism** used to describe the public shaming of another individual who has offended against an ever-narrowing definition of **appropriate** public conduct. In the era of identity politics, it is deployed by activists who wish to humiliate someone they believe has **disrespected** their identity (be it racial or sexual) and offer the process as a warning to those who might consider trying. The term and the divisive activity it describes are slowly gaining currency in Britain, but most people are blissfully unaware of either.

Capital and **Capitol**   The former word has many meanings, as an adjective (as in 'he's a capital fellow' or 'he made a capital transfer', to cite two very different ones) and as a noun meaning an accumulation of financial resources – 'he could only pay the fees by breaking into his capital' or 'there was no scope for additional capital spending that year' – or adjectivally in a different sense as an indication of a penalty necessitating loss of life, such as with 'Japan has yet to abolish capital punishment' or 'the jury was reluctant to convict in case he received a capital sentence'. It is perhaps most frequently used as a noun to indicate a place that is a nation's seat of government and principal city – 'Canberra is the capital of Australia', nominalising the adjective from the phrase 'capital city'. In America, the term 'capital city' is also used to describe the seat of government in each of the states. It is not to be confused with *Capitol*, which is the noun used to describe the main government building in the United States in Washington, DC – 'the riot took place outside the Capitol' – and the administrative headquarters of each of the states. Thus: 'The Minnesota State Capitol is in the capital city of St Paul, and the North Dakota State Capitol is in the capital city of Bismarck.'

-cation   A recent vogue among tabloid writers has been to coin words describing the types of holidays some people take. It became especially frequent during the Covid-19 pandemic, when many people failed to take any sort of conventional holiday. Those who don't go away at all are said to take a 'staycation', and those spend their holiday serving others supposedly have something charmlessly called a 'volunteercation'. So far this joke – which appears to have worn thin quite speedily – has not caught on so virulently as **-athon and -thon** or **-gate** or **-ification** or **-nomics** or **-shame**, but these are early days.

Centred around   If you are going to use the verb *to centre* either literally or metaphorically, then it has to be in the form of something centring on or upon something else: this is entirely logical, as a centre is a specific point. *Centred around* is therefore obviously always wrong, and at best questionable is a usage such as 'the clothing industry, centred in the north of Portugal', which appears on page 174 of Professor Tom Gallagher's highly interesting life of Salazar, the Portuguese dictator. It would have been neater to say 'the clothing industry, whose centre was in the north of Portugal'.

Chaos This term, which the dictionary defines as 'a state resembling that of primordial chaos; utter confusion or disorder' is almost always used today to signify a relatively mild disruption or failure: 'Chaos engulfs US House' the BBC reported, hysterically, when in January 2023 the Republican party could not agree on a new Speaker. The matter was settled within hours, and with no loss of life or obvious impediment to the US constitution or the country's governance. When a word with a specific extreme meaning starts being used routinely to mean something much less, it becomes, like a currency reliant on printed money, rapidly devalued. *See also* **word inflation**.

Chase up and **chase down** Both these usages are examples of **prepositions, superfluous**. Somebody who is 'chasing up' an invoice achieves the same end as were he simply to chase it. And cricket commentators have become very fond of saying that a side in the last innings of a match is 'chasing down' a total of 300, when for decades, and to no different effect, they simply chased it.

Choice This is another of those terms whose usages frequently defy logic. In July 2023 Imelda May, a singer and actress (*see* **actor and actress**), gave an interview to the *Irish Independent* in which she said: 'There are two choices when you have kids. One, you f★★k them up, or two, you don't.' What in fact you have is a choice: implicit in the idea of a choice is that the chooser has **alternatives**, or when there are three or more courses of action, options. To say that a chooser has two choices is to suggest that he or she has two separate choices to make about two or more distinct things – such as what food to pick from a menu, and what to drink with it. What Miss May had was not two choices, but a choice.

Chronic Something that is *chronic* is of long duration. Because the adjective is often used to describe some sort of malady many people seem to apply to it a range of other meanings associated with indisposition, varying from 'unpleasant' to 'irritating' – when they hear that someone has 'chronic backache' they assume it means 'bad', 'severe' or 'acute', rather than that it is a long-lasting backache. As a consequence of this misunderstanding of the meaning of the adjective, one sometimes hears people or things that are unsatisfactory described as 'chronic'; such usage is entirely wrong.

Churn In **corporate speak** this does not refer to the vessel in which milk is stored, though it does have some tangential connection to the verb meaning to turn something over. If you hear a big boss talking about his company's 'churn' it is not churning up the ground, but is a reference to the rate at which employees come and go. Normal people should avoid it.

Circle back This is a nonsense phrase. On 4 August 2023 the Japanese English-language news service the *Asahi Shimbun* reported: 'Vicious typhoon set to circle back, threatening Okinawa'. It could *turn back*, but a circle is a continuous and unbroken line; one circles round, or around. The phrase is also, equally preposterously, used in **corporate speak**, where it means that someone incapable of giving another an answer when asked a question will give it later, when he or she has had time to think about it – or, rather, to be told what to think: 'I will circle back to you on that.' It would be far easier to say 'I'll get back to you', and more comprehensible.

Clichés A cliché is a phrase that not only shows no originality of expression, but also, as a consequence, shows no originality of thought. When one reads prose packed with clichés, or hears someone whose speech abounds in them, one knows one is not in the presence of a thoughtful or original mind, and that the speaker or writer cannot be bothered to try to communicate a specific idea or circumstance other than as blandly and lazily as possible. In recent years several popular clichés have come to prominence, notably 'the elephant in the room', used to describe a subject that needs to be discussed but, at the time of uttering the cliché, has not been – as in 'it's all very well saying that John is paid too much, but the elephant in the room is that he's often drunk and is having an affair with his secretary', for example. There are perhaps three stages of the cliché: novelty, when people are struck by its brilliance and are perhaps not entirely clear why it means what it means; general acceptance and the recognition that the cliché, being relatively new, serves a useful purpose; and then boredom or tedium, when everybody seems to be using it, whether relevant or not, and the fight for its survival is on. Use of cliché in that state of decay indicates that the speaker or writer would rather use ready-made phrases rather than think afresh about what needs to be described or reported. This is especially prevalent in **corporate speak**, something founded on cliché and that has the additional function, like most **jargon**, of seeking to exclude outsiders by making the language of those inside largely incomprehensible to them. During the apparently annual crisis in the National Health Service in January 2023 I heard a distinguished medically qualified professor, who should have known better, describe the shortage of social care not simply as the pre-eminent cause of delays in admitting the sick to hospital, but as being 'the only game in town'. This was despite his desperately wanting to be taken seriously; perhaps he was too defeated and tired to think of an original way in which to describe the problem. Sports commentators, perhaps because of the speed with which they have to think to describe an event on the field, are especially prone to cliché;

and there are circumstances such as those in which it is excusable, or in the most routine speech where only a general idea needs to be communicated. It has no place in elegant writing or speech: when one hears outside the closed world of corporate speak that someone has **stepped up to the plate** and **thought outside the box** in order to **push the envelope**, one suspects the speaker has no desire to be taken seriously. Distinct from clichés, even though that is technically what they are, we have proverbs and sayings – 'a stitch in time saves nine' and so on – which as well as being familiar also convey some degree of wisdom: a claim that cannot be made for 'pushing the envelope'.

Close up The verb comes under the category of **prepositions, superfluous** – one can close a house just as meaningfully as closing one up. The noun *close-up* is an entirely blameless usage to indicate a detailed view of a person or object, normally by a photographer or videographer.

Coarse and **course** These homophones – the former an adjective typically meaning rough (whether of a material or a character), the latter a noun having a number of uses including indicating a direction or a programme of formal study – are occasionally confused, usually in someone being described as a 'course individual', which one might interpret as meaning he hangs around racetracks, when in fact his general rudeness and vulgarity are what the writer is seeking to emphasise.

Collide For things to collide, or to have a collision, both have to be moving. So two cars can be said to collide if they hit each other while driving along a road; or two ships can collide at sea or, more rarely, two aircraft in mid-air. But if one hears that a car has 'collided' with a tree or a lamp-post, it says something remarkable about either of those two usually inanimate objects, either of which would have to have been in motion to cause a *collision* with the vehicle. What has happened is that the moving vehicle has simply hit the **stationary** object.

Comedic This pretentious adjective first appeared, according to the dictionary, in 1639: and then hardly again until 1864, when an anonymous contributor to the *Ladies' Companion* wrote that 'the comic element . . . soon associated with itself a *comedic* element, manifested in the representation of manners and characters of the current age . . . I ask pardon for coining this word *comedic*; but *comic*, in the signification which it has gradually assumed, does not express what I mean.' Had she thought harder she might have seen that, in fact, it did. Then George Bernard Shaw, writing in 1897, justified the use of this odd word as follows: 'Speaking of the masters of the comedic spirit (if I call it, as he does, the Comic Spirit, this darkened generation will suppose me to refer to the animal spirits of tomfools and merryandrews).' In their different ways both writers made the excuse that the low connotations of *comic* or *comical* were unsuited to their more refined purposes; but it is quite clear that either would do, without causing any confusion at all, and *comedic* has no need or cause to replace either. For most of the twentieth century the existence of the word was barely obvious; its usage rocketed from about the 1990s, and it has become a self-regarding adjective for those who feel comedy needs to be elevated in serious discussion. Therefore they say someone has 'comedic' talent, not 'comic' talent or talent as a comedian or as a comic actor; or someone is said to have written a 'comedic' script and not a 'comic' one; or is a 'comedic' actor and not a 'comic' one; or a series of events were 'comedic' when properly they were 'comical'. The word in its new ubiquitous incarnation has been imported from America, where the earnestness of many of the inhabitants forces them to take even comedy seriously. It has been readily adopted by speakers of British English who wish to impress others by showing that they are *au courant* with the **jargon** of the Hollywood film industry. *See also* **filmic**.

Community   This word has throughout time had various distinct and useful meanings, such as to describe a group of people living together under common rules (for example, 'a religious community'), a distinct geographical grouping of inhabitants ('the local community') or a group of a secular sort who live as a minority within a majority (such as in 'London's homosexual community' or 'a French community'). But in late years it has been used lazily to describe any group of people at all – 'the caravanning community', 'the gardening community' and, absurdly, I have even heard 'the criminal community'. In each of these examples the straightforward appellations *caravanners*, *gardeners* and *criminals* would have done just as well, and without the stench of cliché.

Compare   Difficulties persist for some people about whether the preposition after this verb should be *to* or *with*. After all, if Shakespeare wrote in a sonnet 'Shall I compare thee to a summer's day?' then he must be right; however, we realise that in *Paradise Lost* Book II Milton wrote 'to compare great things with small' but then in Book X wrote 'if great things to small may be compared', which suggests that in the seventeenth century at least these things were interchangeable. Usage, according to the dictionary, does appear to have regularised since then. If one is using *compare* in the sense of to liken something to something else, then one uses *to*. If one is simply establishing a comparison – 'I wouldn't compare prosecco with Pol Roger' – one uses *with*.

Comparisons, unfinished One too often sees these in advertising slogans. For years a successful sales campaign professed that 'Persil washes whiter'. Whiter than what? Similarly, we used to be told that 'everything in America is bigger and better', and we were never told than what it was bigger and better, doubtless because it was assumed we realised that everything there was bigger and better than everything on the planet, so no detail had to be entered into. These are unwise assumptions. If you are minded to use a comparison, finish it.

Complacent and **complaisant** The former is an adjective meaning a lack of understanding of the possible shortcomings or even dangers of a situation or of a person. The latter adjective is applied to a person unduly willing to fit in with the wishes or demands of others. *Complacent* is sometimes confused with *complaisant* but not, that I have seen, the other way round.

Complement and **compliment** These two words, whether as nouns or verbs, are constantly confused. A *complement* is something that completes another or an experience even to the point of perfection, as in 'the perfect complement to a piece of Stilton is a glass of claret', or, as a verb, 'her social skills complemented his intelligence perfectly'. Or it can signify the full composition of something, as in 'the ship has a complement of nine hundred passengers and crew', or 'the class had reached its complement of twenty pupils and there was no room for another'. A *compliment* is an expression of praise to someone, as in 'he paid her a compliment about her dress', or it can serve as a verb: 'She thanked him for complimenting her on her command of French.'

Compound verbs, pointless   *See* **prepositions, superfluous**.

Comprise   This verb can sometimes cause confusion between its active and passive usages. Without the preposition *of* it means 'to constitute', so one may say 'the membership of the club comprised a thousand people'. With the preposition, it means 'composed of', as in 'the membership of the club was comprised of a thousand people'. Either is correct, the former more economical.

Connect   This is often used in **corporate speak** to mean 'meet', as in 'Can we connect and talk about this?' It has the smell of **jargon** about it and should be avoided by those who would rather not be thought pretentious; it may, however, be a valuable usage to those in the corporate world who wish to indicate that they have gone native, and ceased to have minds of their own.

Consult   The etymology of this verb includes the anglicisation of the Latin preposition *cum*, meaning 'with': it is therefore a tautology to say, as the BBC did in November 2023, 'British Steel to consult with public over plans to shut furnaces', and for the *Star*, a Sheffield newspaper, to write that 'Sunak says councils must consult with communities before trees are felled'. It would be enough to say that British Steel would consult the public, and that councils would consult communities. No preposition is necessary. A similar but not identical problem is encountered with **meet**, and 'consult with' is becoming almost as common.

Continually and **continuously**   These do not have the same meaning. The former describes an occurrence that happens repeatedly, as in 'he continually asks me for money'.

The latter means a process that never stops, for example 'the heating is on continuously'. If it were on 'continually' it would mean it kept going on and off; if the importunate man 'continuously' asked for money he would be doing it twenty-four hours a day.

Contractual and **contractural**   The dictionary gives the latter as a variant of the former, itself an adjective not apparently seen before 1861, but it is not a satisfactory or necessary alternative, rather one used in confusion. *Contractual* is the correct term to use in relation to a contract or similar document that defines obligations between two parties, as in 'I have a contractual duty to oversee the induction process'. The noun *contracture* is a medical term used to describe rigidity in the muscles or joints, and *contractural* is the adjective related to it.

Coronated   In the meaning of 'crowned', as at a coronation, the dictionary offers only four examples between 1623 and 1847, since when it had not been spotted – and with *crowned* such a straightforward and familiar verb, there was absolutely no need why it should be. However, on 21 February 2023 MailOnline, its writer perhaps showing a careful knowledge of early-seventeenth-century English, announced that the King would be 'coronated in a grand ceremony on 6 May'. As this historic ceremony approached, several other manifestations of this daft word were spotted, but never used by anyone whom one would indeed regard as an authority on the subject.

Corporate speak   This is the **jargon** used by people who run, or help to run, big businesses, and is especially beloved by people who run human resources departments (what earlier generations quite happily and comprehensibly called 'personnel'). It can prove highly contagious to those who wish to suck up to their superiors, or just wish to be sure to fit in with them in order not to be ruled out for promotion: something that, paradoxically, seems to occur easily to those who otherwise exhibit a mind of their own. Frequent use of it may assist a bonding process within a closed environment; but it suppresses the individuality of those who use it, and may even encourage others to think them somewhat moronic and parrot-like. Its frequent repetition, like that of all clichés, diminishes the effectiveness of communication in businesses that otherwise claim to pride themselves upon it. Much of it originates from that cradle of modern corporate culture, the United States, and therefore contains many references that are metaphors drawn from American life, notably from sport and particularly from baseball. It is a jargon often unintelligible to those outside, but it enables the frequently pointless people who speak it fluently to pretend they are accomplishing something useful, and to appear impressive to underlings who have developed insufficient reserves of cynicism. *See* **bandwidth, churn, circle back, connect, diarise, drill down, escalate, glass ceiling, going forward, going the extra mile, not a problem, offline (take something), onboarding, oriented, own, park it, pivot, punching their weight, push the envelope, reach out, resurface, revisit, run it up the flagpole, stakeholders, step up to the plate, talk live, talk to, think outside the box, tools, touching base, utilise, walk back** *and* **walk someone through** and for a peerless example of corporate speak, *see* **people**. *See also* **clichés**.

Coruscating A thoughtful article in the *Observer* in September 2023 pointed out that *coruscating*, from the Latin verb *coruscare*, meaning to 'vibrate', 'glitter' or 'sparkle', and which the dictionary always used to define as meaning 'glittering' or 'sparkling', has now come to be used when a speaker or writer probably ought to have used *excoriating*. That word, from the Latin verb *excoriare*, to 'strip off the hide', similarly in English means to remove the skin from something, and has had a figurative meaning for three hundred years. So if someone delivers an 'excoriating attack' it is a metaphorical flaying, whereas a 'coruscating attack' is a sparkling or glittering one. The politics.co.uk website, for example, described the testimony Dominic Cummings gave to the Covid inquiry in November 2023 as 'coruscating' in the way it savaged his former Downing Street colleagues during the 2020 pandemic. Never wishing to cause offence to those who simply can't, or won't, speak English properly, people were quoted in the *Observer* article saying that change was a wonderful thing and should be celebrated, and that there should be no complaint about this new usage of an old verb, never mind that it arose out of confusion. Surely, though, that depends on the reason for the change? A word that changes its meaning because it comes to describe something that never used to exist is one thing; one that changes because people cannot be bothered to check its genuine meaning is quite another. *See also* **flaunt and flout** *and* **pristine**.

Could of   In speech, this is an ignorant coinage by those who do not realise that they are meant to be saying 'could have'. It is a straightforward grammatical error in writing and must be avoided. A similar error is made with **should of** and **would of** and even **might of**.

Counsel   The plural of this noun is *counsel*, not, as I heard a BBC reporter say in December 2023, 'counsels'. One correctly says that 'Mrs Mary Smith KC and Mr John Brown were counsel representing the accused'. It should not be confused with the noun *council*, which is a deliberative body with some powers of governance. *See also* **Privy Council**.

Cowardly I recall a comedian some years ago making a somewhat tasteless, but nonetheless telling, joke about a newspaper headline that read 'worst plane crash ever', and asking what, therefore, was the best? A similar thought occurs when one reads headlines about 'cowardly attacks' on people by criminals who rob them. One such example was this story from the *Yorkshire Post* in 2016 about a pair of thugs who attacked a defenceless woman in the street, causing her serious injuries, purely to steal some goods: '"Cowardly" Sheffield robbers who attacked woman for £15 of shopping are jailed'. To be fair to the paper they were quoting a policeman who dismissed what happened as a 'cowardly attack'; and doubtless the policeman meant that the two thugs chose a soft target, rather than try to attack two men their own size who might have given as good as, or better than, they got. But it does, like the 'worst plane crash', raise the moral question of whether there can ever be a courageous or brave robbery – whether it would have been in some way noble for them to have attacked two hulking great men instead. *Brutal*, *vicious* or *cruel* would have served better as adjectives, even though the thugs were certainly behaving in a cowardly fashion in picking on a single woman. It is unfortunate, however, that the usage remains frequent, especially when the victim of a violent crime is a child, woman or a disabled person.

Crackdown This word – or rather words, for it was originally *crack down* – is cited in the dictionary as first appearing as a noun in 1935, to mean an instance of 'legal or disciplinary severity' or 'repression': 'the government has ordered a crack down on tax evasion'. It later became hyphenated and then finally joined in the 1960s. The verb followed in 1940 and, pending revision, remains two words according to the dictionary – 'the school said it would crack down on drugs use'. As a phrase it was doubtless originally useful, being coined to describe an act by authority on the criminal, lax or decadent. Now, however, it is ubiquitous: everyone appears to be having crackdowns, or is cracking down, on just about everything else. On one day in September 2023 the media reported 'crackdowns' by the EU on 'big tech', global regulators on decentralised finance, the IRS on 1,600 millionaires, Pakistan on hoarders, Israeli police on predatory taxi drivers, Durham police on illegal dirt bikes, Italy on youth crime, Australia on AI-created child porn, Norfolk County Council on under-age vape use, Pakistan (again) on illegal dollar trade, China on fraud, Snapchat on age-inappropriate content, New York on reckless driving, Iran on dissent and Greater Manchester police on criminals. And that was only the start. One wonders two things: first, whatever all these headline writers would have done before 1935, other than find some non-clichéd way of communicating the idea freshly and originally; and second, whether, with this saturation usage, the noun *crackdown* or the verbal usage *to crack down* (which will doubtless soon merge into one word) actually means anything to any reader any longer, or just goes in one ear and out the other.

Credible and **credulous**   The former is applied to something that is believable; the latter to someone who will believe anything. For example, a Middle East pressure group, CAMERA, wrote on its website in November 2023 that 'Reuters legitimizes wild conspiracy theory with credulous headline'. The headline was, in fact, *credible*: it would be anyone who believed it represented the whole story who was *credulous*. In the same month the LabourList website said the Conservative government's autumn financial statement was 'stretching credulity to breaking point'. Since the article appeared to be about the government's alleged dishonesty, not the public's alleged stupidity, the writer almost certainly meant *credibility*. *See also* **incredible and incredulous**.

Crescendo One often hears or reads of something 'rising to', or increasingly 'hitting' a crescendo. These are absurd phrases that betray an ignorance of what a crescendo actually is. It is not the loudest point in a piece of music; it is the process of the music getting louder over a sequence of notes. The Italian word translates literally as 'growth', 'rise' or 'escalation'.

Curb and **kerb** The former as a noun is a limit, and as a verb means to limit or restrain – 'curb your enthusiasm'; the second, which is only a noun (for the moment) is the edge of a pavement. Perhaps some confusion arises from the fact that, in American English, the pavement edge is spelt like the verb. On 5 December 2021 MailOnline reported the prospect of a 'draconian kerb' on freedom being introduced to restrict the spread of the coronavirus. The imagination runs riot.

Currant and **current** The former is a noun and refers to a small edible fruit, either a berry or a raisin, that has been desiccated; the latter, as a noun, refers to the flow of some continuous force, be it a water course or electricity – 'the river's current tended to be strong' or 'there was no current coming through to the kitchen from the mains'. As an adjective, *current* means 'of the moment', as in 'current affairs' or 'he was not her current boyfriend'. On 28 November 2023 the Egypt Today website failed to make the distinction, saying about the Israel–Hamas conflict raging at the time that talks took place in the hope of 'the extension of the currant ceasefire', which seemed to offer a new insight into weapons technology.

D

Daily basis, on a This is another tediously popular phrase that includes three entirely redundant words out of the four it contains and betrays the gormlessness of those who use it. There is, if one pauses to think about it, no difference in meaning between 'they saw each other daily' and 'they saw each other on a daily basis'.

Data This is a plural noun; its singular is *datum*. 'The data is interesting', written by the normally precise Michael Atherton in September 2022 about an investigation into the quality of cricket, is as wrong as writing 'the referenda is interesting'. However, anyone today who utters the entirely correct phrase 'the data are rather worrying' is likely to be regarded as a dangerous intellectual. *See also* **bacteria** *and* **media**.

Debate When one reads about two people debating each other one has encountered an American usage consistent with that variant of the language's attempt to abolish the preposition. One debates a motion, an idea or a point; but one debates against another, each other or an opponent. This can cause ambiguity: 'Smith wanted to debate Jones' suggests to British ears that Smith wants to take part in a debate on the subject of Jones, or of some aspect of him. To American ears the phrase indicates that Smith wishes to take part in a debate against Jones. *See also* **prepositions, missing**.

Decimation   This was a punishment in the Roman army, whereby one man in ten (the Latin for *tenth* being *decimus*) was put to death *pour encourager les autres*. In metaphorical usage something reduced in scale by a tenth could correctly be said to have been *decimated* : but it now is used to describe any circumstance in which some serious degree of destruction, carnage or wreck has taken place (usually far in excess of a tenth of the whole), and therefore is on the road to becoming meaningless. MailOnline proved the point on 7 August 2023 when writing that 'Russians are looking to buy cheap apartments "with sea views" in Mariupol a year after Putin's forces decimated the city'. The report goes on to say that the siege of 2022 had ended up 'damaging or destroying roughly 90 per cent of its buildings'. Surrender seems to have happened on this abuse of the language, with perpetrators sneering at those who insist on the correct usage as deranged pedants: it is as though it has been weaponised (to deploy a very popular verb recently created from a noun) in some variant of the class war, with those who believe that anything goes thumbing their noses at classically educated purists.

Deliver   As with the verb to **warn**, this is one that requires an object. One delivers the post, or the milk, or a blow. However, since politics has become a branch of the social services the verb *to deliver* has come to mean that somebody in public life has done, or more usually promises to do, his or her job properly in ensuring the efficient commission of whatever service he or she is responsible for. A noun is seldom involved, as we are all supposed to understand this statist **jargon**: and the absence of a noun also helps achieve the aim of many politicians, which is to avoid detail. The Politico website on 6 August 2023 gave a typical example when it asked: 'Is Italy's Meloni failing to deliver for women?' Deliver what, one might ask? And Priti Patel, the then Home Secretary, said of a former chief constable to whom she was paying a tribute: 'He was passionate about delivering for the people of Leicestershire.' It will come as no surprise to many that some politicians are incapable of thinking about the meaning of what they say. *See also* **passionate** *and* **political language, misuse of**.

Demoralised   This adjective is used to describe a person or a group of people who have been drained of their spirit or enthusiasm. It does not mean they have been drained of their morals. *See* **moral and morale**.

Deprecate and **depreciate**   The latter (an intransitive **verb**: *see Appendix*) is sometimes mistakenly used in place of the former (a transitive), though I have yet to spot an example of this happening the other way round. In the sentence 'Mary deprecated John's attitude towards their neighbours', Mary is registering her disapproval of the way John feels about the people next door. When she says that 'the car's value depreciated by 10 per cent the moment it left the showroom' she means that the value of the vehicle declined by that amount. I suspect people misuse the verb *depreciate* – 'she depreciated the way he treated her' – because they may think it is the opposite of *appreciate*. In the sense of an asset, *depreciate* is the opposite in meaning to *appreciate* ('his investments had appreciated by several thousands during the year'). However, in the sense of offering esteem ('I really appreciate his talent for diplomacy'), it would not be correct, let alone idiomatic, English to indicate a lack of regard by saying one *depreciated* another.

Desert and **dessert**   The most frequent usage of the former is to describe a vast geographical area of complete aridity, as in the Sahara Desert or the Kalahari Desert, or metaphorically to describe another form of barrenness – 'the local town was a cultural desert'. But *desert* spelt in the same way, though pronounced in the same fashion as *dessert*, can act as the noun derived from the verb *to deserve* – if one deserves something it is one's *desert*, as in the phrase 'he had his just deserts'. The word, pronounced in the same way, also acts as a verb meaning to leave a place, a person or an institution, and often not with honourable connotations; as in 'he decided to desert his wife and children', or 'he had had enough of fighting and decided to desert from the Army'. It is idiomatic in British English that, when the verb is used about abandoning an institution, it requires the preposition *from* – one may *desert* one's wife and children, but one *deserts from* the Army, Royal Navy or Royal Air Force. In culinary terms, *dessert* is a late or final course of a meal, usually but not exclusively comprising sweet foods.

Devastation   If the tabloid press (and sometimes other media that should know better) have to report either a personal calamity for someone (especially, it seems, a celebrity) or a regrettable incident of any severity, the people concerned are inevitably 'devastated' and the result is 'devastation'. Anyone who suffers as a result of such a calamity is inevitably 'devastated'. Both words have legitimate and valuable usages: in August 2023 Reuters reported how 'Typhoon Doksuri cuts path of devastation across China', and results were in keeping with the main dictionary definition of the verb from which the noun derives, which is to 'lay waste, ravage or render desolate'. At around the same time the *Manchester Evening News* reported that the parents of a small child 'were given the devastating news' that he had leukaemia. The news was certainly awful, distressing, shocking, sad and deeply worrying: but even when one accepts that the term is being used figuratively or metaphorically (and usage statistics suggest its deployment in this way has increased since the invention of the tabloid press) *devastating* does have near-apocalyptic connotations. In the sad case of this family, the use of the term suggests that this grave predicament would have wiped out the child's poor parents – rather than leave them determined to help him fight the terrible affliction and care for him during a debilitating programme of treatment: which is exactly what they did. *Devastation* is another symptom of **word inflation**, and it prevents readers from grasping the reality of unfortunate matters such as the story related, because the routine use of an exaggerated term devalues its effect.

Dialects These are not the same as accents, a term with which they are sometimes confused – 'he spoke in a broad Yorkshire dialect' ought to mean he used elements of vocabulary distinct to Yorkshire, but some people mean it to indicate that he simply sounded like the late Fred Trueman or Sir Geoffrey Boycott, the celebrated cricketers and cricket commentators – although one dialect will usually be spoken in an accent different from that of another dialect. A *dialect* is a distinct vocabulary used in a locality, sometimes with its own variations of grammar, while an *accent* is the fashion in which non-dialect words are pronounced and sound different from when spoken in other accents. Accents remain, but as mass literacy and mass communications have standardised British English to an extent since the late nineteenth century, so dialects have been marginalised: but dialect words still exist in some regions of the country that have been incorporated into standard English, and it is not wrong to use them in speech. Using them in a written communication to a non-dialect speaker might, however, lead to incomprehension.

Diarise A correspondent to *The Daily Telegraph* in October 2023 asserted that the verb *diarise* existed: he knew, he said, because he had 'googled' it, thus wittily making the point that nouns become verbs – and *googled* is an ideal example of the legitimate evolution of language, because a generation ago Google did not exist, and its arrival and the significant place it has assumed in the lives of billions of people necessitates a new language around it. Diaries, by contrast, have existed for centuries: and when an appointment was what some people now call 'diarised', it was what was then called 'scheduled'. *Diarised* is part of **corporate speak**, which rather likes **nouns used as verbs**. Those who use it can decide whether they are embodying linguistic progress, or are simply wrecking the English language through laziness.

Different   Just as one thing differs from another, so something or someone is always different from something or someone else. I have yet to hear or see anyone say or write that this differs than that, or differs to that. Perhaps I have led a sheltered life. However, one is besieged by the incorrect usages 'different than' or 'different to'. The *Investors' Chronicle* in July 2023 ran an article entitled 'Why the UK's mortgage chaos is different to everyone else's' (*see also* **chaos**); the following month the *Guardian* ran a feature under the headline 'When my son got his first job, I was faced with a different world than the one I grew up in'. Americans are fond of 'different than', not that the *Guardian* is an American newspaper; but in correct British English it is always *different from*. See also **prepositions, wrong**.

Disapprove   *See* **approve and disapprove**.

Discrete and **discreet**   The use of *discrete*, from the Latin *discretus* and the French *discret*, dates back (according to the dictionary) to the late fourteenth century; and, like the words from which it derives, means 'distinct', or 'separate'. Its frequency of usage appears (according to the statistics published by the dictionary) to have multiplied greatly during the twentieth century, not least in academic (and especially scientific and technical) writing as the learned showed off to each other, but also because a regrettably large number of people thought it was simply a fancy, alternative spelling of *discreet*. That word, meaning 'behaving or speaking in a fashion to avoid causing shame or embarrassment for oneself or for others, and exhibiting delicate judgement', also dates from the late fourteenth century, and is likewise derived from *discretus*, but in its post-classical sense of meaning 'prudent', and from *discret* in its sense of meaning 'capable of keeping secrets'. The two English words are not interchangeable today, despite occasional appearances to the contrary. The website Hospitality.net confused them when writing a puff for a business's new artistic director in November 2023, saying that 'Maxime constantly works with a more discrete and demanding customer base on sophisticated, modern projects'. It was quite clear from the context that it should have said *discreet*.

Disinterested and **uninterested** The *Daily Star* in July 2023 announced that Roméo Lavia, a footballer, was 'disinterested' in playing a friendly match for Liverpool. He wasn't. He was *uninterested* in doing do. *Disinterest* means objectivity: a judge hears a court case with complete disinterest, in that he does not take sides but listens to the arguments presented by each; the word indicates a lack of partisanship or prejudice. *Uninterest* is a state of simply not caring, or of having no interest at all – as in 'he was entirely uninterested in football', meaning the sport was of no interest to him whatsoever. When thunderstorms obliged Ryanair to divert a planeload of passengers bound for Marrakech to another airport 120 miles away, one of them complained bitterly to the *Daily Record* alleging that there was 'zero care or attention from

Ryanair – no planning for emergency situations like this – disinterested staff', when he meant they were 'uninterested'. The airline was said in another newspaper report to have displayed 'uninterest' in the fate of its customers, the use of which noun was correct.

Disrespect   While the noun *disrespect* and the adjective *disrespectful* have long been in frequent and normal usage, the verb *disrespect* – though first cited in 1638 by the dictionary – was quite infrequently used until towards the end of the twentieth century, when statistics show that its deployment increased dramatically. By the early 2000s it became fashionable for many people (and quite often those who merited little or no respect at all, such as criminals and gangsters) to talk about others who had 'disrespected' them by not treating them with the regard or ceremony they felt (almost inevitably wrongly) was theirs by right. Perhaps they used this odd word because it was quicker than the phrase 'showed me insufficient respect', of which we ought to be in favour as economy of expression. But what is wrong with the good old-fashioned words *insulted*, or *offended*, or *affronted*, or possibly even the phrase 'was rude to', the flourishing over the centuries of all of which kept *disrespect* as a verb at a distance? The term is now in slang shortened to *dis*, as in 'he dissed my girlfriend', to be strenuously avoided by anyone who is, and wishes to remain, unfamiliar with the internal workings of the criminal justice system.

Dive   It is doubtless only a matter of time, but for the moment the past participle of the verb *to dive* is *dived*, not the American *dove*. See **Americanisms**.

Divide up   There is no difference between dividing up a sum of money and dividing it, except that the former phrase contains an entirely pointless word that adds nothing to the meaning. *See* **prepositions, superfluous**.

Do   The past tense is *did*, not *done*, which is the past participle. One occasionally sees ex-convicts interviewed on television and saying how 'I done five years inside' or the even less savoury 'I done him in'. 'Done' in this respect is not a usage for civilised people. *Do* has, in the manner of **get**, become a catch-all verb, used rather too often when a more precise verb would be better: such as in 'he was done for drink-driving' when we mean 'he was prosecuted for drink-driving'.

Double down   This is a popular **Americanism** that means to dig one's heels in, or to stand by something one has done or said. It has infiltrated British English thanks to the assiduous efforts of those who enjoy speaking in the manner of an American film or television character. Where once they would have said 'he stands by what he said' they now say 'he doubled down on what he said'. The dictionary traces its use back to the card game pontoon, and gives its first figurative usage as 2004, in the *New York Times*. Should one crave to appear American, affecting such idioms is as good a weapon as any.

Double genitive   In an article in the *New Yorker* (22 November 2021) about H. G. Wells, the writer stated: 'P. G. Wodehouse, who was, improbably, a good friend of Wells's . . .' However, this usage raises the question 'A good friend of Wells's what?' The preposition is enough: the writer could simply have said 'a good friend of Wells'. The apostrophe and extra 's' are redundant. Similar mistakes are made with all sorts of other objects or people who belong to someone – 'it was an idea of John's', for example, though it would be idiomatic to say 'it was John's idea', in which the possessive is essential. 'Friend of' seems the most promiscuous cause; though one also hears 'a sister of Jack's', or 'a symphony of Mahler's', or 'a novel of Dickens's' when in each case the final possessive could, and should, be dispensed with.

Double negative Members of the 'anything goes' sect of English specialists say that these are perfectly all right, because a second negative adds emphasis to the first. This is a little like saying that the sun rises in the evening, for it is not and cannot be true. 'I didn't do nothing' or 'I never did nothing' quite obviously mean 'I did do something'. It patronises and disadvantages those poorly educated people who use such a construction when those who consider themselves their intellectual superiors pretend otherwise. Where would that leave us with the equally familiar 'I didn't do nothing to no one'? While the proverbial blind eye might be turned to such phrases in casual speech, they are entirely unacceptable in formal writing, and inconsistent with the best style.

Dove This is a bird, and rhymes with 'love'. For the American verb form, which rhymes with 'Hove' and is expressly not how the verb is conjugated in British English, *see* **dive**. *See also* **Americanisms**.

Drill down This is what, until fossil fuels are history, oil prospectors do to find their liquid gold. However, it has become a term of **corporate speak**, and means to investigate a problem or state of affairs more intensely. Outsiders will wonder why *analyse* does not work just as well. One reason is that it does not exclude quite so completely those who have not been initiated into the private language.

Due to and **owing to** These two phrases have become interchangeable and both are now widely regarded as adverbial. However, purists insist on a distinction between them. Traditional usage has had it that *due to* can only be used adjectivally, whereas *owing to* is adverbial. Therefore, one would write 'she divorced her husband owing to his philandering' but 'her divorce from her husband was due to his philandering'. A test of correct usage is when *owing to* can be replaced by 'because of', and *due to* can be replaced by 'caused by': as is the case in these examples.

E

Edgy   This adjective was always used to signify someone in a highly nervous or sensitive state who might lose his or her composure at any moment, and the dictionary has defined it as having had that meaning since the early nineteenth century. It has now become a term used to describe the metaphorical cutting edge of fashion. In August 2023 *Hello!* magazine shared with its readers news that 'Reese Witherspoon's lookalike daughter Ava showcase [*sic*] bold tattoos in edgy selfie', and went on to say how 'the 23-year-old has an edgy sense of fashion'. A few days earlier the American edition of *Elle* ran a feature with the title 'Symbols of Courage: 5 Edgy Jewelry Pieces'. This adjective, whose now common meaning seems to have originated in America in the 1970s, has reached saturation levels of usage, being applied not just to fashion or personal appearance, but to plays, works of art, books and indeed anything that might be described as new, original or radical. Like all saturation usages, it suggests a severe lack of imagination on the part of the writers in looking for a more precise and less anaesthetised adjective, and an unfortunate predisposition to the herd mentality.

Effect   *See* **affect and effect**.

Effeminate and **effete**   One often sees or hears the latter where the former is intended. *Effeminate* is an adjective applied to a man who displays characteristics usually associated with a woman, though the dictionary rules some usages as 'offensive', and context and taste are important when deploying the term. So one should regard sentences such as 'the manner in which he walked seemed somewhat effeminate' as statements of fact rather than judgements. *Effete* is defined by the dictionary as describing something that 'has exhausted its vigour and energy', or persons who are 'weak, ineffectual, degenerate'. This is not remotely the same thing as 'effeminate', but despite that the dictionary adds 'more recently, effeminate', which may be interpreted either as the editors noting a recent usage of a word in a different way, or simply pandering to ignorance. One wonders what all those effeminate men who are not 'weak, ineffectual, degenerate' or anything of the sort choose to make of this new definition.

Either When used as a pronoun, this should be singular – 'Is either of you prepared to do this?' Such a question is addressed to two people (*either* cannot logically be used with more than two) and it demands a response from each as an individual. 'Are either of you' is colloquial. The use of *either* in such a question is distinct from the use of *both* – if the question was 'Are both of you prepared to do this?' it would invite an answer from both people as a couple, not each of the two as an individual. *See also* **neither** *and* **none**.

Eke out This term is correctly used to describe the idea of 'making do' financially until more income arrives – 'she eked out their living by repeatedly mending her and her children's clothes', for example, or other means of stretching out resources. It does not mean 'to earn', a context in which one too frequently hears it used: for example, the football website Breaking the Lines ran a headline in September 2023 describing 'How Arsenal Eked Out a Narrow Win against Manchester United at the Emirates'. Nor does it mean 'to extend', which is what is intended in phrases such as 'they managed to eke out their holiday until the following Monday'.

Elder and **younger**   One sometimes hears proud parents speak of their 'elder' son or 'younger' daughter when one knows they have three or more of each gender; or of an 'elder' or 'younger' child when they have at least three children. These comparative adjectives can be used only when there are just two sons, daughters or children at issue. When there are three or more, the most senior is the eldest, the most junior the youngest. *Eldest* is idiomatic but there is nothing wrong with *oldest*, though its idiomatic use has come to be in descriptions of superlatives – 'the oldest man in Britain', 'the oldest house in England' and so on. For use as a noun it should always, idiomatically, be *elder* and not *older* – 'of my two sons, the elder is the more stupid' – whereas for adjectival use *older* is usual – 'I wore my older coat to the match'. *Eldest* or *oldest* may only be used when referring to three or more people or things: to say 'the eldest of our two sons' would be entirely wrong. *See also* **former** *and* **latter**.

Emergency   We have reached the stage where any chronic state of affairs that is objected to by pressure groups becomes an 'emergency', presumably in order to encourage others to worry or even to panic about it. We hear daily about the climate emergency, though unlike most emergencies this is not going to end in a rapid disaster if not addressed – the terrible effects widely predicted will take decades at least, so the situation would, rather, seem to constitute a crisis (which can continue indefinitely). An *emergency* is a predicament that demands urgent attention, or catastrophe will follow imminently: but even then the word is occasionally used in a preposterous context, such as the footballer Wayne Rooney being described as suffering 'a fashion emergency' before having to appear in a defamation trial when he discovered that none of his suits fitted. It is a term best saved for such genuine horrors as children being about to starve in a famine unless others intervene, or men trapped underground in mineshafts having to be rescued before their oxygen supply runs out.

Emotional   This tiresomely overused adjective is deployed to describe almost any expression of feeling, and therefore has become meaningless. Simply saying 'hello' to a casual acquaintance is the product of some small degree of emotion – if one had no fellow feeling for the person at all one probably would not bother – and therefore it might feasibly be labelled *emotional* just as a howling display of grief at a funeral might. If one wants to describe the latter, then adjectives such as *distraught*, *tearful* or the good old-fashioned *grief-stricken* or *bereft* should be used. There is an even wider lexicon of words that can be used to describe joy; Sky News in January 2024 spoke of 'an emotional moment' when Emma Raducanu, the tennis player, won a match in New Zealand. Joyous? Uplifting? The possibilities do not require a thesaurus. *See also* **evocative**.

Enamoured in   One is enamoured *of* something ('his waistline suggested he was enamoured of cream cakes'), not enamoured *in* it, though the latter solecism occasionally occurs. I was surprised to see that the *Oxford Learner's Dictionaries* suggest the usage 'enamoured with', which is just as wrong. As for 'enamoured by', someone who is 'enamoured by dogs' suggests he or she has dogs madly in love with him or her.

Enormity The death of Queen Elizabeth II in September 2022 prompted a number of commentators to lucubrate about the 'enormity' of the event. The word has since the fifteenth century meant, according to the dictionary, 'deviation from moral or legal rectitude. In later use influenced by enormous. Extreme or monstrous wickedness.' The death of this 96-year-old woman was deeply sad, the end of an epoch and something that occasioned a moment of profound reflection: but it was not an extreme or monstrous wickedness. The dictionary also says that the noun's use to describe something of hugeness or vastness is incorrect, and so it is: those who described the late Queen's death as an 'enormity' were presumably seeking to convey its 'enormousness' in the history and consciousness of the British people and indeed of many others around the world who held her in special regard. This again is an American disease. President Obama, a highly educated man, in his victory speech in 2008 used it in the sense that is wrong to British ears, but his fellow Americans perceived no problem with his diction at all.

Ensure This verb means 'to make sure that something happens', as in 'he tied up his dog to ensure it would not run away' or 'she left early enough to ensure that she caught her train'. This verb appears to play little part in American English, where its place is mostly taken by **insure** – 'she insured her daughter was kept safe'. To avoid confusion with similar verbs, *see* **assure, ensure and insure**.

Epic Examples of the great epics were *The Iliad* and *The Odyssey*, long poems that depicted heroic deeds by great people. Then in the early twentieth century Hollywood stole the adjective and the noun to signify films that were about heroism and, while usually being of long duration themselves (in cinematic terms), covered a long period of time. In another case of **word inflation,** *epic* has come to mean anything large or of long duration, and therefore the impact of its original meaning risks becoming devalued. For example, the *New Yorker*, on 8 August 2022, talked of Britain's 'epic heatwave' of the previous month; a year later the Arsenal Football Club website offered '55 epic photos from our Community Shield win', which seemed to take the adjective to even wilder shores of definition: the notion of how a photograph can be 'epic' would defeat most of us. But then *Hello!* magazine told readers that 'Halle Berry reveals epic hair transformation', so clearly anything is possible on this word's epic journey to utter meaninglessness. *See also* **adjectives, hyperbolic.**

Erstwhile This is an archaic and now rather pompous way of saying 'former'. 'He is an erstwhile teacher' means he is a former, retired, or ex-teacher. It is a word much beloved of those who feel that such affectations make them appear intelligent.

Escalate When dissatisfied with the services of a company of whom I was a client (and paying handsomely for the privilege) I telephoned the customer services department, where the person who took the call agreed that her firm had behaved with a lack of professionalism. To make the point that those in charge would be made aware of the various failings, she said she would 'escalate this to management'. This is now common **corporate speak** to create the impression that one's grievance is being sent on a precipitate upward journey. The dictionary says the figurative use of the verb means 'to increase or develop by successive stages', and refers to the idea of a conventional war developing into a nuclear one. This does not help us with 'escalating' a complaint to management. The speaker isn't developing the complaint, he or she is simply ensuring it reaches a place where something might actually be done about it. This used to be called 'bringing it to the attention of the right person', and it would be better if it still were.

Euphemism English has often reflected a desire for euphemism, or what might most plainly be termed not calling a spade a spade. However, it reached a peak with the Victorians and has enjoyed a revival with the young generation of today, who feel they need to avoid being upset by the mere mention of certain specific words. They have that in common with their great-great-grandparents. Past generations were obsessed with suppressing straightforward discussion of anything concerning sexual organs or the reproductive functions, and indeed with anything to do with the lavatory and what might go on there, and therefore devised terms to refer to such things if any such reference should become necessary. Thus fornicators and married couples 'slept with each other' rather than engaged in sexual intercourse; and all sorts of names were devised for the sexual organs, though some of these were slang and even more offensive than the anatomical terms they replaced. Those urinating were 'passing water' (which sounds like a coach ride along the shore of Lake Windermere), those defecating were 'having a movement' (perhaps experiencing some Beethoven, or devising a political organisation). One of the principal areas of euphemism today is death, one presumes because in our secular age so many people would rather pretend it doesn't exist (which, as Wittgenstein argued, it didn't): so rather than *died* we have 'passed away', 'passed on', 'passed over' and also simply 'passed', which brings us back to matters connected with defecation; or 'taken', or 'gone before', or 'fallen asleep' (all of which risk confusion with more literal interpretations). And a dead person becomes 'the departed' – 'the departed left me well provided for' – as if he or she has gone on holiday or moved to a different part of the country.

A branch of euphemism is the thin disguising of words deemed unacceptable, the selection of which changes with each new era. Until recently, when these words began appearing on television nightly, the most common were f★★★, c★★★ and s★★★, which was how they were written, other than when editors dared not even use the initial letter. But now these are decreed by contemporary scriptwriters as acceptable or, as they would doubtless put it, **appropriate** (except in anything directed at children – for the moment); and the most offensive and literally unspeakable word in the English language is now deemed to be n★★★★★ (as often now written, or as it is increasingly known as, 'the n-word'), a term of racial abuse that was already regarded as beyond the pale nearly eighty years ago, when Eric Partridge deplored it in *Usage and Abusage*. The euphemising of such words is as political as it is polite, and changes from era to era as part of what Solzhenitsyn called 'the censorship of fashion'. For words that are neither political nor impolite, and unlikely if used undiluted to cause public outrage – such as 'dead' – euphemism is increasingly absurd, and suggests a despairing desire to avoid facing unpleasant facts.

Evidence The dictionary shows that the use of *evidence* as a verb – as in 'I can evidence that you are wrong' – began in the early seventeenth century and occurred occasionally over the next two hundred years, but then offers no citation between 1806 and 2011. For the passive participle, *evidenced* – 'his crime cannot be evidenced' – there are slightly more frequent citations, but nothing is shown between 1913 and 2015. This therefore appears to be a resurrection, helped by the vogue of **nouns used as verbs**. Most people would say 'I can prove you are wrong' or 'his crime cannot be proved'. *See* **proved and proven**.

Evocative Everything evokes something, even if only banality or stultifying boredom, so this adjective needs to be used with extreme caution if it is not to be pointless. *See also* **emotional**.

Ex- This is an immensely useful prefix when it comes to conveying succinctly that something or someone is no longer what it, he or she was. Hence 'ex-husband', 'ex-minister', 'ex-convict' and even 'ex-king'. But be careful how you use the prefix when an adjective is involved. In September 2023 Sky News spoke of an 'ex-British soldier' who had been found dead in Ukraine. The poor man was British to the moment he died; but he was an ex-soldier. The correct way to describe him would have been as 'a British ex-soldier'.

Exit The use of this word as a transitive verb (*see Appendix*: **verbs**) is reaching an extreme. During the scandal about the institution closing Nigel Farage's current account in July 2023, Coutts Bank talked of the decision to 'exit' him. This was not about them leaving a place called him, and certainly not about the bank leaving Mr Farage's physical person, but a reference to their forcing him to leave their bank. The dictionary recognises the American usage of *exit* as a transitive verb to mean to leave a building (as in 'we exited the cinema' – most people would say 'left') or an abstract ('she decided the time had come to exit her marriage'), but this usage meaning to force someone to leave something – in this case your customer base – appeared unprecedented, and another of Coutts's many improprieties in this incident. More rational people would have used verbs such as *drop*, *exclude* or *remove* rather than pointlessly mint or abuse one in this way.

Experience *See* **life experience**.

Eye-watering   In its summer 2023 number the journal of the Queen's English Society quite rightly expressed vexation at the seemingly ubiquitous use of the adjective *eye-watering*, applied to something that causes the wrong sort of astonishment to someone – 'he was invoiced for an eye-watering sum of money' or 'the abuse she received was eye-watering'. The writer in the journal compares it with the ubiquity of 'incredible', but the hyperbolic qualities of that adjective seem limited by comparison. It strikes me also that there is a subtle difference between 'an eye-watering rise in interest rates' and 'a rise in interest rates to make one's eyes water'. The latter, if one has to resort to a hackneyed metaphor, is surely logically more accurate, as the former might imply that it is the rise whose eyes are watering. *See* **incredible and incredulous**.

F

Failing and **failure**   A *failing* is a trait that represents a shortcoming, which even the most successful people cannot usually avoid – 'he was a superb manager, but his only failing was a bad temper', for example. It can also be a specific act of negligence or dereliction, as in 'the car crashed because of a failing on his part to check the tyres', though it would be more idiomatic now to say 'a failure on his part'. A *failure*, when the term is applied to a person, is someone who simply cannot succeed either in a specific pursuit or generally. Therefore, 'as a husband, he was a complete failure', or 'he had five jobs in two years, but because of his drink problem ended up a failure'. The noun is more generally applied to a specific act by a person – 'his failure to wear a helmet caused him to suffer catastrophic injuries' – or of machinery, as in 'a power failure left them without electricity for the evening'. In the statement 'Nicola Sturgeon is using independence as a "political shield" for her failings', *The Daily Telegraph* in May 2022 was reporting a comment by Alex Salmond, her predecessor as leader of the Scottish National Party. As Mr Salmond appeared to be referring to failed policies rather than to supposed flaws in Ms Sturgeon's character, he perhaps should have said 'her failures'.

Fall pregnant   The climate of encouraging people to take no responsibility at all for their actions, and have someone else bear the consequences, has encouraged the continuation of this appalling term. One falls ill by catching a virus, which often happens irrespective of any precautions one might take. One becomes pregnant either by taking no precautions at all, or by a failure of contraception, except in cases of parthenogenesis, which are rather rare. Paradoxically, in French one entirely respectable and venerable way to describe a woman becoming pregnant is to use the idiom *tomber enceinte* – to 'fall pregnant'. But we are not in France, and our idiom appears to have been of much more recent origin.

Farewelled When the estimable Australian comedian Barry Humphries died in April 2023 a report on MailOnline said of his funeral that his family and friends who had attended had 'farewelled' him. Ryan O'Neal, the late Hollywood actor, was similarly described a few months later, again by MailOnline, as having been 'farewelled at intimate ceremony in Los Angeles'; though the piece was written for the American edition of the website for which, therefore, normal British rules may not apply. The obsession with minting verbs despite the abundant availability of existing alternatives (*see* **nouns used as verbs**) seldom gets more preposterous than this. If the writer felt an aversion to saying the mourners had 'paid their last respects' he could have used 'bade farewell', 'said goodbye' (we should, I suppose, be grateful that he avoided the non-verb 'goodbyed') or 'saluted his memory' or something similar.

Farther and **further** The current ubiquitous interchangeability of these two words, with a preference now very much towards the latter, suggests that any ancient distinction between them has been lost – though consultation of the dictionary suggests that the loss of that distinction has been happening for centuries. *Farther* was meant to indicate physical distance – 'London is farther from here than Birmingham is', or 'if you walk farther along that path you will see the lake'. *Further* was meant to suggest metaphorical progress or advancement – 'she has gone further in her career than anyone would have imagined' or, as an adjective, 'he was a typical product of the country's further education system'. As an adjective the two words seem to have become identical ('he sat on the further bank of the river' or 'the summer house was at the farther end of the garden') but as a verb it now seems to fall uniquely to *further* to fulfil that function ('you will not further your cause by using language such as that', for example). One has to be an extreme pedant these days to worry about the distinction otherwise, as no one else appears to. Americans generally seem to prefer *farther*.

Fast foodspeak (or possibly **fastfoodspeak**) There is a whole new language, its origins apparently entirely in demotic American English, that one is expected to use in order to communicate comprehensibly when buying fast food or other low-grade takeaway items, and which among other things promises to construct a link between poor diet and language abuse. Such food has brought into existence a language of its own: 'fries' (a term confined to potatoes, though logically much else can be and is fried at these establishments), 'shakes' (something done to milk, allegedly), 'burgers' (not the inhabitants of a German town), 'sides' (which do not refer to certain areas or faces of an object but to items eaten as a complement to the main food), 'to go' (in other words, 'to take away'), 'hold' (an instruction not to include something, as in 'hold the sauce', rather than to grasp it) and 'can I get' ('Can I get a macchiato, please?'). The especially absurd 'can I get' amuses because of the suggestion it makes that the enquirer is seeking permission to go into the kitchen either to collect his selection of cholesterol or, possibly, even to cook it himself: which we know is unlikely to be so. Sadly, customers of such establishments seem to believe that unless they speak in this peculiar argot they will not make themselves understood to those who serve them, who presumably have to leave any proficiency in standard English behind before they come to work. And 'can I get' now has such an infectious toxicity that it has spread far outside the seedy world of burger bars and fried chicken dives: one even hears the phrase uttered by diners in respectable restaurants, on the principle, it seems, that ignorance is bliss.

Fed up of One is always fed up *with* something or someone, never fed up *of* them. A usage such as 'I am fed up of your nagging' is vulgar, which is fine if one is setting out to be vulgar, or simply can't help it. In intelligent speech or writing it must be avoided. *See also* **prepositions, wrong**.

Fewer and **less** The rule is simple, apparently deceptively so. One has fewer of a number of things or people and less of a single commodity. Therefore 'I saw fewer people at the match today than usual' but 'we drink much less vodka than we used to'. So when Professor Gallagher wrote in his biography of Salazar that 'Ferro had no less than 131 meetings with Salazar' he was, I am sure, factually correct but grammatically mistaken: it should have been 'no fewer than'. The reverse mistake seems never to occur. *See also* **many and much**.

Fill in In British English one fills *in* a form; in American English one fills it *out*. Imitation and not clarity leads to the American usage being deployed in the United Kingdom.

Fill up If a good writing style is in part contingent on economy of expression, then looking for words that serve no purpose is a good discipline. *Fill up* is so universally known a term in colloquial English that it seems foolish to criticise it in the written language; but it is often used where it is not necessary. One routinely says 'I filled up the car' and the listener knows that means putting fuel in the tank; if one writes 'I filled up the car with petrol' the 'up' is unnecessary. Similarly, one can write about filling a glass, or a bottle, or any other vessel, without recourse to *up*. There is no need to indicate that the contents reach *up* to the top of the vessel: the verb *to fill* means just that. See **prepositions, superfluous**, and also **full**.

Filmic   Like **comedic**, this is a pretentious adjective coined in America during the silent era. There were sporadic uses of it in British English towards the end of the twentieth century, after which it became a vogue word among those who, however tenuous their connection with the film industry, wished to show off their mastery of, or at least their familiarity with, its critical **jargon**. A perfectly good adjective has long existed that renders this unnecessary, and it is *cinematic*.

Finish up   There is no difference between 'I finished up the drink' and 'I finished the drink', apart from the pointless word. See **prepositions, superfluous**. A similar stricture should apply to *finish off*, though that phrase also has a slang usage that means 'kill' or 'put out of its misery', where in order to convey the exact meaning the *off* must be retained.

Firing line, the, and **the line of fire**   These two phrases are increasingly used interchangeably, which is ridiculous when one reflects that they mean entirely opposite things. The former is the line of armed soldiers with weapons who fire on an enemy; the latter obliquely refers to the enemy, who are in the way and liable to be hit by the fire. It requires less than a moment's thought to see the distinction. Yet in July 2023 the

Guardian, which ought to know better, said: 'As Hollywood actors strike, here's why A-listers are next in the firing line', the headline on a story about how the top actors might be targeted for being overpaid. The reverse mistake – using *the line of fire* to mean 'the firing line' – seems not to occur.

Fiscal and **financial**   *Fiscal*, according to the dictionary, has come to mean 'pertaining to financial matters in general', in other words a synonym for *financial*. This usage dates only from the nineteenth century; back to the sixteenth century (and the usage correctly persists today among the cognoscenti) *fiscal* was a word used in specific relation to the tax system or what the dictionary calls 'pertaining to the public revenue'. The distinction is a useful one if one can be bothered to remember it.

Fit   In American English, the past tense of the verb *to fit* is *fit* as in 'workmen came in and fit a kitchen for her'. In English it is *fitted*, as in 'he fitted his car with a sound system'. The Americans form their past tense as in British English we form the past tense of the verb *to hit* – it does not change, as in British English's usage 'I saw him bothering my girlfriend and so I hit him'. *See also* **knit** *and* **spit**.

Flair and **flare**   *Flair* is the style or panache that one brings to an undertaking – 'he hosted his parties with great flair' – whereas a *flare* is a distress signal sent up by those stranded at sea, or sometimes in a wilderness on land. The ludicrously broad-bottomed trousers worn in the 1970s were called *flares*.

Flaunt and **flout**   A minor improvement lately is that the dictionary's online edition no longer records without comment the ignorant use of the verb *flaunt* to mean 'flout'. It now says that 'this usage clearly arose by confusion, and is widely considered erroneous'. The former verb means to make an ostentatious display of something – 'she flaunted her new boyfriend all over the resort'. The latter means to show a blatant disregard for rules or laws – 'he flouted the law by driving at 95mph'. The mistake – and it is never, or at least not yet, made in reverse with *flout* meaning 'flaunt' but typically in a usage such as 'the team blatantly flaunted the rules throughout the match' – appears to have been something of a craze before the Second World War, since when there are fewer examples. To allow the confusion of two such different words to become entrenched illustrates the wrongness of the supposed embarrassment of correcting children and other impressionable people when they abuse the English language.

Floundered and **foundered**   These are two more easily confused verbs. The dictionary suggests most usages of the former are now obsolete, but it is used (and has been since the late sixteenth century) to indicate something proceeding with clumsy movements, or with difficulty, or tipping over into a swamp or quicksands. It borrowed some of the meaning of its near-homophone *founder*, which for at least six hundred years has meant to stumble violently or collapse, or in the case of a ship to sink to the seabed; and it easily admits of figurative usages – one often hears of a business foundering, for example. The distinction is that someone *floundering* is staggering along and may or may not reach his destination, whereas someone *foundering* is finished.

Flout   *See* **flaunt and flout**.

Focus around   One occasionally hears this illogical phrase. One focuses *on* or *upon* something else; focusing *around* something is a physical impossibility.

Focused   The British English spelling is thus. *Focussed* is American.

For ever and **forever**   *For ever* is an adverbial usage and *forever* an adjective. 'I want to stay with you for ever' is an example of the first, 'the boy will be forever stupid' an example of the second. One should be careful to avoid tautology with either construction; although circumstances can revert or change back, a phrase such as 'my life changed for ever' seems logically to be a tautology, as the change brought by experience cannot be undone. The Americans know only *forever* and use it in all circumstances. Authorities still claim that *for ever* means 'eternally' and *forever* 'continually': regrettably, the terms have become interchangeable now.

Former   This pronoun can, like its companion **latter**, be used only to refer to one of two things or people, as in 'when John and Mary saw the film, only the former enjoyed it'. If there are more than two people or things then the reference to the first has to be precisely that – 'the first'. *See also* **elder and younger**.

Fortuitous and **fortunate**   I was sent a press release on behalf of some 'experts' telling me that these two adjectives did not mean the same thing: that something that was *fortuitous* had happened by chance, and that something that was *fortunate* had happened as a result of luck. The dictionary categorises the former as something 'that happens or is produced by fortune or chance', the latter as applied to something 'favoured by fortune'. A deep and protracted philosophical discussion could be launched on this question, but it seems to be clear (if the dictionary is to be believed, which it probably should be) that there is no real difference at all between these adjectives when used in the sense of good luck or good fortune. Events that occur by chance might, to those affected by them, be a question of luck; however, sometimes that luck will be bad. *Fortuitous* certainly has the implication of good luck, as does *fortunate*: no one sane would say it was fortuitous that someone was struck by lightning, but it certainly would be a question of luck – the bad luck to be in the wrong place at the wrong time. Given that there is no skill whatsoever required in pulling the handle on a fruit machine and three oranges coming up, the financial gain might be considered both fortuitous and fortunate. It would be wise not to be unduly proscriptive about any distinction.

Foundered   *See* **floundered and foundered**.

Fraction   Usually, when writers say that someone had 'a fraction' of someone else's wealth, or talent, or good looks, they mean very little indeed. But 99/100ths is also a fraction, so logically it can mean an almost identical amount. If you must use this **cliché** to evoke paucity, qualify it with an adjective such as *small*. Bloomberg did not realise this when it advised in August 2023 on 'where to find super-old Scotch Whisky at a fraction of the price', whereas the *Waterloo Region Record* in Canada ran a headline the same month saying that 'census data captures tiny fraction of cycling activity'; it was right to qualify the noun *fraction*, but failed to grasp that **data** is a plural noun.

Full   This is a prime example of an incomparable adjective (that is, one such as *dead* or *circular* that cannot have *more* or *most* added to it) but people often struggle to avoid comparing it. It feels natural to say that a glass that is half full is 'more full' or 'fuller' than one that is only a third full. Pedants, of whom I am one, feel happier saying that the one glass has more, or less, in it than the other. *See also* **adjectives, incomparable**.

Further   *See* **farther and further**.

G

-gate In 1974 the President of the United States of America, Richard Nixon, became the only holder of his office in history (so far) to resign, which he did as a result of a burglary on behalf of his campaign and against the interests of his Democratic opponent that took place at the Democratic Party's offices in the Watergate building in Washington, DC. 'Watergate' as it rapidly became known, was the greatest political scandal in living memory. It started the tiresome trend that persists to this day of suffixing *-gate* to the subject matter of any scandal in the English-speaking world to produce a new label by which it becomes popularly known. Thus we have had 'Irangate' (otherwise the Iran-contra scandal of 1987), 'Bunga Bungagate' (almost anything to do with the depravities of the late Silvio Berlusconi) and 'Partygate' (the decision by Boris Johnson and his staff to ignore the pandemic restrictions he had imposed in 2020–21 on the rest of the United Kingdom). For similar boring coinages using other ubiquitous suffixes, *see also* **-athon and -thon, -cation, -ification, -nomics** *and* **shame**.

Get For 'Can I get a pizza, please?' *see* **fast foodspeak**. *Get* is also a catch-all verb that can be used to describe a vast range of functions, but in doing so makes any phrase in which it appears less exact than it could be – whether it is 'get a drink' (fetch), 'get drunk' (become), 'get over' (recover), 'get dressed' (dress) and so on. Precision is always preferable. See also **do**.

Gifted This is an excellent adjective ('she was a gifted child') but a rotten verb ('I gifted her a diamond ring'). One supposes people use it instead of the perfectly serviceable *gave*, or the other relevant part of the verb *to give*, because they wish to emphasise that what was given was some sort of present. However, that is usually clear from the context – 'they gave Mary a bottle of wine when they went to her dinner party' has a sense that is perfectly clear without needing to use *gifted*. See **nouns used as verbs**.

Gifting season, the Although in minority use, this has become a peculiarly repellent way of referring to Christmas by those whose secularism is so obsessive that they cannot bring themselves to utter a word that appears to recognise the existence of Christianity. Many in America have this problem – or are terrified that others have it and do not wish to offend them – and have long called this period of the year 'the holidays', a word British English speakers associate with the summer, buckets and spades, and hideous delays at overcrowded airports. For such anti-Christian extremists the idiom 'the festive season' has long existed in British English, and is far more suitable.

Glass ceiling This phrase was popular at the turn of the century, and is still used by those resistant to being bored by it. It was frequently used in the **corporate speak** of firms who wished to advertise that they placed no limits on the progress that women, or people of colour, or any minority could make provided they had the ability to advance. The glass ceiling was supposed to be the hard but invisible barrier above them against which their aspirations crashed, on the grounds that they were not white men. Since any institution that refuses to promote genuine talent is cutting its own throat, better expressions than this tired cliché might be *bigotry* or *prejudice*.

Going forward This is a particularly sickening and ridiculous way of saying 'in future', as in 'going forward, we shall end our accounting year on 31 December' or 'it would be appreciated if staff did not eat sandwiches at their desks, going forward'. Quite often it is completely redundant, being used as a form of mindless rhetoric; it is part of **corporate speak**, the **jargon** that comes with much professional life, and is used as a verbal tic by many who deploy it. Since the past is usually of no interest to those who keep the phrase in their vocabulary, not least because no order can be given about it that will enable it to be controlled or changed, we have yet to endure 'going backward'.

Going the extra mile This cliché is another manifestation of **corporate speak**, and it is used to describe an employee, or a group of employees, who has provided service beyond what might legitimately have been expected – 'Mary went the extra mile and pulled in dozens of new customers as a result', for example. 'Worked exceptionally hard' would have communicated exactly the same idea and would not have been so hackneyed a phrase. Logicians might also point out that someone 'going the extra mile' will end up beyond the supposed destination, perhaps inconveniently so. *See also* **punching their weight**.

Good and **well** When applied to a human being the word *good* instinctively suggests a moral quality. One would expect someone who says 'I'm good' to be observant of most of the Ten Commandments, if not all of them; but the tendency to use it to describe a state of well-being has become increasingly ubiquitous, and to many people simply sounds odd. When asked how they are, people routinely say 'I'm good' when they really mean 'I'm well', and if a group of people – say when travelling or simply dining out – are asked whether all is to their satisfaction, someone on their behalf is now likely to respond 'we're good' when what he or she means is 'everything is **all right**'. It is another **Americanism** imported into British English without those who use it stopping to think not just whether it is necessary, but whether it improves accurate communication and understanding.

The word is most often an adjective, occasionally (and usually in the plural) a noun ('he sold me some goods' or 'public spending is not a good in itself') but never an adverb. 'Doing good' is a phrase that refers to someone or a group of people acting in a way that benefits others; 'good' in such a phrase is a noun. To do something to a high standard is to do it *well*. However, a radio presenter in May 2023 was heard to say that 'I used to do really good at exams': though not, one presumes, at English.

Gotten   This is the past participle of the American version of the verb *to get*; it is not used in British English except by those incapable of distinguishing between the two variants of the English language. The American usage is historic and was imported there with the early colonists, but it had changed in British English and most of its dialects by the nineteenth century, and was finally eliminated in the United Kingdom by universal literacy and compulsory basic education. Nonetheless a story on MailOnline on 15 January 2023 about an accident involving a motorcyclist and a car passenger 'who had gotten out of the vehicle' in fact described unfortunate events in Manchester, England, not in Manchester, New Hampshire. See **Americanisms**.

Gourmand and **gourmet**   These two French words are used by writers, in attempts to display *savoir faire* and sophistication, as nouns in English and as if they were interchangeable. They are not, though it is a mistake the French themselves make when using them as adjectives. A *gourmet* is a connoisseur of food; a *gourmand* may well be that too, but he is also greedy. *See also* **bon vivant**.

Grow   Historically, this was both an intransitive verb ('I have grown three inches in the last year' or 'that tree has grown several feet since we planted it') and a transitive one applied to physical objects ('I grow tomatoes every summer'). Since the late twentieth century it has become used as a transitive for abstracts, most ubiquitously in phrases such as 'the Chancellor promised to grow the economy by 3 per cent in the next year'. Earlier he would have promised 'that the economy would grow', but now financiers and economists and the people who write about them use this phrase in order to be at one with the **jargon**, and thus appear to be insiders, even if it conjures up images of tomatoes, roses or cabbages.

H

Hang   Perhaps the abolition of capital punishment has accentuated the widespread ignorance of the different passive voices of the different meanings of the verb *to hang*. Game birds are hung before being cooked; pictures are hung and indeed re-hung on walls; but until 1964 in the United Kingdom murderers sentenced to death were, if that sentence were executed, *hanged*, not hung.

Hangar and **hanger**   The former spelling is used to describe a building in which aircraft are housed. The latter is used for an implement on which clothing is stored, and other suspensory items; but it also has a rarefied usage meaning a wood on a slope, and Housman deploys it in *A Shropshire Lad*: "Twould blow like this through holt and hanger / When Uricon the city stood.' The website of a firm called Pembs Steel Buildings Ltd – 'we are a leading supplier of steel aircraft hangers in the UK' according to its Google listing – contains a section 'Steel Aircraft Hangers in the UK'. So even the experts get it wrong sometimes.

Head up   It has long been the case that if someone is leading or directing an organisation then he or she is said to be 'heading' it – 'she has headed the governing body for five years', for example. What is unnecessary is the pointless preposition *up* in this context – yet one too often sees expressions such as 'he headed up the business in its most profitable phase'. The *up* adds nothing. The BBC perpetrated this pointlessness in a badly punctuated sentence on its website in September 2023, writing that 'the cabinet office is headed up by Ms Rayner's opposite number the deputy prime minister Oliver Dowden'. It should not be confused with the slang *heads-up*, which means to alert someone to something – as in 'his boss gave John a heads-up about the meeting the following day'.

Heartbreak   This has always been a metaphor, and a very useful and even a powerful one – 'she suffered years of heartbreak while her husband was held captive' – but it has become a tabloid exaggeration, applied to even the mildest misfortune, and to things that in the warp and woof of life are not a misfortune at all. 'Family's heartbreak as dad finds daughter dead in her bed' was unquestionably a legitimate use by *Plymouth Live* in August 2023: but the *Mirror*'s observation the same day that 'England must take Lauren James lifeline after Women's World Cup heartbreak' fell into the category of hyperbolic drivel. *See also* **word inflation**.

Heave   For some reason the **cliché** 'heave into view' – which is what ships of the line used to do – became enormously popular in the late twentieth century, often being used for comic effect to suggest that a portly, fat or obese person was arriving. Some of the more erudite practitioners of this metaphor know that in this context the past participle of the verb is *hove* (pronounced as in the Sussex resort) and not *heaved*. Others did not, and they were wrong: and although *wrong* is an incomparable adjective, one might be forgiven for concluding that they were not quite so wrong as those labouring under the idea that the past tense was *hoved* (*see* **adjectives, incomparable**). It most certainly is not. The past tense of the transitive verb is *heaved*: 'I heaved the sack of potatoes out of the car.'

Helm   As a noun it means the part of the ship from which the vessel is steered, or a piece of ancient headgear. As a verb it has a long heritage, but according to the dictionary was barely used after the late nineteenth century, and usually and quite rarely in poetic contexts. In the twentieth century, with the advent of the cinema, it was used by the sort of American who utters pretentious words such as **comedic** and **filmic** as a synonym for the verb *to direct*. Inevitably, it has caught on over here among those who believe the only legitimate way in which to discuss the cinema is to do so in fluent American. Thus the Cineuropa website announced in March 2024 that 'on average, film directors in Europe helmed only 1.4 pictures between 2015 and 2022'. But helming goes way beyond film now, with *The Scotsman*, also in March 2024, lamenting the death of a clergyman 'who helmed BBC's *Songs of Praise*', and *The Straits Times*, days later, announcing 'Louis Vuitton's Bangkok restaurant helmed by superstar chef Gaggan Anand'. What is wrong with 'directed' in the context of films is unclear, as is the problem with 'run' in the other two examples.

Hike   The word ought to conjure up an image of people in shorts, long socks and walking boots striding through countryside bearing rucksacks and, possibly, singing. However, it is now used frequently to describe a rise, usually in costs but sometimes in wages, and according to the dictionary's statistics this usage has led to an exponential increase in the frequency of the word's occurrence in the last half-century. The verb meaning 'to go on a long walk' dates to the start of the nineteenth century. The noun with that meaning comes a little later. *Hike* as a rise seems to have begun as a metaphorical usage in America, arising out of the distinct meaning 'to be raised up' – as in 'her skirt was hiked up indecently high'. The first verbal use related to the now common subject of prices, rates or costs is cited from an American newspaper in

1904, but seems to have taken until the late 1960s to reach Britain either as a verb or a noun, by which time it was being used routinely in that sense in America. If its intention was to convey an idea of magnitude greater than that suggested by *rise* or *increase* – 'there has been a massive hike in interest rates' or 'he asked for a serious hike in his salary' – then overuse and familiarity have probably done away with that.

Historian   Correctly, the indefinite article to precede this noun is *a*, not, as is now usually seen, *an*. The 'h' with which the word begins is not silent, as in *hour* or *honour*, but sounded, as in *hysteria* or *hobgoblin*. One would not write 'an history of England' or 'an historical fact' so one should not write 'an historian'. *An* is common in colloquial speech, but that does not make it correct. *See also* **aitch**.

Hoard and **horde**   A *hoard* is a store of things, traditionally money (before the days of retail banking), that goes beyond normal needs – 'he had a hoard of tins of baked beans in case the Russians invaded', for example. A *horde* is a vast number of people, famously but uniquely Mongol, and usually one that is out of control in some way. It is a word Turkic in origin. They are homophones but are sometimes used by mistake for each other by the unwary. For example, the *Mirror* reported on 22 July 2023 that 'hoards of young people scour Irish beach as £3.4m of cocaine washes ashore'; but then the horde [*sic*] of young people might hitherto have been stored away in cupboards against that moment.

Home and **house**   These two words are used increasingly interchangeably, and in certain contexts they are indeed interchangeable – 'he asked me to his house' conveys more or less the same meaning as 'he asked me to his home'. But there are philosophical differences, and more, between the two terms. A *house* is merely a building; a *home* is a specific place where a person or a family lives, and being asked into someone's home suggests an extra degree of intimacy and hospitality than being asked into their house – which is what one might do to a travelling salesman or a visiting policeman. Someone who speaks or writes of his or her 'home' is referring to something of close and perhaps long-standing association with his or her family, compared with when speaking of his or her 'house'. Thus when the *Independent* wrote in August 2023 that 'a third of English homes are at risk of overheating in the future', it might better have said 'houses', as it was the buildings that were most relevant to the thrust of the story, and not the domesticity.

Honest truth, the   It used to be quite obvious that this was a ludicrous tautology, because the truth, if it be true, cannot but be honest. However, then the Duchess of Sussex came along and spoke of 'my truth' and 'our truth' – facts as she strove to interpret them – and one realised that 'honest truth' might have a use after all. *See also* **political language, misuse of**.

Hopefully   In colloquial English phrases such as 'hopefully, we'll arrive in time for lunch' or 'hopefully, she'll realise what a shocking man he is' are ubiquitous and readily understood even though grammatically nonsensical. *Hopefully* is an adverb and therefore qualifies the main verb in each sentence; so in the first it means that the people will be arriving filled with hope – presumably that they are going to get a decent lunch – and in the second that an abundance of hope would accompany the woman's act of realisation about the rotter in question. However, we are conditioned to this colloquial usage and know what each means, and where in fact hope is apportioned. This usage should be avoided in formal written English as it looks sloppy and gives the writer away as unthinking or ill-educated, though it abounds to the point of saturation in sports writing, and supposedly educated people in that and in many other contexts do not hesitate to use it. One would write instead, in my two examples, 'I hope we'll arrive in time' or 'I hope she'll realise', or even 'one hopes' or, most formally, 'it is to be hoped'. Sometimes it is used simply as a meaningless phrase and can be lost altogether. See also **literally**.

Horror In one of its more vivid definitions, the dictionary describes this as 'a painful emotion compounded of loathing and fear; a shuddering with terror and repugnance; strong aversion mingled with dread; the feeling excited by something shocking or frightful'. It also admits to its use in a 'weakened sense' to describe 'intense dislike'. Indeed, it occurs in an even weaker sense than that, to describe anything vaguely nasty that has happened, and as such is a victim of **word inflation**. For example, MailOnline in August 2023 described a '"horror flight" from Ibiza as footage shows terrifying turbulence'. The same day the *Evening Standard* carried a headline announcing: 'Dulwich prep school fined £80,000 after tables and chairs fall on pupils in "horror" ceiling collapse'. On another occasion the *Mirror* wrote: 'Horror as car valet owner reveals worst vehicle he's ever seen – full of mud and needles'. It appears that in the second instance the word *horror* was included in quotation marks because the mother of one of the children affected by the collapse 'looked like a zombie from a horror movie', which is quite a separate matter altogether. One does not doubt that all these events were shocking, distressing and upsetting, which are probably the adjectives the writers were searching for. How far they were horrifying depends on one's sense of perspective, and how easily horrified one is. The worst devaluers of this particular currency are, perhaps inevitably, sports headline writers, in examples (from ESPN) such as 'Ten Hag praises Man United comeback after "horror start"'. When one read on the same day an account in the *National Review* of a blood-soaked event in the war in Ukraine – 'The Horror in Bucha' – one found a rare example of the word's being used accurately, and a reminder of the damage done to sense and to the language by trivialising it to describe the under-performance of a football team.

Humorous, humourless and **humerus** Most sentient people are aware that each of these words has a distinctly different meaning from the others, but problems often arise with spelling. The 'humour' in *humorous* loses its 'u'; the 'humour' in *humourless* retains it; and the first two syllables of the word to describe what (in a superb exposition of the British sense of humour) is often called 'the funny bone' is merely a homophone of *humour*; it has two 'u's but no 'o'.

I

Iconic I had hoped this highly inflated word would have lost its novelty, but it appears to be even more overused than ever, and unstoppable in its misapplication. From the seventeenth century it was used to refer to an icon or other religious images or figures represented in art. Statistics suggest that until 1950 it was hardly used at all, but since the start of the twenty-first century it has been used to describe anyone or anything, or any cultural representation, that has a moderate amount of fame. So in August 2023 MailOnline ludicrously talked about an 'iconic *Come Dine with Me* contestant' as though he were the equal of a representation of a Russian Orthodox saint or possibly even the Virgin Mary. The same day GB News's website mentioned a 'new version of iconic product', namely Toblerone; and another calorie-rich comestible, the teacake, was said by the *Sun* to be produced by an 'iconic Scottish company'. By using the term to describe anything that is culturally familiar – *iconic* television advertisements, film scenes, street furniture, proprietary goods and so on – the word is driven to meaninglessness. *See also* **word inflation**.

If and **whether** Perhaps indeed I am pedantic, but I believe there remain occasions when the careful writer will use *whether* and not *if* when describing possibilities, and the rule governing this once familiar aspect of good style is distressingly simple. If there are alternatives – if your *if* could be replaced by *whether or not* – then *whether* is required. Therefore, 'if I can spare the money I shall go to the cinema' is correct (though if one were determined to go in any event one would say 'whether or not I can spare the money I shall go to the cinema'). However, one would ask 'I want to know whether you are going to the cinema', not 'I want to know if you are going to the cinema'. And it is perfectly correct to say 'I want to know, if you are going to the cinema, whether it is a good film'; not 'if it is a good film'.

-ification When our American cousins start to express concern about acts of butchery to our supposedly common language it really is time to become worried. In August 2023 the *New Yorker* magazine, not known for its rampant conservatism in any matters, drew attention to the plague of words it has spotted in its native media that end in *-ification*. Charitably, it concluded that these new coinages were words that 'serve as a placeholder for our idea until something better comes along'. Yet in some instances something better had already come along, sometimes centuries earlier; equally, something better seems never to come along. The *New Yorker* blamed the internet, too, which it says meant 'we may have lost track of whom [sic] is leading whom'. Such formations have long been with us, and some have become useful terms that are widely understood and used, because they serve a useful purpose – *gentrification* is an obvious example (unless one had wanted to show off one's polyglot capabilities by saying '*embourgeoisement*'), and *electrification*. However, the verbs *gentrify* and *electrify* were also in wide usage, which cannot be said of the verbs one must impute from some of the other examples the *New Yorker* cited. These included 'the flu-ification of Covid policy', the 'Gen Z-ification of the royal couple', the 'old man-ification' of television, and the 'you're doing it wrong-ification' of TikTok influencers. One has yet to hear, for example, the verb 'oldmanify', though doubtless it is out there. From all of this we deduce that an *-ification* can be minted not just through joining a word to the suffix (such as 'hoax-ification', which it spotted in the *Washington Post*, or 'woke-ification', which it blamed on Ron DeSantis, the American politician), but also by adding two or three words or even a whole phrase (it notes also the 'that's what she said-ification' of humour). The magazine called the practice 'nominalization', a version of **nouns used as verbs**. All of the examples above could have been expressed using traditional forms, and I would try to demonstrate this if I knew for sure what any of them meant (I presume that, for example, 'the flu-ification of Covid policy' simply means 'treating Covid as though it were flu'). This novelty will doubtless turn up on this side of the Atlantic soon, and if and when it does it should be used solely for comic effect, and not if a speaker or writer wishes to be regarded as authoritative. *See also* **-athon and -thon, -cation, -gate, -nomics** *and* **-shame**.

Impact The mangling of this verb has been one of the linguistic horrors of recent times. *Impact* has been a verb since the early seventeenth century: however, it was always correctly used with a preposition, usually 'impacted on' or 'impacted against'. Outside the laboratory – for it was always a word used in physics to describe force – it was idiomatically used in British English in the form 'have an impact on'; but in recent years the pure verb form has increasingly prevailed. Where one used to say 'the downturn had quite an impact on the firm's profits' one then heard 'the downturn impacted upon the firm's profits'. Finally, the preposition died, and it became 'the downturn impacted the firm's profits'. On 11 August 2023 the BBC, for example, reported that 'Health

Cuts will impact public'. The transitive verb is increasingly used to describe feelings – 'his grief impacted him' – where one would usually have said 'affected' or possibly 'hit'. One occasionally sees 'the car impacted a lamp-post' as a pompous form of 'a car hit a lamp-post', and one suspects this is thanks to the dramatic connotations of the noun *impact*. Doubtless in triumph, linguists will portray this as a successful evolution of language; some of us will, however, reserve the right to use the traditional constructions associated with this verb, and also to restrict the deployment of the verb to where it makes most sense, and not where it becomes meaninglessly metaphorical. *See also* **prepositions, missing**.

Impactful   This strange adjective has, according to the dictionary, had a cult usage since the late 1930s, and it may be best to keep it that way. It is a contrived way to say 'effective', 'striking' or even 'powerful'.

Imply and **infer**   These two verbs remain almost routinely confused, which is bizarre when one computes how little effort it takes to learn their distinct meanings. To *imply* something is to indicate it or express the likelihood of its happening, or simply to draw a conclusion from it: 'Her stern manner implied he would not get the concessions he sought' or 'that he had run off with another woman implied that his marriage to his fiancée would not now take place'. To *infer* something is to register an implication or to deduce a conclusion from it: 'he inferred from her stern manner that he would not secure the concessions he sought' or 'his fiancée inferred from his having run off with another woman that their marriage would not now take place'. A typical misuse of *infer* was found on the Sky News website on 5 February 2022 when it reported that 'Ms Dorries sought to infer critics of Mr Johnson were those who wanted the UK to remain in the EU'. The opposite error – *imply* for *infer* – is rarely spotted.

Impractical   This is a mangling of the two historically correct forms of this adjective, which are *unpractical* and *impracticable*. It is not cited by the dictionary until 1865 and then for the next hundred years appears to have been used mainly by Americans. 'Impracticable' is cited from the mid-seventeenth century, as is 'unpractical'. It may be pedantic to suggest that *impractical* is an illiterate product of both, but it very much is.

Inappropriate   A weasel word for something we used to term 'shocking', 'appalling' or 'outrageous', as in 'it was highly inappropriate for him to try to grope her at the office party'. However, it can also be used to convey smug disapproval of acts hitherto considered merely foolish, tasteless or ill-mannered, and has developed a close association with the unpleasant cult of virtue-signalling: for example, 'his joke about women was highly inappropriate'. *See also* **appropriate and inappropriate**.

Incomprehension and **incomprehensibility**   The former is the state people are in when they cannot, or will not, understand something – 'she greeted the news of her husband's arrest with utter incomprehension'. The latter describes the state of something that cannot be understood – 'the sheer incomprehensibility of his French had to be heard to be believed'.

Incongruous   This can be used correctly with either *with* or *to*, though the former is more frequent. Thus, in a communication to members in July 2023 the Marylebone Cricket Club was correct when it promised the 'removal of the modern wire-cut brick wall . . . which is incongruous to the Grace Gate and Portland Stone curved walls'.

Incredible and **incredulous**   The former of these two adjectives is applied to something that cannot be believed, though rather like *fantastic* or *amazing* it is hardly ever used in a literal sense but rather to express approval in a rather gushing fashion. 'Her lemon meringue pie was incredible' simply means that it was delicious or exceptional, not that one simply could not believe in its existence. If one hears a phrase along the lines of 'his story was utterly incredible – he was obviously lying' then the word is being deployed in its literal, and increasingly rare, sense. *Incredulous* is applied to a person or people who find it impossible to believe something – 'his teacher was entirely incredulous when asked to believe why he had not done his homework'. The *Express* in April 2023 proved that truth is stranger than fiction when it ran this headline: 'Headteacher denies "cat litter trays in toilets" rumour in incredulous note to parents'. A note, as a non-sentient object, is incapable of belief or disbelief and therefore can be neither credulous nor incredulous: what the writer meant was *incredible*: the note was unbelievable to its recipients. The opposite terms – **credible and credulous** – mean in the former that something is believable, or in the latter that someone would believe anything: 'his story was credible, and they were credulous enough to be taken in by it'.

Infer   *See* **imply and infer**.

Infinitives, split   The prejudice against this formation – characterised by phrases such as 'to boldly go' – dates back to the prescriptive grammarians of the eighteenth century who, schooled deeply in Latin and Greek (languages where the infinitive of a verb is a single word), believed that in English the infinitive, being two words (for example, *to go*), should not be sundered by an adverb (for example, *boldly*). Many, especially Americans, disagree, and split their infinitives with abandon. There is a snobbery in this country about not doing it; however, many of us choose not to do it because we believe it is stylistically unattractive or inferior. I have also yet to encounter a situation in which a split infinitive could not be unsplit without affecting the meaning, nor anyone who has been able to justify that splitting an infinitive enables communication more effective than that in which it is unsplit. 'To go boldly', or 'boldly to go', do just as well as 'to boldly go'. It is interesting to note that although language progressives – those who seek not to draw attention to the failure of the education system, in which some of them work, to teach people how to speak and write English properly – argue for the liberating joy of the split infinitive, the radical publications that they tend to read and in which some of them write are among those who seem to take the greatest care not to perpetrate this usage. It would be all very well to license it in colloquial English, but then it would quickly become utterly ubiquitous. It is not the mark of a reactionary or a pedant, but rather that of a stylist, to persist in avoiding it.

Ingenious and **ingenuous** According to the dictionary, these two adjectives have been the subject of confusion since 1597, when words of Latin origin poured into the language under the influence of the Renaissance. *Ingenious* is from the Latin *ingeniosus*, meaning 'talented' or 'clever', though the English usage implies also inventiveness, originality or a skill at contrivance. *Ingenuous* usually means 'frank', 'candid' or 'honest' and comes from the Latin *ingenuus*, meaning 'noble' – someone of noble birth being in that era associated, accurately or otherwise, with acting honourably and telling the truth.

The form is now more usually found in its negative, *disingenuous*, which one fears is a sign of the times. 'How I now marvel at those ingenuous conversations', wrote a contributor to the *Jewish Chronicle* in November 2023 looking back on happier times, when she clearly implied they were clever and original, not frank and candid. This would have meant those conversations about a bright future had contained harsh and unpleasant truths: which they did not.

Inside   This word does not require a preposition. One says 'they were huddled inside a tent' not 'huddled inside of a tent'. *See also* **outside** *and* **prepositions, superfluous**.

Insure   This verb means to guarantee the payment of a sum of money equivalent to the value of an item – a house, a car, a life – in the event of its being stolen, destroyed or lost. In American English it is also widely used to mean **ensure**. *See* **assure, ensure and insure** to confirm how to avoid confusion between these verbs.

Interesting   Beware any statement in speech or in writing that begins with 'it's interesting', 'what's interesting is' or even worse 'it's really interesting', because what follows inevitably isn't. It is a phrase more often than not deployed as a confidence trick, though in fairness usually an unwitting one, aimed at demanding a listener's attention. Also, the phrase has become a vacuous form of punctuation, in some instances acting as a break or filler in a sentence when not used by people who are setting out to deceive.

Into   Unlike the incorrect **onto**, but like **unto**, *into* exists in this form. Its deployment requires a degree of care by those who wish to be good stylists; its use is often a question of taste, but in some cases is dictated by idiom. The term, as either one or two words, is both literal ('to go into a building') and metaphorical ('to enter in to a partnership'). And it is the distinction between such literal and metaphorical usages that helps settle whether on some occasions to write 'in to' rather than 'into'. In my own writing I make a judgement about whether the verb indicates a physical movement into something; if it does, I join 'in' and 'to', as in 'he went into the room' or 'I put the revolver into the drawer'. If it entails no such physical movement that I do not join them, as in 'he looked in to the room' or 'a number of callers dialled in to the helpline'. One exception to the rule is a usage denoting physical change, as in 'you have grown into a charming young man' or 'that sapling has turned into a really handsome tree'. The young man, by the way, will have 'grown in to' the clothes his mother bought him when he was younger and they were too big for him. In most cases, the correct idiom will be clear from its context.

Irregardless The dictionary says this preposterous word has featured in the English language since 1912, apparently with American origins: and it is described as 'humorous', which is just as well. One presumes some people use it unintentionally humorously because they confuse two words with nearly identical meanings, 'regardless' and 'irrespective'. It doesn't matter whether one says or writes 'I am going to London tomorrow regardless of the weather' or 'I am going to London tomorrow irrespective of the weather': the message a reader or interlocutor receives is identical. However, if one says one is going 'irregardless of the weather', then the reader or interlocutor will think one a twerp. It is, clearly, a double negative, and therefore means the opposite of *regardless*: so it is ironic that in almost every incidence of its use it has been wheeled out to mean 'regardless'. It may be heading towards colloquial use in the United States, for whatever reason, but in British English it is best to pretend it simply doesn't exist.

It goes without saying If it goes without saying, why is one saying it? There may be an excuse for this fatuous remark in colloquial speech, but in writing, never. *See also* **as a matter of fact, at the end of the day, broadly speaking, to be fair, to be honest** *and* **when all's said and done**.

Its and **it's** These appear to be ubiquitously confused – the former is the possessive pronoun of a neutral object ('the heart has its reasons' or 'every dog must have its day'), the latter is the contraction of 'it is', familiar in speech and informal writing ('it's a beautiful day' or 'it's time you grew up' – but certainly not suitable for the most formal communication, such as 'it's with great regret that we have to inform you . . . '). Yet the use of the latter for the former (not usually the other way round) is sadly frequent – 'the town has lost it's charm' and other such horrors. It is quite simple: if you wish to indicate possession, the word to use will always be 'its'. *See also* **apostrophe, misuse of; their, there and they're;** *and* **your and you're**.

J

Jargon The dictionary defines this as a noun 'applied contemptuously to any mode of speech abounding in unfamiliar terms, or peculiar to a particular set of persons'. It causes language to freeze out those who are not conversant in it, and is often used deliberately to exclude outsiders. It is to be avoided by those who wish to communicate effectively with people beyond their circle; and indeed ought to be avoided by those within those circles, because of the element of cynicism and even deceit demanded from insiders who consciously participate in such speech or writing. For examples, *see* **academic speak**, **clichés**, **corporate speak** *and* **fast foodspeak**, though the last of those is, by comparison with the others, relatively harmless.

K

Kerb This word means the edge of a road or of a pavement. It is not in any other sense a limit. *See* **curb**.

Knit In British English, the past tense of this verb is *knitted* – 'she knitted me a lovely scarf last winter'. In American English it is *knit* – 'she knit me a lovely scarf last winter'. *See also* **fit** *and* **spit**.

L

Lady In these undeferential times fewer and fewer people care about the correct address of people with titles. However, enough people still do care, or at least understand some of the more important distinctions, that it helps to try to get things right, not least in some businesses where courtesy to the clientele is important. The title *Lady* is often misused. Lady Jane Smith is only thus if she is the daughter of a duke, a marquess or an earl whose family name is Smith; or the daughter of a nobleman of one of those ranks who has married a Mr Smith. If she is none of those but a peer in her own right, the wife of a peer, the wife of a baronet or the wife of a knight, then she is 'Lady Smith'. If she is both a nobleman's daughter and the wife of a baronet or knight then she may choose how to be addressed, either as 'Lady Smith' or as 'Lady Jane Smith'. She would not normally be 'Lady Jane Smith' if her husband were Lord Smith, though some have chosen so to be styled. When Duff Cooper became Lord Norwich his wife, Lady Diana Cooper (a daughter of the Duke of Rutland), chose to remain thus. This was partly because her name had effectively become a brand, and partly because she disliked her husband's territorial title – on the grounds that it rhymed with 'porridge'. Since the invention of life peerages in 1958 and the right being granted to females to sit in the House of Lords, those women granted life peerages – always in the rank of baroness – have by convention been termed at first reference, for example 'Baroness Smith', and usually thereafter 'Lady Smith'. Some who were well known before their ennoblement often find themselves labelled in the press as 'Lady Mary Smith', which is simply wrong. These simple rules remain beyond many writers, especially in the tabloid press, but there may be occasions on which correct usage may be very good for business or at least for credibility, so it is worth trying to understand it. *See also* **Lord**.

Latter This can only correctly be used when talking of two things or people, as in 'John and Mary came to tea, and the latter praised the cakes highly'. If instead one wrote 'John, Mary and their dog Spot came to tea, and the latter chewed the carpet', that would be wrong: the mischievous Spot, if he is not to be given his name, would have to be referred to as 'the last'. *See also* **elder**, **former** *and* **younger**.

Lay and **lie** These verbs continue to give astonishing trouble. The transitive verb *to lay* is correctly used as follows: 'He lays down a case of wine each month' or 'she lays flowers on his grave regularly'. The past tense is *laid*: 'she laid the table before their guests arrived'. The verb *to lie* – in the physical and not the Boris Johnson sense of 'to tell an untruth' – does not require an object and is often used as a reflexive verb, in other words it describes something one does to oneself, as in 'I lie down each night and go to sleep'. The past tense is *lay* – 'she lay on the couch watching television' – and the past participle is *lain* – 'he had lain in wait for his victim for several hours'. In the Johnsonian sense of the verb *to lie* the past tense and past participle are both *lied*: 'He lied to the House of Commons just as he had lied to everyone else.'

Lead This is not the past participle of the verb *to lead*. That is *led*. *Lead*, spelt thus but pronounced 'led', is a metal.

Learnings This is another abstract noun beloved of bureaucrats and drones who have inserted it, like **behaviours** and even **surgeries**, into their **jargon**, as part of **corporate speak**. In the real world, the noun *learning* cannot have a plural without the person who speaks it or writes it appearing somewhat ridiculous. I once accidentally eavesdropped on a conference call in which one participant said to her colleagues that 'we should make our learnings early', which left me mystified, though I was interested to discern that those who use this absurd form feel that the ideal verbal phrase is to 'make one's learnings'. *Learn* remains far simpler. *See* **plurals, bogus**.

Leisurely This word looks like an adverb but it is in fact an adjective. 'He took a leisurely approach to his work' is correct. 'He worked leisurely' is not. One would correctly say 'he worked in a leisurely fashion'. *See also* **masterful and masterly**.

Less The word refers to a smaller quantity of a single item: 'she started to put less sugar on her cereal' or 'there will be less time for us to see your mother if we go shopping first'. But it is wrong to say or write 'there are less people here than I had expected' or 'I wish there were less trees in our garden': in both statements it should be *fewer*. *See* **fewer and less**, *and* **many and much**.

Lest This useful word, an economical means of saying 'in case', appears archaic but should be absolutely contemporary. However, it requires the **subjunctive** mood (*see Appendix*). It is correct to say 'his mother sewed his name in his coat, lest he lose it', not 'lest he loses it'.

Libel and **slander** These two forms of defamation of character are often confused by laymen. *Libel* is a defamatory statement of which there is a permanent record: say in a publication, an internet or social media posting, or a sound recording. *Slander* is a defamatory statement made in speech by one person about another in the presence of a third party.

Life experience   In this age of real and imagined victimhood, there is a constant appeal for testimony; and no testimony is more valuable than something called *life experience*. What is not explained is how anything can be experienced if it is not part of one's life. This also occasionally occurs as *lived experience*, which makes a more direct comparison with the experience of being dead, one supposes. Those who defend the use of this bizarre term contrast it with *vicarious experience*, which is what one draws from knowledge of the lives of others; but still others would contend, and rightly, that such vicarious experience, being encountered in one's own life, is necessarily part of the sum of one's own experience. Vicarious experience is, by the definition of many people, not experience at all, as experience must be experienced. *Life experience* and *lived experience* are tautologies and show either a poor command of the language or an attempt at manipulation of the feelings of others.

Lightning and **lightening**   The publicity for Professor Julian Jackson's superb book *France on Trial: The Case of Marshal Pétain* described *le Maréchal* as 'the lightening rod for collective guilt'. It was not a unique solecism. The climatic phenomenon is always spelt *lightning*; the adjective *lightening* means, literally, making something lighter, or metaphorically, reducing the darkness of a situation or predicament – 'there was a lightening of the atmosphere after his safe arrival'.

Like   The misuse of this word in various ways has been one of the mounting horrors of colloquial English in recent years.

As I try to make clear throughout this book, colloquial English does not need to be as exact as formal written English; but the various abuses of *like* now prevalent in English are clear examples of when enough has to be enough in the colloquial language, or the speaker (and it is almost always in spoken and not written English that these horrors occur – for the moment) risks being regarded as entirely moronic. Some of the abuses are now penetrating written English, notably in America.

First, there is the use of the word *like* as a form of punctuation, when a person (again, usually if not inevitably a young person and a victim of the failures of our education system) intersperses normal speech with the word *like* in an absolutely meaningless way. Therefore when a good speaker of colloquial English might say 'I saw my friend on the way to the shops, and we decided we'd meet again later today and get a takeaway', an extreme demotic variant would be: 'I, like, saw my friend on, like, the way to the shops, like, and we decided we'd, like, meet again later today, like, and go and get, like, a takeaway.' It seems to have become an addictive habit and apparently some young people grow out of it, having first provided much innocent amusement, but then severe irritation, to the unmoronic.

But a far worse atrocity, and one that has arrived in British English with a heavy prevailing wind from America, is its use as a bastardised form of **reported speech** (*see Appendix*). The normal, unmoronic speaker describing an encounter with another may perhaps say: 'I saw John near the accident and asked him what had happened. He said a car had been going too fast and had knocked a kid off a bike. I said I thought I'd recognised the driver. John said he'd recognised him too – we'd all been at school together.' In moronic reported speech this would translate as: 'I saw John near the accident and I'm, like, "What happened?" And he's, like, "A car was going too fast and knocked a kid off a bike." And I'm, like, "I think I recognised the driver." And John's, like, "I recognised him too – we'd all been at school together."' (I should point out that in those examples I have used quotation marks out of habit and a sense of decency; I have seen such exchanges printed in the American media without any punctuation other than an introductory comma, which reinforces my suspicion that this is designed as a whole new means of conveying the idea of reported speech.) It is precisely the sort of change in our colloquial speech that sends the more patronising end of the linguistics profession into spasms of ecstasy, allowing them to write in beautifully expressed and perfectly parsed sentences, in academic papers in learned journals, about the 'vibrancy' and 'relevance' of street language, and inevitably to have a rapture or two about its 'authenticity'. Such people can perhaps be forgiven for not making a judgement about the primitive and ignorant form of such expressions (for the avoidance of doubt, I seek no forgiveness for my own use of English) but what is harder to forgive is the endorsement it gives to abominable English, and the highly damaging effect it has on a generation that needs to make its way in life through examinations, job interviews, and sometimes by offering some evidence of articulacy.

Like and **such as**   *Like* should be used when making a direct comparison – as in Enoch Powell's line: 'Like the Roman, I seem to see the River Tiber foaming with much blood.' It should not be used when one is offering something as an example, as in 'a woman like my wife would never be seen dead with a man like that', which might pass in casual speech but not in formal writing: there it would be 'a woman such as my wife would never be seen dead with such a man'.

Likely   In British English *likely* is not a synonym for *probably* or *possibly*, though it has become one in American English, and as such is now undergoing an apparently compulsory transfer across the Atlantic thanks to social media, streaming services and, for the few who still watch them, television broadcasts. Naturally, the Americans may do as they wish; in the United Kingdom, a phrase such as 'she was likely the first woman who had ever been allowed inside the club' rather than 'she was probably the first' is, for the moment at least, illiterate. *Likely to* is correct in a sentence such as 'I am likely to take my wife out to dinner tomorrow' but *likely* used in this sentence, from the *Guardian* on 14 August 2023 – 'World Cup shootout TV audience likely the biggest since Cathy Freeman race' – is definitely not. Were the two little words *to be* inserted after *likely*, all would be reasonably well. Similarly, on 3 September 2023 MailOnline reported that 'Putin's regime "likely" sponsored cyber-attack on Britain'.

Linchpin The misspelling 'lynchpin', an American import, is now ubiquitous, despite since 1376 the orthography having been *linchpin*. It remains wrong irrespective of how hard people, by using it exhaustively, pretend otherwise, and irrespective of the dictionary's acknowledging the existence of this illiteracy. The Europe edition of *Strategic Risk* on 11 August 2023 ran a disaster of a headline that read: 'Why data is [*sic*] the lynchpin of climate resilience and reporting.' (*See* **data**.) One can only speculate that the mistake is because of the wide knowledge, and metaphorical usage, of the verb *to lynch* and the nouns *lynching* and *lynch mob*, which are all spelt thus. Spellings of many words have changed over the centuries – only ultra-pedants would for example now write 'shewn' for 'shown' – but one of the main points of a standard dictionary of the language was that spelling itself was standardised. Therefore to write 'lynchpin' rather than 'linchpin' is not striking a blow for creativity or individualism: it is merely displaying one's inability to spell correctly.

Line of fire and **firing line, the**   The *line of fire* is the direction in which ammunition travels once it has been fired by a gun, cannon or other weapon. Some do not understand the difference between that and *the firing line*. They probably would if they were in either.

Literally   The dictionary definition of this abominably abused word is 'in a literal, exact or actual sense; not figuratively, allegorically etc.'. It has had this meaning for six hundred years, since the 1420s. Compare that entirely logical meaning of the word with the following absurdities. 'The night is literally in my hands', wrote a *Guardian* journalist in August 2023, quoting a participant in something called 'an acid house rave'. Perhaps even more ludicrous was an unfortunate man who told Sky News the previous month that his (happily, successful) attempt to escape wildfires on a Greek island 'was literally like the end of the world'. And more preposterous still was *Hello!* magazine's announcement that 'Alexa Chung's holiday wardrobe is literally everything'. The dictionary also concedes the colloquial meaning (with a warning of how obviously it offends against the actual sense of the word), which some may choose to indulge in the way they indulge the colloquial deployment of **hopefully**; though that is not so violent an offence against logic and reason. And the almost randomly idiotic usage of *literally* does handicap those who use it correctly, as was the case with 'he drank so much he literally fell over', or the *Financial Times*'s 'e-bikes should be exploding, just not literally'. Even when one uses the adverb in a legitimate sense one needs to be sure it is not simply stating the obvious, or over-egging the proverbial pudding: in the two correct examples cited, the second is absolutely sound (and makes a good joke as well), the first perhaps mildly unnecessary.

Loath and **loathe** The former word is an adjective and it signifies deep reluctance – 'I am loath to lend him any more money' or 'she was loath to let him into her house'. The latter is a verb that signifies detestation, as in 'I loathe everything you stand for' or 'she loathed the smell of garlic'. The final 'e' is vital for the verb in its present and future tenses, but is never added to the adjective.

Lord This is the normal way to refer to any male in any rank of the peerage except for a duke, who is always 'the Duke of Denver'. The Marquess of Maldon, once formally identified, should then be called 'Lord Maldon', and an earl and a viscount treated similarly. A baron, whether by heredity or a life creation, is hardly ever referred to by his rank, but always as 'Lord': female life peers have by convention been referred to as 'Baroness', then 'Lady' subsequently (*see* **Lady**). Lord John Smith would be the son of a duke or a marquess whose family name is Smith. Had he received a peerage himself, he would simply be 'Lord Smith', or more likely 'Lord Smith of Somewhere', not that many who write about politics seem to grasp this. If they must fulfil their desire to identify him further by use of his Christian or given name, then they should write 'Lord (John) Smith', with his wife (unless a duke's, marquess's or earl's daughter) being 'Lady (Mary) Smith' should further clarification be deemed essential.

Lunch This word is still considered by some to be a vulgar abbreviation of the word *luncheon*, a meal to be taken next after breakfast: but *luncheon* is now used only in the most formal and traditional of contexts, and usually where there is an element of ceremony involved. Also, those who deride the parvenu status of *lunch* should note that it followed *luncheon* into the dictionary over two hundred years ago – the original usage in 1652, the abbreviation of the noun in 1823 – since when it has been in daily usage, so we have all probably had time to get used to it. According to the dictionary the peak usage of *luncheon* was around 1920, with approximately seven occurrences per million English words, against two per million today. This would have much to do with the expansion of the middle classes in the preceding half-century, and the quest for gentility, of which a word such as *luncheon* would be a presumed badge. But even in 1920 *lunch* occurred twice so often as *luncheon* – fourteen times per million words – and after a slump in the 1970s (evidence of a cheerless decade) is now back to twenty-four uses per million: so that battle appears decisively to have been won, though *luncheon* may be deployed according to taste.

M

Mansion In tabloid English, any house (or **home**, as such media would doubtless refer to it) more substantial than a standard property to be found on any civilised housing estate is described as a *mansion*: this is especially the case if there is cause (however tenuous) to assert that the dwelling is worth over £1 million, a sum tabloid journalists peculiarly and rather patronisingly assume to be beyond the dreams of avarice (*see* **clichés**) among their readers. The dictionary helpfully defines a *mansion* as 'any large or stately residence'. In some parts of London flats little bigger than a standard-sized bath sell for well over £1 million: they may be mansion flats, but mansions they are certainly not.

Many and **much** These two words can, in a specific context of indicating quantity, perform a similar function. *Many* always requires a plural verb and is used to describe a large number – often by implication – or a majority of things or people of which there is a multiplicity. Thus one says that 'many people detest criminals' or 'many books are rather boring'. *Much* always takes a singular verb and describes a large amount of something that comes in a single, easily divisible amount, as in 'much of the butter had melted' or 'much of the time was spent travelling'. There is a parallel with **fewer and less**, the former applying to a multiplicity, the latter to a divisible item.

Masterful and **masterly**   These two adjectives (and despite the *-ly* suffix, *masterly* is an adjective and not an adverb) remain deeply confusing to many native speakers of English, judging by the ease and frequency with which they appear to be used interchangeably. The former means 'authoritative', 'imperious', even 'domineering'. Therefore one would write 'his masterful bearing won him the deference of his peers' or 'he was so relentlessly masterful that others began to feel oppressed'. *Masterly* refers to a supreme skill or ability, so one would say that 'her performance of the Rachmaninov was especially masterly' or that 'he had a masterly turn of phrase'. *Masterful* has the corresponding adverb *masterfully* ('he ran the business masterfully') but the dictionary denies the existence of 'masterlily', quite correctly; so one would say 'she played the piano in a masterly fashion'. *See also* **leisurely**.

May and **might**   These two tenses of the same verb have in many instances become interchangeable in modern usage, which correctly they are not. One rule suggested by other grammarians is that *may* is used in the present tense for something with a high degree of probability or possibility, *might* is used for something less probable: it is not that hard to master the idiom. Also, *may* is the present and *might* the past tense of a statement that is a possibility: 'I may go to the beach today, or I may not.' That evening one would reflect: 'I might have gone to the beach today, but I did not.' To say 'I may have gone to the beach today' suggests the speaker cannot remember whether he went to the beach or not. *May* also often asks permission: 'May I use your phone?' To ask 'Might I use your phone?' sounds ultra-polite but is technically the wrong tense, and idiomatically suggests you don't expect to be allowed to use it or, if allowed, you might prove entirely incapable of doing so. If later reflecting on events and having not asked permission, one might perhaps say 'Might I have used your phone?' – in other words, 'Would it have been possible or permissible?' In reported speech, when using *may* to ask a question, 'May I have a drink?' becomes 'I asked whether I might have a drink.' When expressing a wish, 'may his tribe increase' becomes 'I hoped that his tribe might increase'. When advancing a possibility, 'I think the train may be an hour late' becomes 'I thought the train might be an hour late'.

Might has a conditional usage that follows a hypothesis. 'If you take the train you might arrive in time for the concert' is such an example; as is 'had I worn my seat belt I might not have injured myself so badly as I did', or 'if you read that book you might learn something'. *Might* has other specific idiomatic uses, as a form of admonition or implied rebuke over something that has not happened, as in 'you might at least say you are sorry', or 'you might have tidied up the house before our visitors came'; or in making a polite request, as in 'Might you be able to let me know when my order has arrived?' *Might* is also used more widely to refer to something that did not happen – 'he might have been a great cricketer had he practised more' or 'she might have become prime minister had she gone into politics'. *May* can also refer to the past, and to something that is not clear – to say 'he may have been one of our leading writers' suggests the matter is something to be debated, or 'she may have gone to the village' suggests the woman is out and the speaker is unsure where exactly she is.

Meat, meet and **mete**   These three homophones have distinct meanings. The first is a noun and refers to the flesh of animals that one eats. The second is usually a verb that means to encounter someone or something ('he meets his social worker once a week' or 'he met an especially nasty death') – *see also* **meet with**. *Meet* can also be a noun, used to describe a sporting gathering – 'the meet of the local foxhounds was always held at the King's Arms'. *Mete* is a verb, and it means to distribute or hand out, as in Tennyson's 'match'd with an aged wife, I mete and dole / Unequal laws unto a savage race / That hoard, and sleep, and feed, and know not me.' It is a verb seldom encountered in contemporary English.

Medalled   There is almost an obsession among sports commentators to find the vastness of the English language nonetheless inadequate for describing events and incidences in the competitions that they try to describe. The pandemic-enforced delay in the Olympic Games from 2020 to 2021 gave a little extra time to these people to develop and mint new and entirely pointless atrocities, such as *medalled* when somebody finished in the top three in a competition – writing 'Smith medalled in the 400 metres, coming second', for example, rather than expend the minimal extra effort required to use 'won a medal'. A variant of this horror is **podiumed**. *See also* **nouns used as verbs**, **adulting** *and* **netted**.

Media   Because *medium*, unlike *datum* and *bacterium*, is in such popular and regular use as a singular noun, most people realise that *media* is plural, and that the singular is *medium* – as in 'television is a less powerful medium than it was'. Robert F. Kennedy Jr, who at the time was aspiring to become President of the United States of America, was quoted in the *New Yorker* on 26 June 2023 as saying that 'podcasts are a good media for me, because my weakest media is the short soundbite'. It was perhaps a sign of grace that at least he realised 'podcasts' required a plural form of the verb *to be*. *See also* **bacteria** *and* **data**.

Meet with   It is now routine for people to say or write that they have *met with* another. The usage has been imported from America and the preposition *with* is unnecessary. All that need be said is that one has *met* someone else. This usage seems to have developed to create a distinction, with *meet* referring to the first time two people encounter each other and *met with* referring to subsequent occasions. Thus, 'I met my wife when we were both twenty-one and happened to be on holiday in the same resort' but 'I met with my bank manager for another discussion about my overdraft'. The distinction is unnecessary because the context usually makes clear what sort of meeting is being described; 'I met my bank manager' does just as well. This did not stop the *Daily Express* writing in August 2023: 'King Charles to meet with Prince Harry for "peace talks" without Megan'. Even the most blithering of idiots would be aware that the King had already met his son on innumerable occasions, so the removal of *with* would have created no ambiguity. And *met with* has not yet infiltrated various idiomatic phrases such as 'she met me off the train at 7.30' or 'meet me in the pub after work'. There has long been a demotic idiomatic usage of *meet with*, such as 'he met with a sticky end' or similar phrases, but even here the preposition is pointless.

Metaphors, mixed In 2022, when resigning her position as a parliamentary private secretary in the collapsing administration of Boris Johnson, Claire Coutinho, a Conservative MP, spoke of the need for the government to obtain a 'laser-like grip' on public services. A moment of reflection would have told her (as it tells us) that lasers do not grip anything, and that a grip cannot be laser-like. Metaphors, if they are not also **clichés**, at least show an originality of mind; but sometimes that originality can suggest a lack of thought or even a mild insanity. A Tasmanian politician said in 2019 that 'in terms of the thin edge of the world, if you want to use that old-fashioned sloganism, I'm definitely the meat in the sandwich'. One of the most famous in modern political history was coined by a genuinely great man, Ernie Bevin, then Foreign Secretary, who in dismissing the idea of a Council of Europe in 1948 said: 'When you open that Pandora's Box, you will find it full of Trojan Horses.' It is well to recall that even metaphors require some logic.

Meter and **metre**   A *metre* is a foreign unit of measurement. A *meter* is a device that measures consumption, though it is also the American spelling of the foreign unit of measurement. A 'gas metre' is an absurdity.

Might of   An ignorant near-homophone of *might have*. See **could of, should of** *and* **would of**.

Militate and **mitigate**   These two verbs remain easy to confuse among people who only think they know what they mean. The dictionary defines *militate* as 'to run contrary to' or to act in opposition to; hence a statement such as 'his heavy drinking militated against the idea of his promotion'. *Mitigate*, by contrast, means 'to alleviate or give relief from', or to lessen the trouble caused by something – 'she mitigated the pain from her arthritis by taking a selection of drugs'. The word is most frequently seen in the context of court cases, notably criminal ones: 'His barrister said that, in mitigation, the accused was pleading guilty to the charges against him and had offered to make restitution to his victims.' The common confusion is seen in the phrase 'this mitigated against the very idea of transparency'; it should be *militated against*.

Minuscule   The word is spelt thus, but too often – even in reputable books and publications – manifests itself as 'miniscule'. The *Evening Standard*, reviewing a film in August 2023, wrote about 'a bizarre, miniscule, silly cross section of culture that doesn't get nearly enough attention', which is something it apparently has in common with the correct spelling of *minuscule*. A few days later the *Daily Star*, perhaps because of explicable over-excitement, wrote: 'Rita Ora hailed "hottest woman ever" as she showcases washboard abs in miniscule bikini'. As with **linchpin** there is no excuse for running up the white flag on the correct spelling, which has been standardised ever since the advent of the dictionary.

Mischievous This is a word of three syllables, but has in recent years become a common mispronunciation in spoken English, with the interpolation of an 'i' so it is rendered 'mischievious', with four syllables, to rhyme with 'previous'. Clearly, not all words are pronounced as they are written – which is, I am told, one of the joys of learning English as a foreign language, and which is partly why the pronunciation of many proper names changed with the advent of universal literacy – but normally this entails contracting the written word rather than extending it by interpolating a syllable. A rare perpetration of this horror in print was found in July 2023 in the normally pitch-perfect *Times of India* (whose command of English is often far superior to that of many British publications) when it reported: 'Shahana Goswami opens up about Vidya Balan's mischievious side'.

Mislead The past tense of this verb is *misled*. *Mislead*, pronounced 'misled' with the second syllable imitating the sound of the metal, does not exist.

Moral and **morale** *Morals* are ethical standards by which one chooses, or does not choose, to live – 'he took a moral stand against racism' or 'many of her friends said she had no morals at all'. A *moral* is also a piece of ethical learning demonstrated in the outcome of a fictional, or sometimes a non-fictional, tale: 'The moral of the story was that crime doesn't pay.' *Morale* is a condition of enthusiasm and attitude: 'the morale of the employees was high after the company released its latest trading figures', or 'as the tide of the battle turned in their favour, the soldiers' morale rose'. To be *demoralised* does not mean to be stripped of one's *morals*, but to suffer a blow to one's *morale*: 'The enemy's advances left the troops demoralised.'

Mutual   This adjective does not mean something one has in common with others, though that has been the widespread assumption since Charles Dickens's 1865 novel *Our Mutual Friend*. From the early sixteenth century the word had meant 'reciprocal', and is correctly used in a statement such as 'even after their divorce they had a mutual affection and respect for each other' or 'the two clubs had a mutual arrangement by which they offered hospitality to each other's members'. What is often called a 'mutual friend' is in fact a 'friend in common'.

Myriad   This was the Greek word meaning 'ten thousand', and since the sixteenth century it has been used as a noun in English to indicate a large number or multiplicity of people or things – 'a myriad insects burst out of the ground' – and it has often been seen in the plural, conveying even greater numbers. It can also be used as an adjective, without an article, as in 'he had tried myriad times to get his son to change his ways'. Misuse frequently occurs where the adjective is used as though it were a noun: 'Expectations of a "myriad of consequences" from royal race allegations' was a Sky News Australia headline in December 2023. It should simply have said 'of myriad consequences'.

N

Named for　This is an **Americanism** that is increasingly being adopted to replace the perfectly satisfactory and comprehensible British English idiom *named after*, as in 'she named her daughter after her grandmother' or 'the new building was named after its benefactor'. *Named for* – as in a *Philadelphia Inquirer* headline about a woman 'heartbroken at the state of the Philly school named for her mother' – sounds to most British ears as though someone is naming someone or something on behalf of another rather than in honour of another.

Naturalist and **naturist**　It is a good idea not to confuse these two nouns. The former is used to describe someone with a special interest in the flora, fauna and other phenomena of the natural world. The latter is used to describe a habitual nudist, or someone who prefers not to wear clothes.

Neither　When used as a pronoun this must be singular, as logically it refers to one of two people or objects: as in 'neither of the men was armed' or 'neither of the bibelots is to my taste'. 'Neither are to my taste' is a solecism, though one heard routinely in spoken colloquial English. The construction *neither . . . nor* also works only with two subjects and requires the singular – as in 'neither John nor Mary was free that afternoon'. To say or write that neither of them 'were' free would be wrong. Additionally, the *neither . . . nor* construction may apply only to cases where there are just two subjects: one occasionally sees sentences such as 'neither John nor Mary nor their mother was in the house', which are wrong. It would be correct to say 'not John, nor Mary nor their mother was in the house', but it would be stylistically and idiomatically more comfortable to write 'John and Mary were not in the house, and nor was their mother.' *See also* **either** *and* **none**.

Netted In the 2022 football World Cup it became habitual for the scoring of a goal to be described by desperate commentators – desperate in their search for novelty, one supposes – to say that the player who had scored it had 'netted'. It was probably superior to 'goaled', which one presumes will come in time for the 2026 competition. *Netted* has long had a respectable idiomatic use derived from fishing, to describe an accumulation of objects – 'he netted £500 from his concert' or 'the children netted a vast amount of toys at Christmas'. Its appropriation by vacuous football commentators is not a respectable idiomatic usage by any means. *See also* **medalled**, **podiumed** *and* **nouns used as verbs**.

Nightmare We all know that this is a bad or frightening dream, but it is also a tabloid favourite to describe anything from a delayed flight to a lost credit card, and as such has become entirely devalued both as a noun and as an adjective, having turned into the latter quite ubiquitously. On one day in August 2023 the *Mirror* ran a report about a woman's 'nightmare neighbour' who played music too loudly; the *Independent* told how a 'nightmare' alligator had turned up in Mississippi; the *Irish Times*, referring to an air traffic control breakdown, said that 'tomorrow is going to be a nightmare'; the *Daily Record* wrote about 'nightmare tenants' in a Glasgow flat; the *Guardian* spoke of the 'plague of zombies that's making dating a nightmare'; the *Express* had a report about a 'nightmare transfer trade' of footballers. The word has become almost inescapable; as such, its effect on readers is rather like that of an anaesthetic. A half-good thesaurus offers many other options. *See also* **word inflation**.

No worries   *See* **not a problem**.

-nomics   It was during the presidency in America of Ronald Reagan, and his attempt to improve the prosperity of his country and its people, that the term 'Reaganomics' was coined. It appears to have been the first such coinage, and it immediately spawned various imitations, such as 'Thatchernomics', used to describe the policies of his British counterpart. The novelty did not wear off and in the intervening decades this usage has become increasingly boring: in 2022, briefly, in Britain, there was 'Trussonomics', doubtless in an attempt to codify and explain the uncodifiable and the inexplicable. Then in June 2023 the *Spectator*, which ought to have known better, wrote about 'Rishinomics', a cause taken up within days by the *Guardian*. Enough is enough. *See also* **-athon and -thon, -cation, -gate, -ification** *and* **-shame**.

None   For so long as the word *none* has existed writers and especially speakers of colloquial English seem to have used it with a plural verb rather than the logical singular – the logic being that the word is a contraction of 'no one'. Thus we have 'none of them were there' instead of the correct 'none of them was there'. It is a typical colloquial English usage: but the best stylists avoid it in written English, which, with its smell of elitism, is perhaps why progressives detest it so much and are so mordant in their denunciations of those of us who insist on the traditional usage. We do feel logic is on our side: one would not contemplate saying 'no one were willing to put their names forward', instinctively saying instead 'no one was willing to put his name forward' – though to avoid gender specificity the speaker would probably say 'no one was willing to put their name forward' (*see* **their, there and they're**). The dictionary, which locates the word well before the Conquest, notes that it appears 'in later use commonly with *plural* agreement' (its italics), which one takes as an indication that it remains preferable to cling to its origins and have singular agreement. *See also* **neither**.

Normalcy I heard on an English radio station in April 2024 an apparently English person (and an educated one at that) talking about the need for a 'return to normalcy' in an international conflict. This is another **Americanism**: in England and indeed the rest of the United Kingdom (and, I believe, among our cousins in the Republic of Ireland), speakers of British English refer to a state of 'normality'. It should be normal for the British to use their own word, and not to sound as though they are participating in an American conversation in America.

Not a problem Like **no worries**, this fatuous phrase is a modern form of presumed politeness by people – mainly young people, who are recent victims of our education system – working in retailing or our service industries. They have acquired the habit, when responding to a request from a customer, of automatically replying 'no worries' or 'not a problem', when 'yes', and perhaps a smile, would suffice. Apparently it is also becoming common to hear such people reply 'one hundred and ten per cent', which simply boggles the mind as to what might be involved in fulfilling the request (this is also a staple of **corporate speak**, indicating toadying agreement to do whatever one has just been ordered to do). Perhaps if one asks for a pint of beer one is given a pint and a tenth, though I doubt it. Equally, 'May I have a cheese sandwich, please?' elicits the response 'no worries', prompting one to try to imagine what possible cause of worry there might be, and which of the parties involved – the customer or the server – is more liable to endure the worry. Similarly, 'I'd like a gin and tonic, please' is met with 'not a problem', when no possible source of a problem can begin to be detected. The pub is open, the drinker is over age, not behaving in a manner likely to have him (or her) refused service, and there are ample supplies of gin, tonic and empty glasses visible behind the bar, even quantities of ice and slices of lemon. However, if one lingers near the bar one soon discovers that 'not a problem' – like 'no worries' and perhaps 'one hundred and ten per cent' – has become a robotic response to any question, whatever a customer might ask. One can get away with much in colloquial spoken English, but there are limits, especially when one risks unnecessarily presenting oneself to the world as inarticulate. These phrases should never be used in written communications. See also **fast foodspeak**.

Nouns used as verbs Many of the most basic nouns in the language became verbs centuries ago – for example, *dog* was a noun in Old English, but the dictionary dates the verb ('to follow like a dog') from 1519. Similarly *power* as a noun dates back to around 1300, but the verb *to power* something – meaning to move or drive it – is not found for almost another three hundred years. In the past it was logical for some nouns to become verbs because those verbs were needed in the language: and that remains at times true today, not least because of the advance of technology: until there was a *fax* machine (1946) there was no need for the verb *to fax* (1979) as shorthand for 'make a facsimile transmission'. However, in recent decades there has been a vogue of manufacturing verbs out of almost any noun one cares to mention: as noted elsewhere, despite the verb *to write* having given centuries of excellent service, for some reason books now have to be **penned** or **authored**: doubtless in the seventeenth century they would have been 'quilled'. See also **adulting** and, as the world of sport is a grave and serial offender, **medalled**, **netted** *and* **podiumed**. Generally, if there is a perfectly good, familiar and comprehensible verb already in existence, it is rather attention-seeking and fatuous to invent another one. It cannot be long, perhaps, before some people reject the satisfactory word *dine* and write (or 'pen') that they have 'dinnered': after all, *breakfasted* has been with us since 1679, just over two hundred years after the noun from which it derives, and *lunched* since 1823, a mere 232 years after the noun **lunch**. And we cannot be too far from 'carred' (the relatively recent invention *motored* now having a rather period feel, and *drove* becoming rather boring), 'festivalled' and the especially unlovely 'toileted'. If someone plays a practical joke on another he or she is now said to have 'pranked' the victim; it is easier to say 'I pranked Mary' than 'I played a practical joke on Mary', which is doubtless the excuse of those who use this unusual verb, although it is probably preferable to avoid using a rather ugly neologism. However, the need to coin one of these new usages is usually far less than one might imagine, and avoidance of it often requires little other than a dip into a thesaurus. More often than not, because of the existing richness of our language, there is no justification to invent a new verb. A correspondence on this subject in *The Daily Telegraph* in October 2023 included a claim by a reader that New Yorkers say 'there ain't no noun that can't be verbed', which certainly seems consistent with American practice. Talking of which, a favourite means of 'verbing' [*sic*] a noun is to suffix it with *-ise* or *-ize*. (This habit originated in America, where they would use only *-ize*.) Sometimes it ingrains itself rapidly into the language, as with 'weaponise'. This is certainly more concise than saying that something has been 'turned into a weapon'; whether it is stylistically acceptable must remain a matter for debate. *See also* **diarise, evidence, farewelled** *and* **gifted**.

Number This can be treated as a singular or plural noun, like other **nouns of multitude** (*see Appendix*) such as institutions or corporations. However with number, the idiom suggests that following the definite article it should be treated as a singular – 'the number of people out of work has fallen by fifty thousand'– but after an indefinite article it tends to be treated as a plural, hence 'a number of people wish to attend the meeting'. Stylistically, the important consideration is consistency, and not varying between singular and plural in a piece of writing when referring to the same noun.

O

Obligated This ugly participle and adjective has become increasingly common in recent years as yet another symptom of the influence of American media and culture: 'Congress obligated to launch Biden impeachment inquiry after he "clearly lied"' announced Fox News on 28 July 2023. In British English, Congress would have been 'obliged' to launch such an inquiry, just as one says 'I felt obliged to buy him a drink', not 'I felt obligated to buy him a drink'. *Obliged* as a verb – 'he obliged me to stand aside' or 'she obliges her visitors to pray with her' – indicating a sense of moral obligation, dates back seven hundred years. It can also indicate an imputation of obligation to others – 'I'd be obliged if you wouldn't smoke in here', for example. Doubtless it is the noun *obligation* – 'he said he would fulfil his contractual obligations before resigning' – that causes some people to think it relates to a verb *to obligate*, but it relates to *oblige*.

Obscene The dictionary defines this venerable adjective (which, like so many, came with the rise of classical scholarship in Tudor times and dates back to the sixteenth century) as referring to something 'offensively or grossly indecent, lewd', with a clear link to sexual impropriety and indecency. The Romans referred to the genitals as *partes obscenae*, which gives the tenor of the meaning of the English derivative. However, according to a report in the *Sun* newspaper in June

2023 a British Airways jet encountered 'obscene turbulence' over the Bay of Bengal on a flight from Singapore to London. The following month the *Guardian* said that 'Shell's "obscene" $5bn profits reignite outrage amid climate crisis'. We also hear of people earning 'obscene' sums of money, presumably sums that, when we learn of them, the writer assumes provoke in all decent people the same feelings as we might have were we to witness a man standing up in a public place and exposing his private parts. It would be far better, if one feels such a grievance at another's earnings or good fortune, to describe them as 'outrageous' or even 'offensive', both being adjectives that cover a multitude of provocations rather than purely the sexual or carnal.

Of course Although this phrase is a standard filler in colloquial speech – 'of course, you know Mary', or 'of course, you'll have a drink', it is extremely hard to justify its use in written English. If something happens, or just simply is, *of course*, then what is the point in saying so? Thus when one reads 'of course, he never had the slightest intention of giving up drink' just what does *of course* add to the statement? There will be very rare instances where the phrase does add a necessary rather than an unnecessary emphasis, or to reassure someone – 'of course I shan't forget to do that' – but they are the exception and not the rule, and it should be treated with extreme caution otherwise.

Off of The preposition is unnecessary – and, indeed, ugly and illiterate – and can be deleted from the following examples without in any way impairing their meaning: 'they feed off of dead animals', 'they live off of social security', 'the house stands off of the main road' and 'he jumped off of the bus'. It seems to be a frequent intruder into American prose, such as when the *Omaha World-Herald* in August 2023 reported that 'Creighton men's soccer looks to build off of last season's momentum'. *See also* **prepositions, superfluous**.

Officiate   On 8 July 2023 MailOnline reported that a clergyman had 'officiated a wedding'. He had not. He had officiated *at* a wedding. The reporter presumably confused the verb with *conducted*. *See* **prepositions, missing**.

Offline, take something   A term from **corporate speak**. It has nothing to do with the internet but it is used to indicate the initiation of a private conversation: 'I think we had better take this matter offline.' Presumably it sounds far more authoritative to the cognoscenti than 'May we speak privately?'

Older   *See* **elder and younger**.

On the weekend   This usage is an **Americanism**, and in British English includes a misused preposition. This side of the Atlantic we say 'I am seeing Mother at the weekend', not 'on the weekend'. Should we wish to indicate that we are seeing Mother for the entire weekend and not just for tea on Sunday, we would say 'for the weekend'. *See* **prepositions, wrong**.

Onboarding   This new atrocity was recently detected in an astonishing piece of **corporate speak**, used in the context of someone who had recently joined an organisation being reported to have settled in well: 'his onboarding has been successful', derived from the metaphor of the employee's having 'come on board' the enterprise. Whatever is wrong with 'he has settled in well', or something similar, must remain a mystery. It is also clear from reading various trade journals and websites that one can also carry out *onboarding* with customers, to ensure they keep coming back. In July 2023 a website called Customer Think ran an article one week on 'Employee onboarding' that apparently caused such excitement that, the following week, the same writer treated its readers to an essay entitled 'The benefits of proper customer onboarding'. One almost feels like an intruder in this secret world, with its private and largely incomprehensible language. *See also* **nouns used as verbs**.

One   One [*sic*] is often mocked or taunted for using the impersonal pronoun – 'one gets up in the morning and one has one's breakfast' – and indeed it is possible to overdo it, even in formal written English. The French have no such trouble with their equivalent, *on*, as in *on mange le petit déjeuner tous les jours* – 'one eats breakfast every day' – or their much-used phrase *on verra*, which translates colloquially as 'we'll see'. Our own impersonal pronoun has no place in colloquial English, and the tabloid press deploys it only, it seems, when emphasising the elite nature of the royal family – 'One likes one's football!' for example, in a cringe-inducing story about Prince George attending a football match, designed to point out that even in childhood these people are different from the rest of us; and a token means of indicating this is by suggesting they use a starched form of English, which they certainly don't. The late Queen, out of a natural desire to be self-effacing prompted by her impeccable manners, would use *one* in some of her public speeches to convey the idea of generality, rather than make it sound as though a speech was all about her. Indeed, generally one of the more frequent usages of this construction is to project a sense of modesty rather than the self-obsession that is all too evident with many people today. Hence one occasionally hears someone say 'one does what one can' when paid a compliment for a service, or thanked; or 'one would like to think so' when agreeing with a statement and not wishing to impose one's own character on the sentiment. It also creates a distinction from the otherwise ubiquitous *you*, which is often used ambiguously. An example of this is when a speaker says 'one expects better things of a prime minister', which clearly presents a general aspiration, whereas if he said 'you expect better things' an interlocutor, believing he was being spoken for, might well answer 'no, I don't'. The form is stylistically rarefied these days, but many will see nothing wrong with that.

Only This extremely common word must be treated with great care, for a thoughtless placement in a sentence can make a great difference to its meaning. Consider the difference between 'he went to the only [i.e. sole] petrol station' and 'he only [i.e. merely] went to the petrol station' and 'he went only [i.e. solely] to the petrol station' to see the various usages.

Onto George Orwell famously claimed that *onto* should not exist, yet scholars have found its use in some of his early writings. He spoke of his 'archaic horror', when reading the proofs of *Nineteen Eighty-Four* and seeing *on* and *to* printed as a single word. Orwell then seemed to backtrack and try to define circumstances in which the 'horror' might be justified. He used the sentence 'the cat jumped on the table' and suggested it meant the cat, already on the table, jumped up and down on it, whereas (he implies) 'the cat jumped onto the table' makes it clear that the cat arrived on the table after jumping from somewhere else. However, the cat could just as easily have 'jumped on to the table', which stylists (including, one would have thought, Orwell himself) would recognise and prefer. In his defence, Orwell was seriously ill at the time. He drew the distinction with a usage such as 'we stopped at Barnet and then drove on to Hatfield', and idiomatically he is right: *onto*, if one concedes it should exist, creates a notion of physical presence, of one thing on top of another, such as the cat on the table, rather than of progression – as in 'drove on to' or other such phrases including 'he walked on to the stage', 'she passed the book on to her nephew' or 'he went on to study German'. Fowler is deeply unenthusiastic about the word *onto*; the dictionary remains clear that the correct form is *on to*, and has been since 1581, which it calls the *alpha* form; but it also has citations from 1715 of what it calls the *beta* form, with the word as a compound. The meaning of none of the citations would be altered by the division of the word. Those seeking to perfect their written style should avoid *onto*. *See also* **into** *and* **unto**.

Oracy   This is now popular in academic speak, and is therefore a word unknown to the general public if they were educated in the early twenty-first century or earlier. It means, according to the dictionary, 'competence in oral language' and also 'the oral transmission of culture, ideas etc.': so at once context is essential to know exactly how the word is being used. Why people can't say 'articulacy' in the first instance or refer to 'the spoken word' in the second is for them to explain. *See also* **academic speak**.

Oriented   A vogue of recent years in both **academic speak** and **corporate speak** has been to suffix a noun – and it seems any noun will do – with the adjective *oriented* to describe some sort of aim. The adjective was traditionally used to indicate a physical, not a metaphorical, direction of travel, as in 'the telescope was oriented on an east–west axis'. Now we have, for example, in November 2023, 'it's time for a future-oriented pharmaceutical policy' on the Politico website; in December 2023 we were told by the myRepública website that 'COP-28 was effective, result-oriented'; *Psychology Today* wrote of 'Goal-Oriented Challenges'; the *New York*

Times ran a report of 'Youth-Oriented marketing'. There are examples daily that embed any such phrase ever more deeply in the realms of **cliché** and therefore of meaninglessness. We are, one presumes, a short step from baby-oriented nappies and geriatric-oriented Zimmer frames. Choosing to say, as *Outlook* did in December 2023, 'woman-oriented promises' is strange when one could simply write 'promises directed at women' or 'aimed at women'.

Ought and **should**   One senses that the useful auxiliary verb *ought* is becoming rarer these days, supplanted by *should*. There is no difference in meaning, after all, between 'he should be more civil to his friends' and 'he ought to be more civil to his friends'. *Ought* carries with it, however, a sense of obligation or duty, which perhaps *should* does not quite convey even today. It also acts as a synonym for *should* when conveying a notion of expectation, as in 'it ought to take only ten minutes to walk from here' or 'it should take only ten minutes'. The fundamental value of *ought* in contemporary English is to imply a sense of duty only a shade below the use of *must*, as in 'you ought to visit your mother on her birthday', whereas 'you should visit your mother' is simply advice. To use *should* in such contexts dilutes the meaning and undermines the intention.

Outside   This word does not require a preposition. It is enough to say 'outside Shanghai, no one has heard of him', not 'outside of'. *See also* **inside** *and* **prepositions, superfluous**.

Overwhelm   To most of us this word is a common verb ('he aimed to overwhelm her with love') or may be developed as an adjective ('she said she felt overwhelmed'). However, it is also one of those increasingly frequent examples of a verb that becomes a noun, rather than vice versa (something similar has happened in recent years with **ask**, as in 'he felt it was a big ask on their part'). *Overwhelm* as an alleged noun indicates a state of being overwhelmed, as in 'overwhelm may last for a brief period . . . overwhelm is more than stress . . . overwhelm at work is a particular form of overwhelm' – all found in an article on the blog My Online Therapy in December 2021. This may be how the psychiatric or psychotherapeutic professions talk among themselves or to their clients or patients: it would not be a good idea for lay people to imitate them, but rather to stick to traditional and entirely expected and therefore comprehensible forms such as 'feeling overwhelmed'.

Owing to   *See* **due to**.

Own   As an adjective – 'his own dog' or 'her own dress' – it is often, but not always, superfluous; it is usually clear whose dog, and whose dress, is being discussed. It has a valid application in phrases such as 'he offered to lend her his car, but she said she preferred to use her own'. As a verb – 'they had owned their house for years' or 'she had never owned a dog' – it always used to be straightforward. But it has now entered **corporate speak** in an abstract sense. Instead of 'he told John he would be responsible for the new project' we now have 'he told John he would own the new project', as if it were a personal possession, or, worse, that he would 'have ownership' of it. As with most corporate speak, it is best avoided by civilians unless they are striving to appear unintentionally amusing.

P

Paedophile and **pederast**   It is alarming that some view these terms as interchangeable, which they are not. In July 2017 the *Boston Herald* reported that 'survivors decry decision to free pederast priest' before a news story which illustrated that the (defrocked) priest was in fact a *paedophile* who had abused children of both sexes. A *paedophile* is an adult of either sex who craves sexual relations with children of either or both sexes. A *pederast* was, according to its earliest usage, a man who sought sexual relations with a boy, but by the eighteenth century had come to be used as a term for homosexual men, and is now considered by the dictionary to be a derogatory synonym for such a person. *See also* **survivor**.

Park it   This has nothing to do with cars, but is another piece of **jargon** from **corporate speak**. If one is having a frightfully important corporate conversation and someone raises a point that threatens to take the discussion off at a tangent, one does not say 'May we come back to that?' but instead 'let's park that for a moment', rather like a car being driven off the road that represents the main discussion, and left in a side road until it is needed. It is a pretty ugly phrase and best confined to the company meeting room.

Park up   'Police spot stolen car parked up with cloned plates', reported the *Express and Star* in August 2023. What is the point of the *up*? None whatever: the sense of the sentence is the same without it. *See* **prepositions, superfluous**.

Partake of   The correct usage signifies consumption of something, and not participation in something. So one might *partake of* light refreshments, or of a rest cure, but one does not 'partake in' a game of football; one *participates*, or *takes part*, in it. MailOnline quoted a retired footballer saying of Sydney's City2Surf run that 'in order to gain an Australian citizenship this is something that you have to partake in'. He meant 'take part in'. Matters are perhaps made worse by the fact that it now sounds old-fashioned, pompous or arch to use the construction *partake of*, as in 'Would you partake of some tea and biscuits?' instead of the simpler 'Would you like?' or 'Would you have?'

Participles, hanging   This linguistic horror has become increasingly promiscuous, as those who perpetrate it seem incapable of understanding the lack of sense of what they are saying (it is a rarer occurrence in print, though still appears more often than one would think plausible). An example is 'being one of the great tourist sites of England, Mary was delighted to see Buckingham Palace'. The logic of the sentence is that Mary was one of the great tourist sites of England. The problem would be solved by inverting the sentence to 'Mary was delighted to see Buckingham Palace, since it is one of the great tourist sites of England'. Another example is 'sitting in front of the fire, the doorbell rang'. The doorbell was unlikely to be sitting in front of the fire; and the problem can be solved by changing the sentence to 'while we sat in front of the fire . . .'

A ubiquitous example for train passengers is the announcement that 'on arrival the first set of doors will not open', implying that the first set of doors alone and not the entire train will arrive. A slight modification to 'on the train's arrival, the first set of doors will not open' solves the problem. In an otherwise informative article about a man who had spent his life fighting the Mafia, Sky News reported in August 2023: 'Born the third of five children in the small Calabrian town of Gerace in 1958, the 'Ndrangheta was a presence in Mr Gratteri's life from the start.' However, it was not the 'Ndrangheta that was born in Gerace in 1958, but Mr Gratteri. To that substantial number of people who believe logic has no place in language, this solecism will continue to give no trouble at all.

Pass   As a verb and a noun this word already has a multitude of meanings, but it is increasingly a confusing **euphemism** for 'die'. It has been around in this context back to even before those masters of euphemism, the Victorians, when it used to be rendered somewhat clearer by being 'passed on', 'passed away' or 'passed over'. It has somewhat arch connotations about the avoidance of harsh reality, and is best avoided itself. And there is always the danger that, when a woman remarks that it has been some time since her husband 'passed', one is compelled to ask: 'Passed what?'

Passionate   The increasingly frequent, and therefore devalued, use of this adjective in recent years does not appear to be a consequence of the spread of the permissive society, but of the intensely competitive nature of some aspects of the modern world. Someone applying for a place at a university is instructed to demonstrate in a personal statement that he or she is *passionate* about the prospective course of study. Someone applying for a job is urged to appear *passionate* about the business or trade conducted by the prospective employer when going to an interview. And, in the climate of tabloid hyperbole, people are said to be *passionate* about their football team. Long before this, the adjective was used to describe more than simply strong feelings for another human being:

one was said to feel *passionate* about music, about one's country, about one's hobbies. The death of a fine old man in August 2023 caused even *Horse and Hound* to bid 'farewell to [the] passionate carriage driver and countryman'. The devaluation is such that the word has become a straightforward synonym for *enthusiastic*, and before too long this is likely to be reduced further to 'interested in'. At the same time, MailOnline wrote of an actress that she was 'passionate about intimacy coordinators', a reference to a curious brand of specialist who advises actors and actresses how to appear to be having sexual intercourse with each other without, apparently, actually either committing the act or giving the impression they would never wish to commit the act with that other person. Therefore *passionate* seemed an unfortunate choice of words. There are cases where it might be legitimately used (it would be odd to describe a man as in an 'enthusiastic' relationship with a woman, and might indeed create the wrong idea), but they are few and far between. *See also* **word inflation**.

Penned   An affected, and somewhat clichéd, means of saying 'wrote' or 'written': 'She penned her first novel in her early twenties' or 'he had penned the article well before the deadline'. In July 2023 the *Evening Standard* wrote about an 'open letter penned by Sinéad O'Connor to Miley Cyrus'. Not the least obtuseness of this usage is that it is entirely metaphorical. The verb usually applies to a professional writer, hardly any of whom has used a pen in his or her work since the invention of the typewriter, let alone that of the word processor. *See* **authored**, **clichés** *and* **nouns used as verbs**.

People   This used to be a noun and, indeed, a verb as a substitute for the perfectly sensible 'populate', but has become a familiar adjective in recent decades: not least with the phrase 'people person', which one assumes exists as an antonym for 'psychopath'. But the website for the accountancy firm EY shows how much further all this has been taken: it has something called 'People Advisory Services' that describes the pressure to 'build agile people cultures' and commits itself to 'helping our clients harness their people agenda'. With a promise also to 'work with clients to create holistic, innovative answers', it would be hard to find a finer example of **corporate speak**, and the conspiracy it represents against most of the rest of the human race.

Perpetrate and **perpetuate**   These verbs mean two very different things, yet because (one presumes) of their similarity they are often confused. The former means to carry out or commit something, usually a crime, or it is used comically as in 'he perpetrated the mistake of supporting Tottenham Hotspur'. To *perpetuate* something is to keep it going – 'at his college they perpetuate the tradition of saying grace'. Confusion occasionally arises and one hears people say that someone has *perpetuated* something when, in fact, all he has done is *perpetrated* it. It can sometimes be hard to tell whether the verbs are correct or not: one looked twice, or three times, at a *Times of India* headline in July 2023 that said: 'Close down temples if they perpetuate violence'. Although a temple cannot itself be violent, the word here could easily have been used as shorthand for those who form the membership of such institutions. To avoid possible confusion the headline writer might better have said 'encourage violence', or if the reference was to *perpetration*, then 'commit violence' would have been preferable. 'Still perpetuated' is a tautology, because the adjective is obvious from the verb. See also **persist**.

Persist   'Still persist' is a tautology. The verb itself, oddly enough, indicates persistence, or something that is still occurring. *See also* **return** *and* **revert**.

Personal friend One often hears a person describe another as a 'personal friend' or even a 'close personal friend'. There are degrees of friendship, as we all know, and 'close friend' is a meaningful usage. But *personal* friend, whether close or otherwise, is an absurdity. If there is no personal relationship, how can someone be a friend of any degree? A similar tautology is heard in the warning to passengers, as a train nears a station, to ensure they have 'all their personal belongings with them'. If the belongings were not personal, they would not belong.

Perspicacity and **perspicuity** These abstract nouns seem to have become interchangeable, which they are not. The dictionary defines the former as 'clearness of understanding or insight' or discernment, as in 'the chairman saw the root of the problem with immense perspicacity'. *Perspicuity* is the quality of easy comprehensibility – 'the perspicuity of her writing made her book easily understandable to all'. *Perspicacity* refers to something more exclusive than perspicuity.

-phobe, -phobia and **-phobic** In this era of identity politics the search for enemies, real or imagined, has become highly significant. Whether the enemy is someone of deep and hate-filled prejudice, or simply someone who does not agree with the fundamental contentions of the group that is identifying itself, that enemy is now branded a *-phobe*, or is accused of *-phobia*, or is described as *-phobic*: be it a 'homophobe' (who is perceived as having objections to people who are homosexual) or a 'transphobe' (perceived as having objections to someone seeking to change, or in the process of changing, his or her gender, or who has already changed it). In a different context one hears too of 'Islamophobes', who are people who dislike Muslims. In June 2023 the editor of a small newspaper in the furthest reaches of northern Canada, the *Inuvik Drum*, wrote a thoughtful leader on this subject, which addresses the key point at issue. He asserted that people with phobias always used to be those who feared a certain thing, coming as the English suffixes do from the Greek word for 'fear'. Illustrating how arachnophobics feared spiders (similarly, agoraphobics fear open spaces, and claustrophobics fear confined ones), the editor added: 'Aside from trauma survivors who could very well develop legitimate fears of people who resemble someone who hurt them in their past, I'm pretty sure the vast majority of people who claim they're homophobic or transphobic have not seen a doctor about it. They're using politically correct terms to mask their discrimination.' In the context in which 'homophobe' and 'transphobe' are used it is about people who dislike or feel a prejudice against, rather than fear of, the persons of whom they are said to be *phobic*. These suffixes should be avoided except in cases where there can be no doubt that genuine fear is involved, and the fact that the problem is actually one of straightforward loathing should not be disguised.

Picket This is the correct noun to describe a person who protests at the scene of a strike, usually trying to dissuade others from entering the premises. A wave of strikes in America in 2023 caused the transatlantic form *picketer* to appear on the airwaves in the United Kingdom. But it has also, as such infections do, gained a foothold on British websites, such as Yahoo!'s British 'Movies' page, where an actress was described in October 2023 as having been an 'active picketer' during the Screen Actors' Guild strike.

Pivot This is what people used to call a volte-face, as in 'he made a volte-face and announced that he did, after all, like his son'. It is used in **corporate speak** to indicate a change of strategy or of policy, usually by someone responsible for having instigated a failed one in the first place – 'he's pivoted on the strategy'. The term is often used in an attempt to conceal the earlier failure and to limit the humiliation of the person responsible.

Planning, forward   Since all plans are by definition ideas for the future, what is the purpose of the adjective *forward* before the noun *planning*? How could there be backward planning, or even planning for the present? The phrase is a tautology, and the adjective can be lost. *See also* **pre-**.

Plant up   One often hears on gardening programmes a pundit talking about the need to 'plant up' certain beds at certain times of year. As with **park up**, the *up* is unnecessary, though possibly more excusable in this usage, given the image it may convey to some listeners of a defined space being filled – or **filled up** – with plants. *See* **prepositions, superfluous**.

Plead   In Britain the past participle of the verb *to plead* remains *pleaded* – as in 'the youth pleaded not guilty' – but in America it is *pled*. There is logic in our saying in British English *lead* and *led* – as in 'I shall lead my troops as he led his', rather than *lead* and *leaded* to be consonant with *plead* and *pleaded*. The former is a strong verb and the latter a weak one, which means that in the past tense it simply adds *-ed*. For the moment *pled* will continue to cause incomprehension among most speakers of British English, though a few more years' relentless exposure to American films and television programmes will doubtless change all that.

Plurals, bogus   There are some nouns, mainly abstract ones, that do not have plurals, other than in the imaginations of some of the illiterates (many of them supposedly highly educated, as some of the worst offenders are bureaucrats who have imposed these words into the vocabulary of **corporate speak**) who perpetrate these mistakes. **Behaviours** is a common current offence. So too is **learnings**, things one is supposed to acquire, presumably, from having the gravity of one's bad behaviours brought to one's attention. *See also* **surgeries**.

Plurals, snob These are deemed to be plural forms of nouns used only or almost only by the most elevated ranks in society. *See* **snob plurals**.

Podiumed This particularly offensive and silly recently minted verb is meant to reflect the fact that those who come first, second or third in sporting competitions, notably athletics ones, stand on a podium with different levels according to whether one has come first, second or third. First one *podiums*, but then one **medals** as the gong is hung around the winner's neck. There are plenty of other ways to describe this action, such as 'won', 'came second' or 'came third'. *See also* **netted** *and* **nouns used as verbs**.

Political language, misuse of For centuries politicians have been accused of manipulating the language to avoid precision, in order not to say anything that might prove damaging to them in the future. Some politicians, or people who choose to conduct themselves in the manner usually associated with the political class, also introduce concepts into the language that are, to put it charitably, absurd. One example is the 'alternative facts' idea voiced by Kellyanne Conway, former handmaiden to President Donald Trump; another is the Duchess of Sussex's idea of 'my truth' (*see* **honest truth, the**). One would not like to give the impression, however, that this is purely an American affliction. One has lost count of the number of members of the political class who are asked a straightforward question, decline to answer it, but announce: 'What I will say is . . .' Similarly, they say 'I want to be completely clear' when they want to be nothing of the sort, and one prime minister to whom the truth was an almost complete stranger, Boris Johnson, would preface some entirely dishonest remark with a protestation that he 'fully respected' the point of view of an interlocutor, which it quickly became obvious he did not. When a politician runs out of answers it is 'time to move on'; when one wishes to indicate that something unpleasant may have to happen it has to be preceded by a **robust** inquiry or investigation, leading to a 'robust' conversation and quite possibly a 'robust' decision – in other words, a decision forced on a minister or government by circumstances created either by his or her incompetence, or which are outside his or her control.

Other words when used by such people have become terms of abuse, often useful in passing blame away from themselves as ineffectual politicians to others – elites, for example, or bureaucrats. They are always talking about their desire to **deliver** – Liz Truss, admittedly in a state of shell-shock, used the term three times during her resignation speech – and whether things are 'fit for purpose', which prefaces a supposed determination to rectify deficiencies; a determination that usually remains rhetorical. And, when one hears a politician say that 'the fact is', it almost inevitably is not. Perhaps the most grotesque example in recent years (other than President Bill Clinton's definitive statement about his affair with a young woman with whom he had sexual relations in which he said 'I did not have sexual relations with that woman') of a politician's complete abuse of language – or downright lying – was the aforementioned Johnson's statement on 12 April 2022 on his receipt of a fixed penalty notice for breaking Covid regulations: 'And in a spirit of openness and humility, I want to be completely clear about what happened on that date.' Also, you will note that when any politician is promising the proverbial earth, he or she will articulate an 'overwhelming desire' to achieve something, and good luck if it ever happens. *See also* **tireless**.

Pore over and **pour over**   One *pores over* a book that seizes one's interest, in reading it with great attention to detail and, often, enthusiasm – 'she pored over the latest Jilly Cooper novel'. However, one *pours* a liquid *over* something else – 'here's some gravy to pour over your potatoes', for example.

Practice and **practise**   The former is a noun and the latter the verb, so 'I went to net practice' but 'he has been practising his scales to little effect'. Matters are complicated partly by ignorance of this distinction, but also because in American English the verb, like the noun, is spelt with a 'c'. It would be incorrect to emulate that practice [*sic*] in British English.

Pre-   This prefix is, like **ex-**, a very useful way of describing concisely the status of something – in this case to describe a state of affairs that pertained before something else; *pre-war*, *pre-eighteenth century*, *pre-Reformation* and *pre-Covid*, for example. But it is also increasingly used absurdly: a euphemism for something that is second-hand is the ghastly 'pre-owned' or the even ghastlier 'pre-loved' – and in those cases it is used wrongly, as it is not a synonym for *previously* or *already*. The prefix is also often found in entirely tautologous usages, such as with 'pre-planned' or 'pre-arranged': something cannot be planned or arranged other than in advance, as should be apparent to most rational people. Taking tautology to an extreme is the mintage 'pre-prepared', which the *Manchester Evening News* perpetrated in November 2023 in an article about mulled wine: 'Although these pre-prepared bottles have taken most of the hard work out of it, it's crucial not to boil your wine when heating.' Perhaps an even worse example is 'pre-existing': on 28 November 2023, during a cold snap, the UK Health Security Agency warned people with 'pre-existing health conditions' to take care to keep warm. These people's health conditions simply existed; how they could pre-exist is unclear. *See* **planning, forward**.

Precede and **proceed**   The former verb means 'to go or occur in front of something or someone else', the latter 'to advance or to carry on'. Hence 'she preceded him into the dining room' or 'I always like to precede dinner with a glass of sherry'; and 'he proceeded to take out his gun and shoot the intruder' or 'they decided to proceed with the sale of the house'. *Preceding* is an adjective meaning earlier or former ('they had missed the preceding train') and *proceedings* (usually plural) a noun meaning an event or sequence of events ('they were so late they missed the proceedings altogether'). If, as one occasionally does, one sees a statement such as 'in the proceeding fortnight there had been no such incidents' then one has encountered a confusion of the two words.

Preferable and **preferential**   Something that is *preferable* is to be desired above other similar things, as in 'the butcher's meat was preferable to the supermarket's'. Something that is *preferential* is offered to someone in preference to its being offered to another, as in 'Mary had preferential treatment when it came to being allocated a room'. Because the usage 'in preference to' is common, a phrase like 'they went to France for their holidays in preference to Spain' may lead to the mistake that 'France is preferential to Spain for a holiday', which is entirely wrong. A grammar website on the internet offers 'it is *preferential* to eat healthy food' as a legitimate usage, but it is not; it is *preferable* to eat healthy food.

Prepositions, missing   In British English we have always appealed *against* a decision, approved *of* a policy, disapproved *of* someone's behaviour, debated *against* an opponent, had an impact *on* somebody else, officiated *at* a ceremony, and protested *against* a ruling. In recent years, under American influence, these prepositions appear to have evaporated, and not only in colloquial speech, but also in formal English. The loss of the preposition can create ambiguity and seems to defy logic in some cases, though it is not unprecedented. Many pre-war English novels talk from time to time about one of the characters feeling the need to 'telephone to' another; but after the war he or she would simply 'telephone' someone else. To many English ears the American usages – '**appeal** a decision', '**approve** a policy' (though 'approve of' was an early casualty, and many speakers and writers of British English now see no cause to use a preposition), '**debate** an opponent', '**disapprove** someone's behaviour', '**impact** somebody else' and '**protest** a ruling' all sound wrong ('**officiate** a wedding' is wrong, even in American English, and the preposition *at* is essential). Stylistically, in British English the prepositions are not optional. *See also* **bestow**.

Prepositions, superfluous   There is an increasing tendency to use phrases in which a verb that does a perfectly good job on its own has a preposition tacked on to it that adds nothing to the meaning and undermines any attempt at style or economy of expression. For specific examples, *see* **chase up and chase down, close up, divide up, fill up, finish up, head up, inside, off of, park up** *and* **plant up**. Such phrases are, however, being minted daily.

Prepositions, wrong   A difficulty with verbs that do require prepositions is that writers or speakers may occasionally choose the wrong one. *See* **arriving into, bored of, different, fed up of** *and* **on the weekend**.

Prescribe and **proscribe** These two verbs remain depressingly easily confused. To *prescribe* something is to order, or commend, it – 'the doctor prescribes plenty of exercise' or 'her teacher prescribed extra study of irregular verbs if she were to have a chance of passing her exams'. To *proscribe* something or someone is to ban it or forbid it – 'the government proscribed a terrorist organisation' or 'cocaine and heroin are absolutely proscribed'. Indeed, to *prescribe* drugs is markedly different from *proscribing* them.

Prevaricate and **procrastinate** The former word and the noun that complements it, *prevarication*, have according to the dictionary been used since the mid-nineteenth century to indicate delay or indecision. Etymologically, this usage is wrong and unnecessary, when the verb and the noun both historically indicate a degree of mendacity rather than of delay. 'More weeks of prevarication on the Portuguese leader's part followed', writes Professor Gallagher in his excellent biography of Salazar, when he seems to indicate delay rather than dishonesty. Oddly, the dictionary declares as obsolete a number of other meanings of the verb that indicate deviation from the truth or from honourable practice, though it does concede that the word still means 'to deviate from straightforwardness; to speak or act in an evasive way; to quibble, equivocate'. *Prevaricate* really means 'to lie'; but the dictionary says that the 'usual sense' now is 'to procrastinate'. We are back in the territory of **flaunt and flout** – if a word is used sufficiently often to mean something it does not mean, and used thus because it has certain sounds in common with a word that does have that meaning, then it must through force of habit acquire that meaning too. *Procrastinate* is a perfectly good verb to use to describe a person's postponement of action through indecision or idleness; if one wishes to use *prevaricate*, use it to describe the behaviour of someone who is a stranger to rectitude and honesty.

Prevent and **stop**   If one thinks about the logic of these two verbs they are not quite synonyms. To *prevent* something occurring is to take precautions to ensure that it does not come about – 'he had prevented a more serious injury by wearing a seat belt', for example. To *stop* is to end something that is already physically or metaphorically in motion – 'she decided to stop smoking' or 'the policeman stopped the car in the high street'. To *prevent* smoking, as opposed to *stop* it, means you ensure it doesn't start in the first place; to *prevent* a car in the high street is not remotely idiomatic, but if it were used it would mean to bar it from entering that location. You cannot *prevent* something that is already happening, but you can attempt to *stop* it. When *prevent* is used, it is idiomatic to use the preposition *from*, as in 'I was prevented from entering the room'. To say or write 'I was prevented entering' is wrong. In the active voice 'he prevented me from entering' is correct; 'he prevented me entering' is not idiomatic, 'he prevented my entering' is, but rare. See *Appendix*: **gerunds**.

Principal and **principle**   These two words, the former a noun and an adjective, the latter a noun that can be developed into an adjective, continue to cause immense confusion, as (according to the dictionary) they have done since the fourteenth century. *Principal* means, effectively, chief or foremost – 'my principal concern is that you do not catch cold' or 'the principal actors are no longer under contract'. It has also come to be used as the title for the head teacher in a school – 'the Principal is Miss Smith' – and for the capital sum used for an investment – 'the principal was £25,000'.

Principle has its origins in theology and philosophy to mean a fundamental precept, source or origin, and is generally used today to mean something an individual or a movement recognises as a basic truth or basis for personal or institutional beliefs, as in 'I do not enter betting shops on principle' or 'the free market is one of the principles to which the Conservative party generally adheres'. It gives us the adjective *principled*, in instances such as 'I have a principled objection to eating meat'. To say that 'honesty is one of my principals' is a solecism, as is 'my principle objection to eating meat is that an animal has to die'.

Pristine This adjective is now routinely used to describe something that is immaculate, factory-fresh or what numismatists in referring to a coin would refer to as 'mint condition'. It in fact means original, or belonging to the earliest period. If you want to say a car looks brand new, then say so: to describe it as *pristine* implies it dates from well before the Model 'T' Ford.

Privy Council This body, which in the United Kingdom advises the Sovereign, is composed of *Privy Counsellors*, not *Councillors*. There is also one in the Kingdom of Thailand, and its English-language media always refer to its members as 'privy councillors'. That usage often appears in relation to the UK body, and it is wrong.

Pronouns It has always been polite to refer to people, whether by their names, titles or pronouns, in the way he or she would wish to be addressed. For example, when a man or woman is ennobled through choice he or she ceases to be 'Mr' or 'Mrs' and becomes 'Lord' or 'Lady'. Some people who inherit peerages choose not to use their titles, and instead remain 'Mr' (they are almost always men), as do some baronets who choose to remain 'Mr' rather than become 'Sir'. That is their privilege, and it is not new: as has been noted elsewhere, Lady Diana Cooper, her courtesy title deriving from her birth as a daughter of a duke, chose to continue to be addressed as such even after her husband, Duff Cooper, was created a viscount (*see* **Lady**).

Now, with the debate among activists about gender identity, the matter of what people call themselves when it comes to pronouns that indicate a gender has become intensely, and in some cases aggressively, political. It also provides challenges to those who value sensible grammar, and who deserve just as much respect as any other beleaguered minority. It has long been generally accepted that a person who has had the medical procedures required to change his or her sex is, out of logic as much as out of good manners and common courtesy, thereafter referred to by the pronouns that go with the acquired sex: *he* becomes *she*, *her* becomes *him* or *his*, and so on. Now, some activists demand that people should be accorded these changed pronouns even if they have simply decided to consider themselves of a different gender, rather than undergo the extensive surgery required to change it. Equally, some people now decide they have no specific genders, and someone who looks and acts like a 'he' or a 'she' becomes *they*, even though the person concerned is a singular and not a plural.

This can be highly confusing even to those who take a libertarian view of these questions. A measure of the grammatical difficulties that arise from this sociological development was found in a thoughtful letter in the 15 June 2023 edition of the *London Review of Books*, from a Mr David Book, writing from California. His subject was a review published a month earlier by Dr Erin Maglaque (who specialises in, among other things, 'gender history') about the American academic and literary critic Lauren Berlant, who was born female. The late Professor Berlant did not make matters simple for those who write about her; as her Wikipedia entry says: 'Berlant used she/her pronouns in personal life but they/them professionally.' One infers from that that someone writing about Berlant as a woman would, out of courtesy, refer to her as 'her', but writing about her career as a critic or teacher would refer to 'them' as 'them'. Equally, one might think such a distinction nonsense or an affectation and not bother. That must remain a matter of taste and conscience, and be coupled with the awareness that most people are not activists on this issue, and would find 'them' simply puzzling or wrong.

Mr Book wrote, quite correctly, that Professor Berlant had every right to take the attitude to her pronouns that she did – 'as much right as Queen Victoria had to the use of "we" when referring to herself. Others may have done the same, out of respect, when speaking to or of Berlant. But that is not a compelling reason for Maglaque to do it now, after Berlant's death.' Mr Book surmised that perhaps the reviewer 'feels a bit uncomfortable with the non-binary form and tried to minimise the use of this clumsy contrivance'. He noted, admirably, that 'using one word for two different jobs is always an impediment to clarity'. That, indeed, will be the main concern to people who value good grammar, and who understand that such value is not to demonstrate that one is part of some intellectual elite, but to write English free from ambiguity or misinterpretation. However, it is increasingly clear that ease of communication will not be allowed to impede what has now become a political question.

Matters were not helped by a reply from Dr Maglaque in the following issue of the *LRB*, in which she hoped her use of the non-binary pronoun had helped Mr Book move 'that much closer to loosening his attachment to the fantasy of gender altogether'. Doubtless Dr Maglaque has a well-developed command of irony and was seeking to be mischievously provocative; but since one suspects that a vast majority who speak English do not regard gender, or the long-established idea of a male and female sex, as a 'fantasy' they may well persist accordingly in using traditional pronouns, with the non-binary usage confined to parts of academia, local government and the civil service where dread of causing offence overrules all else, and to virtue-signalling private-sector organisations and individuals who feel similarly. The great majority of ordinary English speakers appear to have little interest in this matter, but they may be forced to alter that view if this question ceases to be confined to rarefied sections of society. As with most uses of language, thoughtful people will exercise their own discretion, and seek to remain clear in their meaning without acting discourteously or causing unpleasantness. *See also* **their, there and they're**.

Prostate and **prostrate** The *prostate* is a gland in the male body notorious for the difficulties it can cause when its owner reaches later life. *Prostrate* is an adjective that refers to someone of either sex lying face down ('he was prostrate with grief'), and gives us the verb in 'she prostrated herself in worship'. 'Another one is prostate on the ground' reported MailOnline of a criminal incident on 28 June 2023, the writer clearly not having mastered the distinction.

Protest In conventional British English, this verb must be accompanied by a preposition, and not deployed in the American fashion of 'they protested the invasion of Afghanistan'. Good style in English requires a usage such as 'the students protested *against* the increase in tuition fees' or possibly 'the staff protested *about* the cuts to the service'. One occasionally hears 'protested over', which is barbarous, but 'the teachers protested in favour of a rise in their salaries' is quite acceptable. *See* **prepositions, missing**.

Proved and **proven**   *Proved* is the past tense of the verb *to prove*, as in 'the police proved he burgled the house'; *proven* is the adjective, as in 'he is a proven liar'. A modern variant is 'it was proved', which is now common, but not strictly correct. 'A proved liar' would not be correct, and not remotely idiomatic.

Punching their weight   This is a tired phrase familiar in **corporate speak**, and is applied usually in the negative to some often well-paid employee who is not earning his salary by making a sufficient contribution to the business's profits or efficient management, as in 'John hasn't been punching his weight for the last few months'. An example appeared in the *Herald* newspaper in May 2023, when a local businessman said: 'If I look at Glasgow, I see a hugely powerful city that I just don't think punches its weight.' It is a form of euphemism, and the tedious **cliché** can be avoided, and the communication made more effective, by saying directly what the problem is – 'lazy', 'idle', 'distracted' or even 'stupid' might serve the purpose far better when describing individuals. 'Punching above their weight' is meant as a compliment: the person referred to is performing better than his or her earlier record suggested was possible. Where this cliché is avoided it is sometimes because the speaker or writer has substituted the equally tedious **going the extra mile**.

Punctilious and **punctual**   These two adjectives are not synonyms, though *punctuality*, which is the habit of doing something on time, may well be an element of *punctiliousness*, which requires the strict observance of the rules of good conduct.

Push the envelope   It is now rather rarer to hear this ludicrous piece of **corporate speak** than it was a decade or two ago, when it still had the merit of banal novelty, so perhaps the vogue for using it has died out, or those who insisted on using it have bored themselves to death. It is believed to indicate that someone should take a more radical or original approach to something, as in 'Mary needs to push the envelope with her marketing strategy'. It would be far better to say that Mary needed to find a more inventive marketing strategy. It is still occasionally spotted, such as on the Motley Fool website in August 2023 when it published the phrase 'T-Mobile pushes the envelope on pricing'. The story was not satirical; but this is a **cliché** that should be vigorously avoided by all who wish to be taken seriously.

Q

Question mark, misused It ought to be clear that one uses a question mark to end a statement in which one has posed a question, as in 'Does he take sugar?' or 'Do you consider yourself a good speaker of English?' Those of us with the misfortune to receive countless emails from people with whom we are not acquainted, but who engage in public relations on the part of commercial interests or lobbyists, find they often begin their communications with a tedious assumption of intimacy, as in 'How are you today?' in which the question mark is used legitimately. However, other such insincere enquiries after one's well-being include 'I hope you are well?' or even worse 'I hope you are having a good day?' These are not questions and therefore require no question mark; they are expressions of esperance, sincere or otherwise.

Quotation and **quote** The former is the noun, the latter is the verb. 'He would show off by dropping quotations from Horace in his conversation' or 'he would quote Horace in his conversation in order to show off'. Ubiquitously, however, *quote* is used as a noun, as in 'Can you remind me of that quote from Shakespeare?' but this usage should be regarded as slang. It still has no place in good style or in formal writing.

R

Rain, reign and **rein** In a publisher's catalogue, of all places, in a notice about a forthcoming work of fiction, it was said that a character in a novel about the Second World War watched 'the bombs begin to reign down on London'. Other solecisms are 'to give it full reign' and 'to lay down the reigns', great favourites of the MailOnline website. Perhaps both are the consequences of the obsession with monarchy as a form of celebrity. Another possibility for the confusion is that the three homophones all have wide metaphorical usages. As verbs, *rain*, literally, means for precipitation to fall from the sky and, as with bombs, has a range of metaphorical deployments, as in 'blows rained down on the defenceless man'. *Reign* means, literally, to occupy a throne ('the late Queen reigned for over seventy years') or to have command over something ('Smith has reigned over United for a decade'). *Rein* (usually *rein in*) is to slow down a horse, but is used figuratively in contexts such as 'he tried for years to rein in his headstrong son'.

Raise and **raze** The former verb means to lift up; the latter to destroy or demolish, often in the phrase 'to the ground', indicating nothing is left standing. In April 2024 MailOnline wrote that a former home of the Duke of York had been 'raised to the ground' – a logic-defying assertion – but to its credit the error was corrected a few hours later. The confusion seldom occurs in reverse: I have yet to read of something 'being razed above the ground', but am prepared to be proved wrong.

Raise and **rise**   As verbs, both of these words mean 'lifting' or 'elevating' something. The former is transitive and the latter intransitive (*see Appendix*: **verbs**). Thus one might say 'I raised the level of the ceiling in the new extension by six inches' or 'she raised her head and acknowledged him when he entered the room'; but 'the storm rose after six o'clock' or 'the sun rises each morning'. In American English as a noun the former is used idiomatically to describe an increase in pay – 'he asked for a raise of five thousand dollars' – but in British English it is *rise* – 'he was given a rise of five thousand pounds'. And the verb *to raise* is not to be confused with *to raze*, its homophone, which means to reduce a building or buildings to rubble. *See also* **arise and rise**.

Rather   Does one say, and write, that 'he is rather a shocking brute' or that 'he is a rather shocking brute'? There is often a complete disregard for word order where the deployment of the phrase 'rather a', to accentuate a noun, is concerned. 'Rather a shocking brute' is preferable to the latter, and to see why, simply remove the adjective. 'He is rather a brute' makes sense; 'he is a rather brute' is nonsense. 'Rather than' means 'instead of', as in 'he put on his thick sweater rather than wear a coat'. Another usage is where *rather*, as an adverb, indicates a preference: 'I'd rather swim than go for a walk' simply means 'I'd prefer to swim'.

Reach out   This is another omnipresent expectoration of **corporate speak,** though it is now also used far outside business. In a climate where the public sector increasingly wants to prove it has regard for those who have no choice but to use its services, instead of simply viewing its clients as necessary evils, 'reaching out' happens all the time. To *reach out* physically to get something is a usage the dictionary traces back to the times of the Angles and the Saxons. A metaphorical usage in this modern sense dates back to the mid-nineteenth century, with an emphasis on expressing sympathy: but now it seems mainly to mean 'connect with' or 'offer support to', both of which phrases are more exact and therefore more satisfactory ways of describing what *reach out* is taken to mean. In August 2023 the *Financial Times* reported: 'EU's new Green Deal chief to reach out to industry and voter'. What this appeared to mean was that he was going to keep them informed of what he was doing. In Scotland, the *Daily Record* reported: 'Hate crime victims encouraged to reach out to police as Perthshire Pride approaches'. It is part of the modern vogue that the corporate speakers now invite people to *reach out* to them rather than initiating the *reaching out* themselves. In America – where this usage seems to have started – a local website announced how 'community leaders reach out with ways you [*sic*] help asylum seekers living on Staten Island' – as with **warn**, no direct object now appears to be required by this phrase. To *reach out* can also indicate not merely a public relations exercise, but a cry for help, and individuals now appear to be as adept at it as groups or institutions. The *Guardian* ran a feature with the headline: 'Living alone is making my anxiety spiral but I'm too ashamed to reach out to friends and family'. In that example, and more clearly in the following one, 'reach out' has come to be a **clichéd** and long-winded way of saying 'ask', or to 'seek aid from': according to *Psychology Today* there is 'The Right Time to Reach Out for Help'. And, in a story with whose veracity we need not, for our purposes, unduly concern ourselves, *OK* magazine reported that 'Kate Middleton [*sic*] "wants to reach out to Prince Harry" amid Royal Family rift'. Perhaps no example quite underlines the dreary absurdity that this phrase has now attained as that fatuous speculation does.

Rebut and **refute** *Rebut* began its life meaning to drive something back, and has come to mean simple denial or contradiction: you can rebut my assertion that you are an idiot, because I can't prove that you are and you probably can't prove you aren't. But if you say you are of good character and I have documentary evidence of your criminal record, I can *refute* your statement by proving that you aren't. In our political life politicians generally rebut; they seldom have the proof needed to refute. The former act only buys time; the latter tends to close the question definitively. The former relies on bluster; the latter on proof.

Regretful and **regrettable** These are not synonyms. Someone is *regretful* when he or she feels sorrow or remorse over an action – 'she felt deeply regretful that she had ditched her husband'. By contrast, 'she had come to regard her decision to ditch her husband as deeply regrettable' would be correct – *regrettable* being an adjective applicable to any act that is susceptible of being regretted.

Reluctant and **reticent** One sometimes hears that someone 'showed enormous reluctance in discussing his achievements' when in fact what he showed was *reticence*. He may have been *reluctant* to speak about them too, which is a related matter, but it is not quite the same thing. *Reluctant* is an adjective that can be applied to a wide range of things that a person might be deeply unwilling to do, speaking being but one of them. *See* **reticent**, *and also* **flaunt and flout**.

Restaurateur This is the correct term for someone who runs a restaurant, not 'restauranteurs', who according to

MailOnline on 30 April 2023 'have today warned the nation's network of Italian diners is at breaking point', which also demonstrates the dangers of failing to have an object with the verb to **warn**: the *restaurateurs* were warning the public and perhaps the government, not the nation's network of Italian diners. Indeed, by also using the **Americanism** for a café or cheap restaurant, the report creates confusion over whether 'diners' are such businesses, or are the people eating in them.

Resurface For most of us this verb describes something that should happen to a road full of potholes; or it might possibly describe what a deep-sea diver does once he has finished his explorations. However, it has now entered **corporate speak** to describe returning to an issue that had been put to one side (or **parked**) some time beforehand – as in 'Perhaps it is time to resurface the possibility of doing a deal with France?' If one seeks a juicy metaphor in this context then *resurrect*, or even that old corporate-speak favourite **revisit** might suffice, if desperate. Most people would say 'look again at' or 'return to'.

Reticent This means to be a man, or woman, of few words. It is frequently confused with **reluctant**, perhaps because it suggests a reluctance to speak. Conservative MP Tobias Ellwood, talking about Putin's regime, said in August 2023 that some Third World nations were a little bit reticent about joining in with the sanctions against Russia. He apparently meant 'reluctant', though it is quite likely that those nations were, for fear of some degree of reprisals, also reticent on the subject.

Return MailOnline in August 2022 wrote of a distinguished scientist, exiled from Nazi Germany, 'returning back' to his homeland after the defeat of Hitler. One cannot return anywhere else but 'back' to the place where one is returning; so it is a tautology. Something similar applies to **revert**.

Reveal and **revelation**   *Reveal* is a verb, and it means to unveil or expose or display something. It is not a noun; that is *revelation*. However, in promoting a new television series in January 2024, Sky News spoke of the 'big reveal' contained in the forthcoming saga. Why this verb had to be 'nouned' when *revelation* serves perfectly well is unclear.

Reverend   One of the most ubiquitous forms of mis-address in England today is to describe someone as 'the Reverend Smith'. It is imported from America, where it is not regarded as a solecism. *Reverend* traditionally requires an honorific or, like the chivalric title 'Sir', a Christian name or forename. So it can be 'the Reverend Mr Smith' or 'the Reverend John Smith' but never 'the Reverend Smith'. D. J. Taylor, in his life of George Orwell, refers to the clergyman who conducted Orwell's second wedding ceremony as 'the Reverend Braine', so it is a mistake made in even the better-educated households. There is also an increasing tendency to describe a man or woman of the cloth as a 'reverend', which while technically accurate is idiomatically absurd – in a phrase such as 'when he finished university he decided to train to become a reverend'.

Revert   'You can revert these changes at any time' said MailOnline on 2 July 2023, in an item about managing a smartphone. *Revert* does not mean reverse, which is what the writer should have said. 'Revert back' is possibly an even greater offence, because a moment's thought and the application of logic would indicate that it is a tautology. Reversion is in any case the act of going back. *See also* **return** *and* **persist**.

Revisit Following the success of the television adaptation of Evelyn Waugh's *Brideshead Revisited* in the early 1980s – indeed, some people might even have gone to the lengths of reading the book – there was a vogue in **corporate speak** to use the verb *revisit*, which had long been rather literal, as a metaphor. So whereas one had hitherto said 'we hope to revisit Cornwall one day' or 'I revisited France for several successive years' we suddenly had an avalanche of 'we must revisit the profitability of that division of the business' or 'it's time we revisited the question of unisex lavatories'. I rather hoped that, forty years later, this silly phrase would have died out, but it hasn't. As with the even worse **resurface**, what is wrong with 'look again at'?

Rewriting history It is now a commonplace of an archaeological discovery, or even the turning up of some long-forgotten manuscript in an archive, that the act will 'rewrite history'. Sky News announced in November 2022: 'Discovery of 2,000-year-old bronze statues to "re-write history"'. The argument was that these statues told us more about the expansion of the Roman empire at the expense of the Etruscan civilisation, which appears to be the case. Individual aspects of history are frequently being revised because of such discoveries or investigations, but to say they are being rewritten means taking the extant history and paraphrasing, editing or making a précis of it. What such statements mean when they use this **cliché** is that new evidence has been found that will make us think again about some aspect of history and perhaps to write it afresh, not to *rewrite* it.

Rife On 30 September 2023 MailOnline spoke of 'rife accusations' being made against an alleged criminal. *Rife*, which means frequent or plentiful, is not an adjective that can be used idiomatically in that way. Accusations *were* *rife* against the man; or there were numerous accusations against him.

Rise   *See* **arise and rise**, *and* **raise and rise**.

Rising to a crescendo   *See* **crescendo** for an explanation of why this phrase is nonsense.

Robust   A political weasel word meaning 'frank', 'unpleasant', or perhaps even 'frankly unpleasant'. An inkling of its traditional meaning of 'rigorous' may or may not come into it. *See* **political language, misuse of**.

Rock up   This term, meaning to arrive or to appear – 'he rocked up just before closing time' – has wriggled its way into our slang quite thoroughly in the last decade or so; but an alarming number of people seem to think it acceptable to use it even in conversations in contexts where they might otherwise wish to be treated with respect. Perhaps it does impress their interlocutors. It has no place in serious written English. That did not stop the technology website TweakTown (which, in its defence, appears to be aimed at the juvenile market, whether in fact or in theory) from running a headline in August 2023 proclaiming: 'Elon Musk says he's going to rock up at Mark Zuckerberg's house today ready to fight'. The two men were planning a cage fight that the website also described as 'highly anticipated', which of course it was not: it was, though, long awaited, much looked forward to, and generating a high level of expectations. *See also* **anticipate**.

Rococo   This term, which signifies an exceptionally ornate variant of the baroque, is in danger of becoming overused in an abstract sense just as **baroque** itself is. As such, it risks becoming meaningless. An example was provided by Tony Travers, who wrote in the *Local Government Chronicle* in January 2023, that 'ministers and officials are trapped by the rococo complexity of their funding system'. The adjective is frankly just showing off, and not in an enlightening fashion.

Run it up the flagpole   This is one of the more ludicrous outpourings of **corporate speak**. It means to put an idea or proposal out for consultation, to see whether others like it. Since the only thing in non-metaphorical life that one runs up a flagpole is a flag, and usually not one that is a subject of debate or of contention, one struggles to see how on earth this phrase came into use.

S

Safe   It is becoming commonplace to be urged to 'drive safe'. *Drive* in such a statement is a verb, and if one is going to do it in a particular way then it requires an adverb. It should be 'drive safely'. *See also* **wrong**.

Sat   In conventional and correct usage, this word is the past tense and past participle of the verb *to sit*, as in 'the cat sat on the mat' and 'no one had sat in that chair since the old man died'. However, it is frequently and wrongly used as the past tense of the passive voice of the verb *to seat*, which means to place someone in a seat or a chair in a particular place. 'If you carry on down the aisle an usher will seat you', one might hear at a wedding, or in the past tense 'I was seated behind the bride's mother'. Yet one too often hears the solecism 'I was sat behind the bride's mother', which shows a profound lack of grasp of the language. A prime example was Holly Willoughby, the television presenter, in June 2023 saying how odd she felt 'sat here' without her former colleague Phillip Schofield. She might have felt odd 'being seated here' or even just 'sitting here' without him, but 'sat here' was incorrect. As well as being used wrongly for 'I was seated' it is also frequently used when one should say 'I was sitting'. *See also* **stood** *and* **took**.

See   It is lazy to write that 'the forecast of snow has seen the Met Office issue weather warnings'. What it had in fact done was *caused* the issue of the warnings. *See* is overused to the point where it becomes meaningless, and good stylists should avoid it in contexts such as 'yesterday saw the highest number of illegal migrants arrive at Dover', writing or saying instead 'the highest recorded number of illegal migrants arrived at Dover yesterday'.

-self and **-selves**   Pronouns ending in *-self* and *-selves* (*myself, yourself, him/her/itself, ourselves, yourselves, themselves*) have specific uses and are not interchangeable with the basic pronouns such as *me, you, him* and *her*. The most frequent correct usage is in direct reference to oneself or to another about an action affecting those people – 'I saw myself in the mirror', or 'you must have thought yourself very lucky', or 'Why didn't they buy themselves some tickets?' However, a sentence such as 'he gave it to myself' or 'Would yourself like some tea?' is always wrong: it should be 'he gave it to me', however emphatic the statement is. 'Would you like some tea yourself?' is a correct usage if one has ordered or requested tea for everyone else but left it unclear to the person pouring it whether you yourself [*sic*] want a cup. Talking of emphasis, one can understand why Vivek Ramaswamy, the potential Republican presidential candidate, said in August 2023 that 'I don't think that there's a relevant race for any two candidates other than Trump and myself', but colloquially he would better have said 'than Trump and me' (*see* **than**). Something such as 'Look at himself!' can only be meant satirically. Correct uses of this pronoun also include emphasis on another person, usually unexpectedly – 'the prime minister himself opened the debate and not, as had been expected, the Chancellor' or 'the children themselves arranged the party without any help from the adults'; or the separation of an element in something larger: 'the starter itself cost £25, and the whole bill was over £200', or 'the houses themselves took three years to build, and it was another two before the gardens were finished'. If using this form of the pronoun, it is always valuable to pause and reflect whether the usage is necessary or correct.

Sewage and **sewerage** Sewage is human waste and other effluent that runs through a system of pipes known as sewerage. Those who speak of our grotesquely polluted inland waterways being filled with 'sewerage' have gone a syllable too far.

Shall and **will**, and **should** and **would** These two forms of the future tense appear interchangeable, but they are not, and they remain greatly confused in both written and spoken English, with the distinction between them these days largely unknown. The simple future – the expression of what is going to happen, is related as follows: 'I shall see you tomorrow; you/he/she/it will see him tomorrow; we shall see you tomorrow; you/they will see him tomorrow.' But when a future verb form relates to a command or a determined resolution, the auxiliary verbs change round. Therefore it becomes 'I will stop all this nonsense'; 'you shall do as you are told'; 'she shall have champagne on her birthday'; 'we will give up smoking'; 'they shall go to the zoo'. The old joke that children used to be taught in order to learn how to handle these verb forms correctly still pertains, about the boy who falls overboard and cries out 'I will drown and no one shall save me', his determination to drown being underlined by the auxiliary verb *will* and his resolve not to be saved underlined by using *shall* for his potential rescuers. Had he cried 'I shall drown and no one will save me' then, presumably, he might have had a chance. Stylists who wish to exhibit the subtlety of their command of the language will continue to notice the distinction of these future forms; others, one fears, will continue to fail to note their existence. The same distinction applies to the conditionals *should* and *would* – 'I should like to play cricket' or 'they would like to play cricket', both statements expressing a simple wish for the future rather than absolute determination; and 'I would like to play cricket' (in response to a suggestion that he would rather do something else) and 'they should like to play cricket' in a similar circumstance – as well as to the past-tense uses of those auxiliaries: 'I should have liked a drink had I not been in a hurry' and 'they would have gone for a walk had it not rained so heavily'. *See also* **should**.

-shame This has become another one of those suffixes (*see* **-athon** *and* **-thon, -cation, -gate, -ification** *and* **-nomics**) that tabloid journalists enjoy tacking on to the end of a noun to indicate something else about which human beings are supposed to feel guilty: as in 'body-shame' when someone is meant to feel bad about not looking like a supreme athlete or film star; or 'fat-shame', which is something similar and unpleasantly implies a failing on the part of the person being 'shamed'. The *Sun*, in August 2023, talked of 'travel shame', which is apparently what is imposed on those who behave badly on aeroplanes, ships or forms of more quotidian public transport. Another coinage, in this age of climate **emergency**, is 'carbon-shame', a term applied to people who fly too much, light too many barbecues or even choose to eat dead cows.

Should This auxiliary verb is most frequently used when advising another to carry out a certain action: 'you should wrap up today, it's cold', or 'he should be careful what he says', or the often heard 'I should do that, if I were you'. Unlike when this auxiliary is used as a future or conditional tense, it remains *should* in all persons. Sometimes, however, such a construction will require a stronger alternative, as it may be inadequate for the job it has to do: *see* **ought and should**.

Should and **would**, **should have** and **would have**   *See* **shall and will**.

Should of   One often hears in demotic colloquial English phrases such as 'you should of told me', where the speaker imagines he or she is uttering the perfect tense – what to most people is 'should have'. This normally escapes going into print, but so ubiquitous is its use becoming that it cannot be too long before it does. *See also* **could of**, **might of** *and* **would of**.

Slander   This is a defamatory statement made orally, unlike libel, which is such a statement published in some form. *See* **libel and slander**.

Snob plurals   This was a phrase used by Eric Partridge, the author of *Usage and Abusage*, an immensely thoughtful expert on words and grammar, and whose observations, albeit many of them made over seventy-five years ago, command respect still. He referred in this instance mainly to plurals used by the upper and upper-middle classes that were not common among the rest of society, and they referred mainly, it seemed, to animals. This was because of the predilection (as he saw it) among such people for shooting game, not just in the British Isles, but in other parts of the then empire. Hence phrases such as 'plenty of tiger in these parts' among those old colonial types who had gone on tiger shoots, or 'not many pig around here' if one was partial to some pigsticking. Such usages went out of vogue at about the same time as the empire itself, and their use now would appear an absurd affectation, not least given the evaporation of most big-game hunting. However, even in the third decade of the twenty-first century game shooting still exists in the United Kingdom, so it is quite usual to hear those familiar with it talking about 'a brace of pheasant', 'a good bag of grouse' or 'we saw plenty of partridge today'. Non-participants must make their own choice: the plural of *grouse* is *grouse*, whether one approves of shooting them or not (if someone talks about 'grouses' they are using the word as a synonym for complaints or grievances – 'he had no end of grouses about the hotel'). *Snipe*, likewise, is the plural of *snipe*. It is not wrong to talk about pheasants or partridges or woodcocks or pigeons, but bear in mind that if you hear people talk about there being 'plenty of woodcock about', they are probably deep-seated country men or women. With cloven-hooved game something similar applies: but even the most urban people seem to realise that the plural of *deer* is *deer*. Despite trying very hard, I have never yet heard anyone talk of 'deers', but 'muntjacs' is not unknown, and not necessarily wrong.

Snuck   This is used as the past participle of the verb *to sneak* only by Americans or by people who find it amusing to pretend to be American. People who are British or wish to pretend to be British should write or say *sneaked*. See also **Americanisms**.

So   This is a pretty tedious piece of punctuation in colloquial speech, and has no place in good written English. One often hears announcers in broadcasts begin their statements with the word: 'So, the prime minister will today . . .' or 'So, the fallout from yesterday's announcement . . .' and so on *ad nauseam*. Some users simply cannot help it. If you can, then please do. However, it is acceptable as a synonym for *therefore*: 'The traffic was abominable and in any case they left late, so they did not arrive until after dinner had started.' A similar offence to that caused by the needless use of *so* when introducing a sentence is often heard in the use, in identical circumstances, of *but*.

Soar The dictionary says that this verb means 'to ascend to a towering height'. It is not a synonym for *rise*, or *increase*, though the financial media seem very much to think it is. 'Soaring costs', 'soaring interest rates', 'soaring numbers of households' and 'soaring inflation' were to be found across British newspapers on the same day in October 2023. It was lucky the weather was simply warm, or we would have had 'soaring temperatures' as well. *Rising* would have done the job well in any of these examples. The ubiquity of *soaring* removes from it any sense of drama and replaces it with familiarity and tedium. Those who care about effective style would be well advised to avoid it.

Soaraway Used in the 1970s as an advertising slogan in Britain for the *Sun* newspaper – 'the soaraway *Sun*' – its usage elsewhere now has become self-parodic, with all that that entails.

Solid and **stolid** These two near-homophones are occasionally confused, with the latter used in place of the former rather than vice versa. *Solid*, which was borrowed either from the Latin or the French, has been in English since the late fourteenth century and refers to a physical substance having a filled interior: a solid piece of metal or wood is one that is not hollow. It is also used extensively metaphorically to indicate something or someone of durability, hardness and reliability – 'he's a solid supporter of the Labour party'. *Stolid* comes from the Latin adjective *stolidus*, meaning motionless, and used in English to mean dull and impassive, having entered the language early in the seventeenth century: 'her reaction to the man's death was one of stolid frigidity', for example. Something that is solid is not necessarily stolid, though someone who is stolid could well, in some metaphorical sense, also be solid.

Sorted   This malefaction has been increasingly common in the last couple of decades. It seems to have begun as part of the cockney argot, as a truncation of *sorted out*, but is now in such universal use that on the increasingly rare occasions when someone hears the correct expression, such as in 'he has sorted out the problem', one almost faints with shock. The *out* is vital. One can *sort* things, but it means to arrange them by type or genre – 'she sorted the beads by colour', or 'he sorted the post'. Whereas the expression used to be the province solely of the uneducated, educated people now find it amusing or even 'liberating' to use it. It is expressly to be avoided in formal written English. If someone wishes to indicate that something is done, then they should say it is done, or has been 'sorted out'; or, if it was a problem, that it is solved.

Speak   One *speaks to* somebody or to others, one does not *speak with* them, which suggests all parties are talking simultaneously, and therefore incomprehensibly.

Spelling, casual attitude towards   I persist in the nakedly old-fashioned view, expressed in my earlier books, that ever since British English acquired a standard dictionary with the publication of the first edition of the *Oxford English Dictionary* almost a century ago there have been no real excuses for playing around with spelling. Other nations and cultures using our language may do as they wish, and the Americans in particular do – not just with orthography, but also with elements of grammar and words (especially slang) that have meanings quite different in other places where English is spoken from those in British English. Some spellings that were debatable at the time of the *OED*'s arrival – such as *shew* and *shewn* for *show* and *shown* – have gradually by custom and practice been settled one way or the other. This is happening all the time, especially with recent coinages. Thus the early-twenty-first century's *e-mail* has become the 2020s' *email*. A debate continues about whether to spell words ending in *-sation* with a 'z', making them end in *-zation* – so *civilisation* or *civilization*. I prefer the former, with the latter increasingly regarded as American orthography, but the matter is far from settled and in publications, websites or newspapers often comes down to a question of house style. Some words in the English language are notoriously difficult to spell, because they defy logic. Some people do not have the sort of memory (inevitably, visual memory) that easily enables them to register and remember the spelling of thousands or even tens of thousands of words. The rise of the spellchecker may convince some of them that they don't need to bother to master a skill that most readers and writers of any language usually find comes with repeated practice. The spellchecker is not, sadly, always available; and human nature has it that people who can spell often take a certain view of people who can't. That said, a distinguished teacher at Cambridge told me years ago that it was possible to get a first-class honours degree in English, never mind any other subject, without being able to spell correctly, which one can put down only to a political attitude on the part of those who mark the papers. Most printed media in this country set a high store by using meticulous spelling, and most of those with websites do too. It is a sensible example to follow.

There is a small group of words in frequent use that many people have trouble spelling correctly. What follows does not pretend to be an exhaustive list, but it is one that contains the most troublesome of the words that cause difficulty in this respect:

accommodation	cemetery	definite
all right	committee	(just) deserts
bellwether	consensus	desiccate

diarrhoea	linchpin	recommendation
drunkenness	manoeuvre	restaurateur
dumbbell	mantelpiece	rhythm
embarrassment	memento	separate
fulfil	millennium	skilful
gauge	minuscule	stratagem
harass	misspelt	succeeded
harassment	possession	supersede
humorous	privilege	tyranny
independent	publicly	weird
jewellery	quandary	withhold
liaison	questionnaire	
lightning	receive	

Spit   In British English this irregular verb imitates *sit* in its past tense, becoming *spat*, as in 'I spat on the floor and did not worry about the mess'. The American English verb does not change: an American would say 'I spit on the floor and did not worry about the mess'.

Stakeholders   This term was once confined to describing people who literally had a stake in an enterprise, specifically investors in a company with a financial holding in it. The financial media still use it in this way, and quite legitimately so. However, it has entered wider **corporate speak** to refer to anyone who is even slightly affected by the operations of anything at all. Therefore a person receiving state welfare benefits is described as a *stakeholder* in the social security system, rather than as a claimant or possibly even a client. A commuter is a *stakeholder* in the transport system. Parents are *stakeholders* in the primary school system, and so on. It is cynically used by impersonal big business to imply a relationship, usually non-existent, either with customers or those whose lives might be affected by its actions. Therefore when it is planned to build a vast housing estate on an open space, the locals used to having that space at their disposal for recreational purposes become *stakeholders*. This means merely that they have an interest in what happens to the open space, and might pretend that they have a say in the matter; but in reality the term is usually meant to flatter, and their objections will simply be heard politely by the developers who wish to make money out of building the housing estate, and by the local authority that wishes to be able to boast about providing more homes. The people who might buy or rent the new properties are also *stakeholders*; as are the council, any private individual or company that might own the land, and so on. It is a term created to suggest empowerment, but as far as most so-called stakeholders are concerned it does nothing of the sort. As an example of the adoption of this increasingly bogus term, a document about Nigerian schools from the United Kingdom's Foreign, Commonwealth and Development Office in November 2021 was entitled 'Stakeholder Perspectives on Improving Educational Outcomes in Enugu State', the perspectives being those of a wide group of people concerned with providing and receiving education in that part of Nigeria. The word becomes an excuse not to define exactly who those people are, but is used as shorthand for all concerned. Like much corporate speak, it avoids clarity, and causes one to fear that its purpose is to confuse.

Stand in line This is a popular **Americanism** that has penetrated ever more deeply into British colloquial English in the last decade or so, and is now creeping into written English. It means to 'queue', 'queue up' or 'stand in a queue', phrases that represent an ancient British tradition and one of the declining number of cultural aspects of British life of which it is possible to be proud. A near-relation in British English is 'stand in a line', which means something different:

it is what people do on identity parades or in the Armed Forces, or what children do in playgrounds when their teachers are trying to get them under control. In the British phrase there is no element of waiting to take one's turn to do something. Unless one is keen to be considered American, or of doing a creditable impersonation of one, there is no need to depart from the tried and tested *queue*.

Stand, take the   The immense popularity of American crime and courtroom dramas on British television for decades did not, for much of that time, cause the phrase 'take the stand' to supplant the British phrases 'go into the witness box' or 'give evidence'. A series of high-profile real-life cases in American courts, shown extensively on British news programmes on television in more recent years, seems to have changed all that, with court and crime reporters from British networks, covering British cases, frequently using this **Americanism** to convey what the two long-serving British phrases mean. It is rarer, for the moment, in written English. Another Americanism, *testify*, is also becoming more common in this context: in Britain we correctly 'give evidence'. Nor should 'take the stand' be confused with a phrase often used both in Britain and in America, 'take a stand', which means to dig in one's heels and fight for something as a matter of principle – 'she took a stand over the rights of women'.

Start over   This is yet another **Americanism** that is taking root in spoken British English, as in 'my girlfriend and I decided to start over'. In British English one would normally say that the couple would 'start again' or 'make a fresh start'.

Stationary and **stationery**   The former means to stand still, as in 'the car was stationary when the lorry hit it'. The latter is something one writes letters on, and other such paper requisites and accessories – 'all the envelopes were kept in the stationery cupboard'. On 3 February 2023 MailOnline lamented the demise of the 'stationary' chain Paperchase, which sold *stationery*.

Step up to the plate   We have probably all heard those fluent in **corporate speak** use this phrase, which will be meaningless and puzzling to many speakers of British English. This is because it is a metaphor drawn from baseball, the *plate* being the place where the man on strike stands with his baseball bat while a pitcher throws the ball towards him. In corporate speak it means that someone must, as a colloquial British idiom has it, 'pull his (or her) finger out'. Thus when one is told that 'John must step up to the plate or he may well be sacked', it means he must work harder, show some initiative and turn in a higher level of performance than he has before. There are a number of metaphors more comprehensible to British ears than this – I have indeed cited one – or the matter can be dealt with un-metaphorically by simply saying he must try harder and do better.

Stood   This suffers from an abuse similar to that of **sat** and **took**. Correctly, it is the past tense and past participle of the verb *to stand* in both its transitive and intransitive usages (*see Appendix*: **verbs**), as in 'he stood the ornament on the shelf', 'I stood on the corner' or 'I have stood quite enough of this rubbish'. It does not work in the uncouth usage 'I was stood on the corner', which is not a past tense except in the event that one has been specifically placed there by a higher authority, as one is when one is *seated*. 'I was standing' is quite correct, as in 'I was standing near the shop when it caught fire'.

Story and **storey**   The first is a tale or an account (its plural is *stories*), the second refers to a floor in a building that has more than one of them (and its plural is *storeys*). In America both terms are spelt the same, without the 'e'.

Strive The past tense of *strive*, which is a strong verb – that is, one that does not form its past tense simply by adding the suffix *-ed* – is *strove*; the perfect tense is *has striven*. Yet one sometimes reads a sentence such as 'we have always strived to keep costs down', which is illiterate. The website of Liverpool Football club, This is Anfield, carried a story on 10 October 2023 with the almost entirely incomprehensible headline: 'Klopp hailed "special" Eden Hazard – but he strived to reach Mo Salah's "level"'. *See Appendix*: **verbs, strong**.

Surgeries I had the misfortune to encounter this bogus plural in a report about a gifted doctor who had saved many lives by performing a wide range of operations in a benighted country: but instead of saying 'operations' the reporter felt the urge to say 'surgeries'. He could equally have said that the doctor had undertaken a wide range of surgery; but he thought worse of it. The legitimate use of this plural noun is to describe the buildings in which doctors work ('the Minister was clear that all the local practices should have new surgeries built') or the distinct sessions of time in which they are available to see patients (Dr Smith held surgeries three mornings a week).' *See* **plurals, bogus**.

Survivor One reason to be careful with the usage of words is that some of them have particularly powerful meanings that become diluted if they are overused or trivialised. This is in danger of happening to the noun *survivor*, which was until very recently used to describe someone who had emerged alive from a situation in which many, or most, others had died. The dictionary dates such a usage as from 1624, in John

Donne's *Devotions*, clarifying the meaning as 'one remaining alive after another's death, or after some disaster in which others perish'. Thus it was entirely legitimate to talk of survivors from Auschwitz, survivors of a great tsunami, survivors of a plane crash, a shipwreck, a huge fire, or of cancer or indeed of a campaign by a mass murderer. Perhaps inevitably, given the national sense of humour, the word was first trivialised to describe anyone who had come through a strenuous experience: the dictionary calls this its 'figurative' usage and dates it from 1859, about a man out hunting who was still in the saddle after a long day 'over a very severe bit of country'. Since then the 'figurative' usage has multiplied: 'survivors' of an all-night ball meet for breakfast, for example, and I have even seen the term applied to those who returned home having watched the England cricket team lose a Test series abroad. Also, there is the general metaphorical sense of the word as in 'he's a survivor', to mean either that he has gone through life getting out of tight situations in his private and professional lives, or that repeated attempts to do him down in some way have inevitably proved unsuccessful.

But now the term is increasingly appropriated in a sense that its users consider, with some justification, not to be remotely figurative, but which nonetheless does not describe those who have always cheated death, as opposed to having lived through a horrific period in their lives. It describes those who have suffered gravely at the hands of others and in events that were without question not remotely trivial. Groups of people in middle age who endured physical or sexual abuse at the hands of teachers or clergy are now routinely described as 'survivors', for example, as the *Irish Times* did in August 2023 when talking of an initiative to help 'survivors of abuse' in schools 'run by religious congregations'. At the same time the Irish government published an announcement that it would set up a National Centre for Research and Remembrance for those who had been in any number of educational institutions, run either by the Irish state or by the Roman Catholic Church, classing as 'survivors' anyone who had the misfortune to attend one. Such people may certainly regard themselves as victims in the strict sense of that word, but others prefer to see themselves as having overcome these horrors and regard themselves as 'survivors'; that is their privilege, and being a 'survivor' is also unquestionably right for those in specific cases where children were killed or victims later committed suicide. Such considerations certainly make a mockery of assertions that someone is the 'survivor of a burglary', or some other unfortunate but usually not life-threatening incident.

Its use in this new sense will affect the overall meaning of the word. The latest revision of the dictionary includes the word in this sense, in an addition dated 2021, and its origins appear to be American, and first used here to describe 'survivors' of rape. In an August 2023 press release from Essex Police the officer in charge of the force's domestic abuse team referred interchangeably to 'survivors' and 'victims' benefiting from the work of a charity that was teaching women how to box. The term must be handled with care to acknowledge the suffering of those who have endured lethal threats, even if the distinction is not always obvious.

Susceptible This adjective may be used, with distinct meanings, either with the preposition *of* or with the preposition *to*. To be *susceptible of* something is to be capable of undergoing or receiving it, as in 'the evidence was susceptible of more than one interpretation'; to be *susceptible to* something is to demonstrate a weakness towards it, as in 'she was susceptible to flattery' or 'he was susceptible to colds'.

T

-t endings in past tense   Such endings – *learnt, dwelt, spelt, dealt* and so on – are not archaic, but they are forms now mostly peculiar to British English – though note the case of 'burned', below. If one reads 'learned', 'dwelled' and so on it is either in an American text, or a text written by someone not acknowledging the difference between British and American English. It is also important to note the use of the word *learned*, pronounced as two syllables as in 'my learned friend', to indicate someone who has been well educated. *Burned* and *burnt* may also be distinct, the former as the past tense of the verb *to burn* – 'Cranmer was burned at the stake' – and the latter as the adjective – 'the room had the smell of burnt charcoal'. *Earnt* is correct as the past tense of the verb *to earn*, but used exclusively in British English and now considered to be archaic. It is important in writing to be consistent about which form of the past tense one chooses, and not to move between the two.

-tainment   This is one of those suffixes that people touting what is now universally known as 'content' stick on to parts of other words to try to elevate or define what exactly they are offering. A programme that aims both to entertain and to educate (and in such estimations, as in much else, beauty is in the eye of the beholder) is branded 'edutainment', and anything pretending to inform as well as amuse is 'infotainment'. There is also 'realitainment', for those decerebrates addicted to reality television programmes, and, for those unfortunate souls who find politics exciting, 'politainment'. Farms where urban people can take their children to pat sheep, pigs and cows on the back are apparently classed as 'agritainment', and there is also allegedly something called 'pornotainment', which would appear to be a particularly gratuitous tautology. According to taste one will find such terms highly illuminating or patronising, and any temptation to circulate or expand these manufactured absurdities should be resisted.

Talk live   This is **corporate speak** for 'meet in person' or even just 'meet', used in a preposterous sentence such as 'John and I are scheduled to talk live at 2 p.m.' In the post-pandemic age of working from home, it is used as a means of indicating that a meeting will be face-to-face and not held by means of a video call. 'Talk dead', its obvious antonym, is patently an occupation of mediums and necromancers.

Talk to   This phrase has always had a straightforward application in signifying simple verbal communication between human beings: 'Mary talked to John about their holiday' or 'I talked to my son about his bad behaviour'. It has now entered **corporate speak** in phrases such as 'could you please talk to the question of our profitability in the last quarter' or 'I am going to talk to the issue of staff pay'. One does not *talk to* these things: one *talks about* them, or addresses them. They are not sentient beings capable of talking back.

Tautology   I have cited several examples of this vice in this list of horrors – such as **life experience** (sometimes rendered as *lived experience*), 'still **persist**', 'still **perpetuate**', '**revert** back' and '**return** back'. The usual form of a tautology, as these all demonstrate, is where an adjective or an adverb echoes or repeats the meaning of the verb or, as in *lived experience*, the meaning of the noun — as would be the case in a phrase such as 'an inebriated drunk', 'a mendacious liar' or 'a dishonest fraudster'. It is fundamentally an error of logic and suggests a speaker or writer is not thinking carefully about the meaning of all the words he or she is using.

Textspeak Older readers will recall how, in the last century, it suddenly became possible to send text messages by mobile phones, but the technology was so primitive that in any single message only 140 characters could be used. Therefore it necessitated mastering a vocabulary of abbreviations, if one were to be able to communicate anything meaningful in a single message. Some incorporated numbers for homophonic reasons, as in 'tlk2ul8er', which is 'talk to you later'. The technology has improved and one can send a message the length of a novel should one wish to do so, even from a desktop computer to make typing easier. However, elements of the vocabulary are persistent; and while this is understandable in rapid communications made while in a hurry, they all too frequently insinuate themselves into other forms of writing where they do not look attractive. They include 'btw' for 'by the way', 'obvs' for 'obviously', 'defo' for 'definitely', 'probs' for 'probably' and 'lol' for 'laugh out loud' — though some people, confusingly, use it for 'lots of love', which may cause someone being offered an endearment to imagine he or she is being ridiculed. Some terms were familiar well before the invention of the text message, such as 'wysiwyg' ('what you see is what you get'). Indeed, some seem positively Victorian, such as 'yr' for 'your'. Others stem from schoolboy humour ('zzz' for 'tired' or 'bored'), and others still have leapt into everyday discourse, notably 'wtf' for 'what the fuck?' On the internet there are several glossaries of this language, which would require some considerable dedication to master in full, an effort perhaps better put in to mastering English in its traditional form as the latter skill has wider applications. What friends say to each other stays between friends: but use this sort of argot for anything designed to be a serious communication, and the recipient's judgement may not be so engaging,

Than Grammarians and pedants have, according to the dictionary, been exercised about one particular usage of *than* since the early sixteenth century: it is whether, when used before a personal pronoun, that pronoun should be in the nominative or accusative. The argument is over whether one says 'I am much better at cricket than him' or 'I am much better at cricket than he'. The former treats *than* as though it were a preposition, the latter as though it were a conjunction. One of the arguments for the former is that in the days when people knew how to use the pronoun *whom* – which it defines as having occurred 'up to the twentieth century' – the usage 'than whom' was accepted and even required by those who thought 'than me' wrong, even though both used the accusative case. Thus they would demand 'he is a blackguard than whom there can be no worse example' but condemn 'he is a worse blackguard than me'. The dictionary is clear that *than*, when it is used as part of a comparison, is a conjunction; but sometimes conjunctions take the accusative, as in 'she showed it to John and me'. The object of the verb, of which the writer or speaker is one, has to be in the accusative case after the conjunction *and*. However, after almost five hundred years the debate effectively comes down to a matter of taste. For those who believe that 'she ran down the hill faster than I' sounds wrong or archaic, and 'faster than me' sounds too colloquial, then there could be no dispute if the form used were 'she ran down the hill faster than I did'. Similarly, if one bridles at 'Mary is a far more accomplished student than he' or 'than him' one can simply say 'than he is'. The world now seems to be divided between those who see *than* as a preposition, in which case it must take an accusative, or as a conjunction, which means in most cases it should take a nominative. Doubtless the battle will continue indefinitely.

Their, there and **they're**   These three homophones are liable to frequent confusion, especially the first two. *Their* is the possessive pronoun of *they*, the third person plural. Therefore one writes 'John and Mary drove to their house'. *There* is usually an adverb ('he sat there until the phone rang'), but may be interpreted as a noun meaning 'that place' ('there is the letter'), an adjective ('he is there') and also an interjection ('There! I told you so!'). *They're* is the contraction of *they are*, as in 'they're so boring'. *See also* **its and it's, them and those** *and* **your and you're**.

Them and **those**   One often hears in spoken colloquial English someone say 'I didn't like them sweets' or 'she couldn't stand them people'. The demonstrative plural pronoun of *this* is *those*, not *them*, which is the accusative of *they*, as in 'he showed it to them'.

Think outside the box   This tedious phrase is both **corporate speak** and a **cliché**. It is most frequently used to urge someone to be more radical or original in his or her thinking – 'Mary needs to think outside the box if she is going to boost her sales figures', for example. Still worse is the phrase 'outside of the box', though both forms should be avoided. The phrase seems to arise from a popular American puzzle in which one joins up the dots in as few lines as possible. It would be much easier and more straightforward to invite her simply to 'think afresh' or something similar, and would also have the benefit of not bombarding her with **jargon**.

Though When this word introduces a subordinate clause it should take the **subjunctive** mood (*see Appendix*), as in 'she is furious with him, though if he were to apologise she would forgive him' or 'I cannot abide Indian food, though if I were starving I'd eat it'. It is not inevitably a synonym for **although**, particularly in some of its other uses where it acts as a synonym for *however*, such as 'I'll have a copy of that book, though'.

Times less One rather too often reads nonsense such as:– 'I'm dating a man who earns ten times less than I do', which appeared in MailOnline on 5 May 2023. It should have taken but a moment's thought, and not necessarily a GCSE in maths, to work out that logically this is absurd. The woman speaking should have said that her date was in fact earning one tenth of whatever she did, or that she was earning ten times what he was: but 'ten times less' is an almost incomprehensible statement.

Tireless Some indefatigable people do genuinely appear to be tireless ('she worked tirelessly for the charity for forty years'), but the adjective and the adverb have been hijacked by the political class to indicate extreme effort where none has actually been exerted, or to invite praise for quite average people and activities. For example: in June 2023 the *Morning Star* lauded Jeremy Corbyn as 'a tireless voice for peace' and the *Daily Record* the following October ran the headline 'East Kilbride councillors recognised for tireless work in the community'. Anyone with direct experience of politicians knows that they certainly do tire of their activities from time to time, but one of their trade secrets is to pretend otherwise. The word is now so overused that it risks having its meaning diluted to 'long-serving'. *See also* **political language, misuse of**.

Titillating and **titivating**   These two words have the misfortune to be relatively rare usages in English and to sound very similar, and therefore they often suffer the indignity of being mistaken for each other. Early in 2023 a news radio broadcast had it that a 'book was meant to be published in August, but it was pushed back, perhaps so that titivating detail from the Coronation can [*sic*] be included'. Apart from the speaker's inadequate grasp of the use of the conditional, the report mistook *titivate* for the verb *titillate*, which the dictionary defines as having since the eighteenth century meant 'to excite or stimulate', and which was used initially in regard to the palate about the response to food and wine. By the late nineteenth century it had also come to mean 'to arouse (a person) to mild sexual excitement or interest'. The verb *titivate*, by contrast, had been used since 1705 to mean to improve one's appearance by tidying up one's hair or applying make-up. However, the dictionary also concedes that since 1833 people have been mixing the two up, so that *titivate* has been used to mean 'to excite or stimulate agreeably'. One trusts this is one of those occasions when the dictionary simply notes a mistaken usage rather than endorses it, for the two meanings are utterly clear to those who look carefully.

To be   One of the most widespread solecisms in the language, the mangling of the past tense of the verb *to be*, is so easy to avoid. It seems compulsory in some circles to say 'I were' (and not in a **subjunctive** sense – *see Appendix*), 'you was' and 'they was'. There have been newspaper reports in recent years of teachers declining to correct such horrors, apparently on the grounds that the meaning is clear and that it would appear unpleasant to the perpetrator to do so, not least because the usage counts as dialect. Doubtless it does; however, whether a potential employer would inevitably be so understanding when a person who believes the usage to be correct English writes a letter or email applying for a job and makes such an error must remain a matter for speculation.

The other issue with the verb *to be* is the understanding that, as in Latin, it always takes the nominative case. This is now almost never observed in colloquial English, in which only the starchiest of speakers will announce 'it is I' rather than say 'it's me', or 'it is she' rather than 'it's her'. However, the strict usage is expected in formal written English, and it is a failure of style to ignore it. One would always write 'it was he who signed the treaty in 1713' or 'it will be she who opens the conference', never 'it was him' or 'it will be her'. *See also* **accusatives, misused** *and Appendix*: **nominatives**.

To be fair This, like **to be honest** and **as a matter of fact**, is a largely meaningless phrase used to fill up the beginning of a sentence to give the writer or speaker time to think of something interesting to say. However, to be fair [*sic*], it has the occasional legitimate usage when someone has just been blisteringly critical of someone or something and wishes to present a positive fact in his or its favour. For example: 'He was a shocking husband but, to be fair, he was very good to his children.' In illegitimate uses it raises the question of whether everything else one has said or written is unfair, which may not be the case. *See also* **as a matter of fact, at the end of the day, broadly speaking, it goes without saying, to be honest** *and* **when all's said and done**.

To be honest To drop in this piece of meaninglessness might encourage your interlocutors to think that everything else you have said is rampantly dishonest. If one does mean to convey something by the phrase – usually a blunt but necessary truth to a third party who is slow to understand a grave and generally unpleasant reality – it would be better to say 'for the avoidance of doubt'. *See also* **as a matter of fact, at the end of the day, broadly speaking, it goes without saying, to be fair** *and* **when all's said and done.**

Tools The English language is rich in metaphor, but the trouble with this rhetorical device is that it can become overused, tedious and eventually meaningless. Not long ago *tools* were metal objects carried in toolbags, or toolboxes, by skilled workers to make items, undertake building work or carry out repairs. With the advance of the digital age they started, in abstract form, to appear on computers and other electronic devices: the software I am using to write this book presents a list of options at the top of my computer screen of which one is 'Tools', and a drop-down menu (another metaphorical usage) tells me all sorts of aspects of the software's functionality that I may use should I wish. Given this technological advance, it is quite understandable and normal that some words in the English language should change to reflect it and to communicate its purpose and abilities, and there is a logic to the application of the word to the functionality of software as it carries out various tasks analogous to those of a workman with his tools. However, the term has now been adopted by an almost incomprehensible range of people and activities to the point where tedium is setting in, which is hardly a key to effective communication. **Corporate speak** abounds with 'tools', and one hears of 'marketing tools', 'advertising tools', 'HR [human resources] tools' and 'sales tools'. One should take care before expanding the toolbox further as it is starting to look overloaded.

Took As some people insist on saying 'I was **stood**' or 'I was **sat**' instead of 'I was standing' or 'I was seated', so they will say 'I was took to the hospital' rather than 'I was taken to the hospital', or that I was 'took ill' or 'took by surprise'. This solecism shows a confusion between the active past tense ('I took a bus to work') and the passive past tense ('I was taken to work on a bus').

Totes   This is slang for 'totally'. I have only ever encountered it in colloquial speech among young people, but one fears it is only a matter of time before it intrudes further. It is another of those terms that one should avoid using if one wishes to be treated as an adult.

Touching base   How seriously does someone in a position of authority, who uses this exhausted **cliché** from the lexicon of **corporate speak**, expect to be taken? Like so much of this argot it is of American origin, and is not unique in coming from baseball. It seems mildly absurd for a British person to speak in a way that affects a familiarity with that game – rather as if one were hearing an American talk about a 'sticky wicket' or 'taking the shine off the ball'. It simply sounds affected and mannered.

Tragedy   We have come a long way since Aristotle, but it is nonetheless a good idea to refresh our memories about how he defined *tragedy*: 'An imitation of an action that is serious, complete, and of a certain magnitude; in language embellished with each kind of artistic ornament, the several kinds being found in separate parts of the play; in the form of action, not of narrative; through pity and fear effecting the proper purgation of these emotions.' The use of this noun broadened out somewhat before the twentieth and twenty-first centuries, the dictionary saying that from 1509 it was used to describe 'an event, series of events or situation causing great suffering, destruction, or distress, and typically involving death (especially on a large scale or when premature)'. It goes on to describe the word as being 'in weakened use' to mean 'a shocking or lamentable event or situation'. Most intelligent people will be able to envisage events that justify the label – a terrible natural disaster, genocide, the cruel death of a young person, and so on. Yet it is a word much beloved of the tabloid press and deployed in situations infinitely less grave, indeed not by normal standards grave at all. *See also* **word inflation**.

Train station If you are in America, and seek to travel by rail, then you catch your train at a 'train station'. If you are in England, or indeed a speaker of British English anywhere, and have the same intentions, you should find it at a 'railway station'. Rather like **taking the stand** and **standing in line**, this has become an intrusive **Americanism**; and it is surprising that it has, considering how little is left of the American rail network. As with those other terms, people who use this one sound as though they are trying to pass themselves off as Americans, and it has no place in formal British English writing. *Time Out*, which has always considered itself to be highly advanced and **edgy**, used the term in August 2023 in the almost ineffable sentence: 'Stratford train station could soon be getting much bigger, with new plans having been revealed for a mega refurb.' Elsewhere on that website one is told that 'you can stay in an old Victorian Train Station in Scotland', which also presents an example of **tautology**. Since Queen Victoria died almost a century and a quarter ago, a 'new' Victorian 'train station' would be quite an achievement.

Trauma This word originally referred to a physical wound, but by the late nineteenth century it had been adopted by the psychiatric profession to describe what the dictionary calls 'a psychic injury, especially one caused by emotional shock . . .

also, the state or condition so caused'. It might legitimately be applied to those who had survived a terrible catastrophe, but witnessed death and other horrors all around them; or indeed those who had witnessed the carnage and brutality of armed combat, or suffered a horrific assault or an attempt on their life. However, by the late 1970s it was being used routinely to describe things that were mildly upsetting, inconvenient or tiresome. It is therefore used in almost any discussion of the unhappiness of the Duke of Sussex. In August 2023 the BBC ran a headline that read: 'Porthcawl disabled woman recalls trauma of night-time arrest'. The English-language edition of the Spanish newspaper *El País* is to be congratulated for running a feature a couple of days earlier asking a highly pertinent question: 'Is trauma the same thing as adversity?' To judge from the promiscuous use of the word, many writers believe it is. Any young person in particular who has a difficult or unpleasant experience, short of some grave assault or injury, is routinely described as having 'trauma', as is anyone who is prone to mild unhappiness or who feels somewhat unstable. Its careless use diminishes the real gravity of the term, and the shocking effects of genuine trauma on those who experience it, as opposed to those who use it to dramatise their own experiences or those of others. *See also* **word inflation**.

U

Under way As a phrase this is two words, not one, and should be written thus. It now hardly ever is. *See* **all right**.

Underestimate When Mary Quant, the famous fashion designer, died in April 2023 MailOnline said that her influence 'could not be underestimated'. If that were so, her influence would have been meagre, which it was not. The writer had meant to say 'overestimated', but used a double negative, giving a prime example of the dangers to meaning and comprehension of doing so, and emphasising the importance of thinking carefully about the use of words. Open Access News on 8 August 2023 fell into the same trap, with a headline announcing that 'the public sector cannot underestimate computing's environmental impact', above a story that described in great detail the vast scope of that environmental impact, almost to the point when one expected it to argue a return to quills, abaci and the cleft stick. One is reminded of the solecism of President George W. Bush on 6 November 2000, just before he won his first election, where he explained that his internal Republican opponents had 'misunderestimated' him.

Uninterested *See* **disinterested and uninterested**.

Unique One often reads or hears that something is 'very unique' or 'quite unique'. If something is *unique* then there is only one such thing in existence. If there are two or three of them, or a handful of them, or it is rare, then say so. Also, some entities – people and places, for example – are by definition unique, so there is hardly any point in saying so. What one makes of the claim by the WorldAtlas website to be offering a feature about 'Seven of the most unique towns in Virginia' one staggers to think. Not only must each of those towns be unique, but how can one be more unique than another, or the whole lot of them 'most unique'? And the science website Earth.com proclaims that 'Europe had very unique plant-eating dinosaurs'. What made them more unique than other unique plant-eating dinosaurs? Or might it be the case either that these 'very unique' dinosaurs were not unique at all, or just straightforwardly unique?

Unto   This word is now regarded as archaic, and finds itself deployed mainly in consciously affected speech or in writing that seeks to create a sense of a past age. It usually means 'to', as in 'render unto Caesar that which is Caesar's', but was also used to mean 'until' – 'we shall be together unto eternity'. Unless one has a strong desire to sound biblical, the word is probably best avoided. *See also* **into** *and* **onto**.

Utilise   This once useful [*sic*] verb has now largely become a pompous way of saying 'use', and is a favourite verb in **corporate speak**. It began life by meaning 'to make something useful', which is a different matter from *using* it – 'he was able to utilise some old tyres to make a life raft', for example. Now it has become an aid to those who think using a short word makes them appear more stupid than using a long one. It is always surprising to read 'utilise' in newspaper or news website headlines because it is such a long-winded way of saying 'use', which is just three letters. Yet in August 2023 Plymouth Live ran a headline which read: 'Plymouth Argyle set to utilise their squad for Crystal Palace clash'. There is clearly something about this word and football, because a few days earlier Sky Sports presented a feature on 'how teams are utilising box midfield'. At the same time, in another sphere, the *Yorkshire Post* managed to use the word in its original sense in a headline that read 'Green belt land could be better utilised for food production', which meant that land currently used for scenic or environmental purpose could be made more useful if it were turned over to growing food. By definition, something that has already been designed to be useful can only be used, not utilised. A headline in Tech Business News about something called 'the Workplace Utilisation Index' is puzzling; one should suggest it ought to be renamed 'the Workplace Use Index', since one presumes that in its creation a workplace has been utilised, and then it only remains to use it.

Utmost and **upmost**   While one admires the principle – however slowly displayed – of anyone who resigned from the catastrophic administration of Boris Johnson and accelerated his and its demise in the summer of 2022, such people cannot be absolved from linguistic horrors (though it may well be that they were suffering such trauma at the time that they were incapable of knowing better). One such was Simon Hart, the MP for Carmarthen West and South Pembrokeshire, when he resigned as Secretary of State for Wales. He told Johnson in his resignation letter that 'colleagues have done their upmost in private and public to help you turn the ship around'. Manifestly there are times when one's *utmost*, or even one's *upmost* (whatever that may be), is not enough.

V

Venal and **venial**   The first of these adjectives is applied to those who are easily corrupted, as in 'the police officer was completely venal and took a number of bribes' or 'the venality of the party was shown by the absence of principle common among its members'. The second, *venial*, is an adjective with a highly specialised meaning, referring normally to a transgression that is not considered especially serious – 'others regarded his decision to eat too many chocolates as a venial sin'. One prominent mistaken use of *venial* is in the television series *The Sopranos*, where one character says to another about his prospective time in prison: 'You add up all your mortal sins and multiply that number by fifty. Then you add up all your venial sins and multiply that by twenty-five. You add that together and that's your sentence.' It is a *venal* sin that is less damaging than a mortal one, though still serious: a *venial* sin would have been forgivable and merited no prison time at all.

Verbs, missing   All sentences require a main verb if they are to be constructed grammatically correctly. Regrettably, quite a lot are not, and it is especially true of political speeches, which in recent years have been composed in an ever more staccato form, of the shortest possible phrases in order to create the much-desired 'soundbite', and because the political class harbours the belief that most people who might listen to them are thoroughly stupid and have the briefest attention spans. A speech by Rishi Sunak in September 2023 contained five successive sentences without a main verb: 'Inflation – down again today and on track to be halved. Fastest growth in the G7 over the last two years. Debt – on target to be falling. The NHS – treating more patients than last year. And small-boats crossings significantly down on last year.' Whatever the factual accuracy of the statements, the grammatical condition was abominable. *See Appendix*: **sentences**.

Vibrant The traditional meaning of this adjective, which was once applied to things that vibrated or resonated, has since 1993 been expanded by the dictionary to mean 'full of vitality, teeming, exuberant, flourishing'. It also expanded further to cover 'objects with an appearance suggestive in some way of vitality or the exotic' and can also be used of colour to mean 'bright and striking'. Perhaps with the emphasis on 'exotic' it is also a consciously or unconsciously patronising term used predominantly by white people to describe gatherings or communities of non-white, and especially black, people. Sky News, commenting on the Notting Hill Carnival in August 2023, spoke of 'thumping bass, vibrant parades and curried goat'. The same week Bdaily News reported about a 'historic East London building to be transformed into "vibrant, accessible hub"', the *Newcastle Chronicle* said how 'thousands brave heavy rain for vibrant celebration of South Asian culture' and the *Guardian* related how 'Leigh were not the only winners at an inclusive, vibrant Challenge Cup final'. The new sense of the adjective is now so embedded that it has almost suffocated the original sense; but in becoming so familiar it has also become a **cliché**, and appears to have turned into a lazy and self-satisfied way for any writer to describe a gathering of people celebrating a non-Anglo Saxon culture. There are plenty of other adjectives to describe a colourful, exotic gathering, and by being more specific they are less insulting to the cultures thus described.

Vow   For seven hundred years the verb *to vow* has meant to give a solemn promise, and for roughly the same span of time the noun has described such a promise. For much of that time what made a vow a vow was that it was taken in the name of God, as in a marriage vow. Now the meaning has been diluted, and the word signifies a promise to do anything without any religious solemnity at all; not least because, being only three letters long, the word is greatly beloved of headline writers, especially in the tabloid press, where *promise*, *resolve* or even *swear* might not fit so easily. Because of what is now its predominantly tabloid sense, it is perhaps best used in formal English only when referring to the taking of some sort of oath, and best avoided in all other senses unless the writer wishes to pass himself or herself off as a tabloid sub-editor. This overuse is not, incidentally, confined to the tabloids: Reuters reported on 31 August 2023 that 'Shapps becomes UK defence secretary with vow to keep up support for Ukraine', and the BBC said that 'Council vows to meet soaring cost of five new Borders schools'. ITV News announced how 'Sunak **doubles down** on "stop the boats" vow as Channel crossings continue'.

W

Waive and **wave**   The first verb means to forgo a right or privilege, as in 'he waived his right to cross-examine the witness'; the second refers to a literal or figurative motion of the hand – 'she waved to her parents from the car' or 'you can wave goodbye to your bonus this year following this performance'. *Waive* and its noun *waiver* are often misspelt, without the essential 'i'.

Walk back   This phrase might appear to describe what someone does when returning from a stroll or a constitutional, but it is a popular American usage that has rapidly infiltrated **corporate speak**, meaning to repudiate or deny something one has said previously – 'he walked back his remark about women footballers', for example. What is wrong with 'changed his mind' or 'altered his view' or simply 'withdrew' is unclear. In August 2023 the CNN website reported that Robert Kennedy Junior, a candidate for the presidency of the United States, was having to engage in this process too: 'RFK Jr's campaign tries to walk back his support of three-month federal abortion ban.' What is wrong with 'undo' or 'reverse' is also unclear.

Walk someone through   This is not, as might be suspected, a gallant act by someone offering to escort another through a sensitive or potentially hazardous situation. It is a part of **corporate speak**, and it means (to put it more clearly and succinctly) to explain something to somebody, as in 'let me walk you and the rest of the board through the annual accounts' or 'let me walk you through the plans for the weekend'. Like all corporate speak, it is the language of the poseur.

Warn   This is a transitive verb and it requires an object. 'John warned Mary that if she didn't stop drinking she would fall over' is correct, whereas 'John warned that she would fall over' is not. If one cannot bear to use an object, one correctly would say 'John gave warning that she would fall over'. The disregard of this point in now nearly universal. In September 2023 the BBC announced: 'Nitrous Oxide: Laughing gas ban could harm users, experts warn'. Warn whom? The assumption all readers are supposed to make is that the recipients of the warning are general humanity, which makes the target somewhat vague too. Tabloid and news media headlines are rife with the formula, with countless examples daily ending in 'experts warn' and 'scientists warn' – to the point, one suspects, where people fail to register what is actually being said. And there is also the danger of ambiguity. The ScienceAlert website said in August 2023: 'Scientists Warn 1 Billion People on Track to Die From Climate Change'. One might imagine they were warning a billion people, with everyone else unaffected; but they were warning the general public that a billion would die out of the whole population of the planet.

-wash   This suffix has become popular in recent years, having originally been confined to *whitewash*, with its metaphorical meaning of making something look clean or innocent when it certainly isn't. The new popularity seems to stem from *greenwash*, which is when an environmentally unfriendly concern seeks to dupe the public that it is quite the contrary, and makes entirely false claims about its activities.

Another variant of this process is 'social wash', used in November 2023 by the marketing data website Kantar, which wrote of 'the impact of greenwashing and social washing on brands'. The latter coinage seems to refer to greenwashing accomplished through social media. The same month the *Guardian* accused Nigel Farage of seeking to 'fun-wash' himself by going on a light entertainment programme and seeking to appear harmless through his irrepressible geniality (the question of his harmfulness must remain a matter of individual judgement). The BBC website home page in December 2023 had a headline that read: 'Saudi World Cup sportswashing claims "very shallow"'. The term 'sportswashing' initially conjures up problematical images of lots of beefy men in the showers, but is explained as follows: 'Critics say unprecedented spending on sport has been used to improve the oil-producing kingdom's reputation over its human rights record and its environmental impact.' These usages are possibly amusing once; repeated use will make them boring and thus futile. If the vogue continues we shall doubtless hear of murderers engaging in lifewashing, thieves in jewelwashing, and arsonists in housewashing.

Weave The passive voice uses the form *woven*, as in 'the tapestry was woven by nuns in the thirteenth century'. One too often hears the solecism 'weaved', which is not even correct for the active voice, where it is *wove*, as in 'the cyclist wove in and out of the traffic'. However, the Limerick Live website in August 2023 had a headline that 'Armed men weaved through traffic on busy Limerick road, court hears', with the solecism repeated in the first paragraph of the report. *See Appendix*: **verbs, strong**.

When all's said and done This is a fatuous phrase used by those lacking anything sensible to say. It is probably used as a synonym for *in the end*, which also rarely means what it says. If it did, we should all be on the verge of the apocalypse. *See also* **as a matter of fact, at the end of the day, broadly speaking, it goes without saying, to be fair** *and* **to be honest.**

Whether This valuable but increasingly unfashionable word is meant to indicate that a statement includes the recognition of a choice. An example is 'she wanted to know whether he had read the book', which allows for the possibility that he had not (in such a sentence 'or not' is always understood after 'whether'). The form usually seen now is 'she wanted to know if he had read the book', which could mean something quite different, such as that she did not want to know if he had not. *See* **if and whether**.

Whimsy and **whimsical** The noun *whimsy* has over centuries developed to mean the same as the noun *whim*: which the dictionary defines as 'a capricious notion or fancy'. It is far more likely these days, and has been for a hundred years or more, that someone would say 'John took Mary to Monte Carlo on a whim' rather than 'on a whimsy'. Doubtless because of its ending in a 'y', *whimsy* has occasionally been mistaken for an adjective, which it is not: that honour falls to *whimsical*, as in 'it appeared to have been a whimsical decision' and not 'a whimsy decision'. And it is certainly not an adverb: that is *whimsically*, as in 'he conducted his relationships with others somewhat whimsically'.

Who and **whom** It is so easy to write or say *whom* rather than *who* when the grammar of a sentence demands it (which it does when the relative pronoun is the object of the sentence) that one wonders why so many people seem to have an almost religious objection to doing so. One senses that for some it seems stuck-up or pedantic, and for others its usage appears to have become associated with English as spoken by a certain class, and by an exclusive class at that. It is unclear whether it was class feeling or illiteracy that prompted the *New Statesman* to ask 'Excessive for who?' in its daily newsletter on 23 November 2022, about disputed housing targets. As the object of the sentence, and following a preposition, *whom* should have been used. Indeed, one could also use it if showing one's freedom from pedantry by placing a preposition at the end of a sentence – one could say 'Whom was it excessive for?' It has largely dropped out of colloquial English, though one does from time to time still hear questions such as 'Whom do you want?' or 'To whom did he speak?' – in both examples the accusative *whom* is used because it is the object of the sentence. It does still occur regularly in written English and, as with the subjunctive, is kept alive not least by our American cousins, who have no shame in using it. In August 2023 the Colorado Politics website asked 'For whom does this government work?' And in Great Britain, *The Daily Telegraph* ran an erudite piece on 'the saintly failure whom Goya admired'. In much colloquial speech, however, the accusative pronoun is missing: people who would never dream of using *he* for *him* or *they* for *them* (for *whom* can serve as a plural too) are heard to say things such as 'Who did he hit?' and 'Who is it for?' not because of ignorance but apparently out of uncertainty or a fear of sounding affected. It is not rational.

Sometimes an excess of zeal can cause *whom* to be used wrongly, when a subject is mistaken for an object. 'He couldn't imagine whom had done it' is wrong because 'it' is the object of the main verb, 'done': it should have been 'he couldn't imagine who had done it'. The pronoun is not the object of the verb 'imagine'. Similarly, 'she is the woman whom I am sure will turn the company round' is wrong. If in doubt, invert the sentence; one would instinctively say 'I am sure she is the woman who will turn the company round', never 'whom will turn the company round'. *Whom* never appears immediately before a verb; it follows a preposition ('the man with whom I wish to live' or 'the women by whom the club was established') or it is the object of a verb – 'the boy whom he saw stealing the handbag' (though 'he saw the boy who stole the handbag') as the boy is the object of the verb 'saw'.

Woman The active minority of transgender activists who flourished in the early 2020s, some of whom regarded the very idea of gender as 'a fantasy' (*see* **pronouns**), were regarded by some of their critics – mostly feminists, not all of whom were female – as trying to erase the traditional notion of women from everyday discourse. They may have had a point, given that one saw and still does see usages such as 'person with a vulva' or, even worse, 'person who owns a vulva', as if one can buy one on the internet or in a showroom, to avoid the speaker's or writer's having to utter the term *women*. *Women* does, however, remain a normal, sensible and inoffensive usage to over 99 per cent of the population. If one wishes to become overtly political, or to avoid causing offence when in the presence of one of these zealots, then one may feel free to go to such lengths to avoid the term. Otherwise, we are not yet in the realms where avoiding this utterly inoffensive word is necessary either in speech or in writing, and indeed a mass audience would find one who did so rather absurd. A report in August 2023 highlighted a related instance in which certain NHS hospitals in England were briefing their staff on ways to avoid using the equally inoffensive and time-honoured term 'mother' and to say instead 'parent'; and other stories talked of NHS Trusts demanding the use of the term 'pregnant people'. Even many NHS staff were outraged, so with luck this fashion will soon pass. To emphasise further that the term *woman* is perfectly acceptable, people should not feel obliged either to use the word *lady* as some sort of euphemism, other than in the most formal of circumstances – as in 'the ladies will now retire'.

Word inflation   A use of words in an exaggerated fashion, long rife on newspaper sports pages but common in the tabloid press throughout the paper. Such hyperbole serves only to diminish the force of the word itself. It is an extension of Aesop's fable about the boy who cried 'Wolf!' If one continues to read about 'tragedies' and 'traumas', even those that really are tragedies and traumas will cease to appear so. If the loss of a football match occasions 'heartbreak', then how does one describe the effect on their families of a young man dropping dead on his honeymoon, a young woman being diagnosed with a terminal illness, or a busload of children going over a cliff? *See* **brilliant, chaos, devastation, epic, heartbreak, horror, iconic, nightmare, passionate, tragedy** *and* **trauma**.

Word order, mangled   It is crucial to consider word order when writing a sentence, or else one is liable to cause ambiguity and therefore confusion. For example, some trades unions put out a press release in August 2023 headlined: 'Protest against ticket office closures at Department for Transport'. One's first thought is that the protest has been provoked by the closure of ticket offices at the Department: but the Department has no ticket offices, which are at railway stations. What the press release should have said was 'Protest at Department of Transport against ticket office closures', which was susceptible of no other meaning. And a satisfactory word order is not enough: a sentence also requires correct punctuation if complete clarity is to be obtained. *See also Appendix*: **punctuation**.

Would of This vulgar colloquialism is a phrase uttered by mistake when the speaker means 'would have'. I have yet to see even the most progressive linguist attempt to defend it, but doubtless that is because I have not been looking hard enough. *See also* **could of, might of** *and* **should of**.

Wrong 'Why we brush our teeth wrong' proclaimed the BBC website nannyingly in July 2022. Nearly a year later MailOnline told its readers 'You've been using your potato peeler wrong!' shortly before advising you that you were also 'eating your spaghetti wrong', 'folding up your clothes wrong', and 'you've been cleaning your shower WRONG' (the headline writer becoming, it seems, so proud of his solecism that he chose to shout it rather than just say it) and even 'sitting all wrong'. *Wrong* is used in all these instances as an adverb, and should therefore be *wrongly*: perhaps the tabloid website is just being amusing, but the BBC ought to be above such things and should have said 'why we brush our teeth wrongly'. *Wrong* is an adjective, as in 'the wrong usage'. *See Appendix*: **adverbs**.

Y

Younger This adjective can apply only to a context in which there are just two people or items; the other is the **elder**. If there are three or more then the least old, or most young, is the youngest. *See* **elder and younger**.

Your and **you're** The former is a possessive pronoun – 'your dog', 'your car', 'your wife' and so on; the latter is the contraction of 'you are', entirely acceptable in speech and informal writing, best avoided in formal writing. Therefore one would say 'you're late' or 'you're beautiful' or might write to a friend to say that 'you're welcome to arrive any time after seven'; but it might cause a little surprise to receive a letter from your bank that says 'you're overdrawn', even though you know you are. Usages such as 'you're dog', 'you're car' and so on are evidently nonsense. *See also* **its and it's** *and* **their, there and they're**.

Appendix of Grammatical Terms

Author's note:
For ease of guidance to readers, this is a list of grammatical terms defined mostly without expression of opinion. Cross-references within this section are to items also within it, and *not* to those contained in the main A to Z.

Accusatives   The accusative of a noun is usually invisible to the eye and ear, as English nouns, unlike Latin or Greek ones, do not decline. It occurs when the noun is the object of the sentence, as the noun *car* is in these statements: 'he drove the car', 'she locked the car', 'they pushed the car into the garage' (in the last sentence *garage* is an indirect object). Pronouns, however, do decline – 'she gave it to him' (not *he*), 'he thanked her' (not *she*), 'she saw us' (not *we*), he wrote to them (not *they*). The accusative pronoun that gives the most trouble, and is frequently ignored doubtless as a consequence, is *whom*, which must be used when it is the object of a verb or following a preposition, as in 'she was the woman with whom I saw him' or 'the man whom I married'.

Adjectives   The adjective appears to have become an ever more powerful part of speech in the last decade or two, not least in the degree to which it has supplanted the innocent but increasingly unfashionable adverb. (*See* **adverbs** for a discussion about why one does not say 'he went too slow'.) Adjectives are used to amplify nouns, to communicate more information about those nouns, be it a living creature or an inanimate object. They come in two forms, which we might term the *objective* and the *subjective*. Here are examples of one of each for both living and inanimate objects: 'The former Home Secretary' is a statement of fact; 'the inadequate Home Secretary' deploys the adjective to register an opinion or a prejudice, however justified that may be. 'The green wallpaper' likewise is a statement of fact; 'the ugly wallpaper' one of taste. In good factual writing, the best style is short on adjectives, and is confined mainly to objective ones in order to convey essential information. The use of subjective adjectives is more prevalent in fiction, especially in comic writing, for effect.

Adverbs The purpose of these is to give extra meaning to a verb, as in 'he sang horribly' or 'she cooked brilliantly'. It is, sad to say, a part of speech that appears to be under a death sentence, having become rarer and rarer in recent years. Many people without blinking would now say that a man sang 'horrible' or a woman cooked 'brilliant' (in fact a common horror now is the degeneracy of the old phrase 'you have done brilliantly' into 'you done brilliant', wrong in so many respects one hardly knows where to start). A television advertisement for trousers that promise to fit proclaims: 'We are all made different'. No, we are not: we are all made differently. The verb *make* requires an adverb, as do all other verbs: but out of idleness or ignorance countless verbs every day are palmed off with adjectives – 'he went too slow' instead of 'too slowly'. As part of its clickbait (a noun whose invention shows the usefulness of an adaptable language in inventing words demanded by new technology and its opportunities) the MailOnline website is fond of telling its readers that they are doing things 'wrong' – storing things 'wrong', cooking things 'wrong', cleaning things 'wrong'. The website is what it would doubtless label using English 'wrong', since in each case all these criticisms should be about things done 'wrongly'. Adverbs cost no more than adjectives, and so it would be a pity were people to become afraid to use them.

Aposiopeses These devices are used more often in fiction than in formal or serious writing, by which a sentence suddenly breaks off – indicated by a dash – or appears to peter out without a full stop but with a row of (usually, by printers' convention, three) full stops, thus . . . A strict classical definition – though the device is used more widely today – is when an 'if' clause is not followed by a 'then' clause, as in 'if I hear you say that again . . .' *See also* **ellipses** *and* **full stops**.

Apostrophes In punctuation, the purpose of the apostrophe is often (but not always – it will become clear from the context) to indicate possession: as in 'John's book', 'Mary's coat', 'the dog's breakfast'. It is also used as a means of indicating possession in the **gerund** construction, as in 'Mary's being present was a great comfort to John', where it shows that the state of being present belonged to Mary. Also, it is frequently found in English to indicate a missing letter; whether in contemporary speech and less formal writing in usages such as 'don't', 'won't', 'can't' or 'wouldn't' (if writing a formal piece of prose it is better not to mimic speech but to write 'do not', 'will not' and so on); and in some older or archaic texts to indicate missing letters such as in 'o'er and 'ne'er'. It survives in certain terms such as 'five o'clock', 'will-o'-the-wisp', 'ne'er-do-well' and 'cat-o'-nine-tails'.

Capital letters In British English these are correctly put at the start of words that begin sentences, or at the start of proper names. Conventions change: a glance at a late Victorian reference book will show names such as

'Whitehall-place' or 'Oxford-street' that we would now write as 'Whitehall Place' and 'Oxford Street'. But the convention about starting proper names and sentences with capitals remains constant. There are schools of thought about titles, and all one can do is remain consistent. Some ancient offices, such as the Chancellor of the Exchequer or the Home Secretary, have acquired the force of proper names; 'prime minister' has come to depend on the house style of whichever publication is referring to him or her. Some publishing houses now talk about 'the king' and 'the queen' whereas others (correctly in my view) mention 'the King' and 'the Queen'. It presumably depends on whether or not the editor is a monarchist. 'A king' or 'a queen' is correct. Some people are tempted to use capital letters to make themselves better heard, such as in writing 'this is NOT the way to speak English'. It qualifies as shouting and, as with shouting outside print, should be avoided. A word in lower case, italicised, is a preferable means of emphasis.

Clauses These are parts of a **sentence**, usually separated from each other by punctuation. In the sentence 'John decided he would leave the house if Mary chose to follow him' the words up to and including 'house' constitute the main clause, those after it the subordinate clause. The subordinate clause is judged as such because it cannot stand on its own as a sentence; whereas 'John decided he would leave the house' can. Also, a subordinate clause does not have to follow the main clause; the sentence makes perfect sense if cast thus: 'If Mary chose to follow him, John decided he would leave the house.' There can be several subordinate clauses, though short sentences are always preferable in the interests of easy comprehension.

Colons These highly useful elements of punctuation are much misunderstood and, as a consequence, frequently either avoided or misused. One is correctly used to introduce a discrete part of a sentence that contains a specific statement, explanation or even a sequence of facts or items. For example, 'he could not attend the dinner: he was too ill', in which it replaces a **conjunction** (*for*, *since* or *because*), for stylistic reasons of emphasis. Or 'it was too late to get him a present: they would simply have to send something on afterwards'. Or 'she knew what she liked: diamonds, champagne, truffles'. If any of those preceding examples had included some sort of introductory phrase or conjunction they would have required a **semicolon**. A colon often precedes a quotation (though some people prefer to use a comma instead): 'Churchill said: "We shall fight them on the beaches."' It can also be used to join two sentences when the second has a direct relationship in sense to the first, usually by continuing its stream of thought. This is the case in 'she could not stand the sight of him: it astonished her he could stand the sight of himself'. This should not become a habitual stylistic trait for a writer, however, or that style will become staccato and mannered.

Commas In the most basic usage a comma gives clarity of meaning to a sentence of two clauses or more, and serves the stylistic purpose of making it easier to read. In this simple two-clause sentence – 'she walked to see her friend, crossing the road at the lights' – the comma comes logically between clauses that describe two entirely separate actions. Were it not there it would suggest she had walked to a specific place with the purpose of seeing her friend cross the road at the lights. Were the sentence to read 'she walked to see her friend and crossed the road at the lights' the conjunction *and* removes the need for a comma. Stylistically, this might not apply to all conjunctions. If one wrote 'she walked to see her friend, but crossed the road at the lights' it would imply a further statement was coming that would describe a consequence of her having crossed the road at the lights: for example, 'she walked to see her friend, but crossed at the lights because she did not wish to be run over'. Commas are also used to break up a list, and this leads to one of the more contentious debates in English style. Were one to write 'he had oxtail soup, fillets of sole, roast beef, apple pie and cheese' one would in my view be using the sequence of commas entirely correctly, since the conjunction 'and' at the end of the list dispenses with the need for a comma after 'pie'. (Although were the sentence to read 'he had oxtail soup, fillets of sole, roast beef, and apple pie with custard', then the sense would demand the comma after 'beef'.) Others, however, particularly Americans, would argue that it is necessary. I don't agree: to me it is redundant and stylistically harmful. It must be a matter of taste. The matter is clearer with lists of adjectives. 'You are a dirty, filthy, deceitful pig' will always be punctuated thus, with no comma between the last term of abuse and the noun.

Commas can also indicate a parenthesis, as in: 'Mary saw her car, which was parked on a double yellow line, being towed away.' The sentence would be a mess without the second comma, with some readers perhaps thinking that the double yellow line was being towed away. The importance of completing a parenthesis with a second comma shows how this device of punctuation has its greatest importance in helping avoid ambiguity. There are other ways in which this happens. Consider the difference between 'I have a colleague who likes books' and 'I have a colleague, who likes books'. The first implies that of the many colleagues the speaker or writer has, he has one who likes books; the second that the speaker or writer has only one colleague, and that colleague likes books.

It used to be the case that certain adverbs required a comma – 'therefore, I have decided to resign', or 'nevertheless,

I refuse to pay' and so on – but this too has become a matter of judgement and context. 'She gave Rover some chocolate. Therefore he died' will seem as correct to many as 'Therefore, he died'. Similarly 'he worked for months on his book. Nevertheless it was a failure' will seem perfectly correct to many. If a long sentence follows the adverb then a comma may well improve sense. Every sentence has its own architecture, and although to many writers punctuation is instinctive, others will need to read back carefully whatever they write in order to ensure that the meaning is clear. Most valuable of all punctuation marks, when it comes to ensuring such clarity, is the comma. Sometimes, however, it is seen wrongly used, as in this sentence: 'He encountered a number of difficulties: relentlessly bad weather, appalling visibility in the valleys and on mountain tops, and the inadequacy of his clothing.' The meaning would be clearer if each comma were replaced by a **semicolon**. There is also a habit in fiction of using commas to link sentences where correctly there should be semicolons.

Comparatives and superlatives These terms apply to adjectives and the degree in which they are used. *Long* is a basic adjective; *longer* ('your arms are longer than mine') is the comparative of the adjective; *longest* ('his arms are the longest I have ever seen') is the superlative. An adjective that idiomatically does not change in these conventional ways, such as *beautiful* or *random* or *particular*, is modified using either *more* or *most*: thus 'the outcome was more catastrophic than he had feared' or 'she was the most pathological liar he had ever encountered'. And a few adjectives modify in an irregular fashion, such as *good, better, best*; or *bad, worse, worst*; *little, less, least*; and *many* (or *much*), *more* and *most*. These forms simply have to be learnt by heart.

Conditionals In some languages conditionality – the idea that something could, should or might happen – is classed as a mood, but in English it is a group of tenses using modal verbs – *can*, *may*, *will* or *shall* – in their conditional forms of *could*, *might*, *would* and *should*. The conditional of *can* is correctly used following the past tense of main verbs. Thus it is incorrect to say 'if I save the money I can go on holiday', but correct to say 'if I saved the money I could go on holiday'. Using *may* it would be 'after work I may go to the pub' (with it being understood that, equally, 'I may not'), but a sentence of conditionality would be phrased 'if I finished early enough, after work I might go to the pub'. Such forms are also used in asking a question, and the tense in any subordinate clause must follow logically from the tense in the main clause. Therefore one would say or write 'Could you please let me know whether you would like me to arrive at eight?' or 'Would you tell me if I might bring anything?' The second example avoids two of the most common mistakes in English, where people say or write 'Would you tell me if I can bring anything?' or, recognising the conditionality of the sentence, 'Would you tell me if I could bring anything?' First, *can* cannot be right after *would*, which establishes conditionality, so if one insists on using that verb it must be *could*. But what that question asks is whether the person being asked it thinks the questioner capable of bringing anything; what the questioner is in fact seeking is leave to bring something – it may even cause offence to do so, or simply not be necessary. His or her ability to bring something is almost certainly not in doubt. As previously noted, it would have been better to say 'Would you tell me if I might bring anything?'

The choice between *should* and *would*, as with that between *shall* and *will*, depends on what person is speaking: therefore such sentences take the form of 'if I finished in time I should go straight home' (the modal verb does not in this case equate to 'ought to', but is simply the conditional of *shall*); but 'if he finished in time he would give me a lift'. With the verb *to be*, 'if' ought correctly to take the subjunctive – 'if I were to meet the right girl I should want to get married', rather than 'if I was to meet the right girl'. Similarly, in the third person it would be 'if he were to meet the right girl he would get married', not 'if he was'. Sentences such as 'if we go to the cinema we will have dinner afterwards' would be better cast as 'if we went to the cinema we would have dinner afterwards', though such formality has been almost entirely lost in speech, if not in written communication. There is also a mistake frequently made when using the perfect tense of the conditional. One often hears people saying 'I should have liked to have done that', which is a double perfect tense and makes little sense. The correct form is 'I should have liked to do that'.

Conjunctions Clauses – the component parts of sentences – are often linked by conjunctions. An example is *but*: 'He wanted to go to the football match but his mother wouldn't let him.' Others frequently used are *and*, *or* and *nor*. And there are yet others that suggest cause or lack of it: *because*, *for* ('he decided to ring his girlfriend, for she might leave him if he didn't'), *yet* ('I had eight hours' sleep, yet was dead tired all day'), *as* ('I was late for work as I overslept'), *since* ('I hate going to see them, since they are always so rude to me'), *although* ('I found him tedious, although he was interesting on the subject of Proust') and *though*. Also, there are *unless* and *until*, and *where*, *when* and *while*. *Which* is a relative pronoun, not a conjunction, even though it links clauses. *See* **pronouns**.

Dashes In pairs these can be used as a form of parenthesis, for example in 'John – who had just arrived – said he had seen Mary', or they can provide a break in a sentence that is stronger than a comma but unsuitable for a colon or semicolon. An example would be: 'I shall meet you at the station – off the six o'clock train.' If being used as a parenthesis it is important to add the second dash, to indicate completion. Long dashes, usually deployed in pairs as parentheses (particularly in America) but also singly in dialogue to indicate an interrupted speech ending suddenly, are known as em dashes, because they suggest the width of that letter; and shorter ones as en dashes.

Ellipses These are used where something is eliminated from a quotation and a series of three spaced full stops is used to indicate the omission. *See also* **aposiopeses**.

Exclamation marks These marks are used in English to indicate, unsurprisingly, exclamations. In written English they most frequently appear in dialogue and in certain sorts of trash journalism. People who use them in formal written English are either being over-dramatic, over-excited or rather arch. 'He said it cost £50,000!' is fine in dialogue but in reported speech the exclamation mark is not required – 'she told her sister that he had said it cost £50,000'. There is a distinct link between serious writing and an absence of the exclamation mark. Fine writers are expected to make their points in other ways: and not by shouting – and an exclamation mark is, effectively, a shout. It also in many contexts conveys a sense of trivialisation, fatal if the subject being discussed is intended to be serious. If the temptation to use one proves irresistible, then stick only to one.

Full stops These are perhaps the most significant of all punctuation marks. They end **sentences**, as is about to be demonstrated with this one. Sometimes in informal or comic writing a sentence will end with an **aposiopesis**, or a row of (usually three) full stops, as in 'she told him she never wanted to see him again. But he had other plans . . .' That device is supposed to create tension or mystery, and good luck to those who try it. In serious writing, the use of **exclamation marks** is likewise to be avoided, so every sentence which does not end with a **question mark** must end with a full stop or, if it is dialogue that has been interrupted, possibly an em **dash**.

Genitives In English there are two ways of deploying the genitive of a noun, which indicates possession. One can either say 'Sally's dog was big and ugly' or 'the dog of Sally was big and ugly'. The former is the more common, especially in speech, though there are well-worn idiomatic uses for the latter – including in phrases such as 'the end of the world' or 'the start of the race'.

Gerunds The use of this grammatical structure is essentially stylistic, but it is dying out, which is to be regretted, because if used correctly it adds a precision to an expression. People now usually say or write 'John having a heart attack was deeply worrying', whereas the traditional construction – the *gerund* – was to make a nominal phrase out of the statement by changing the noun 'John' into a possessive 'John's' before the present participle 'having'. One thus says 'John's having a heart attack was deeply worrying'. Stylists prefer this form because it is technically and logically correct. It tends to be used instinctively with pronouns – we say 'my having gone there on holiday was a huge mistake' and not 'I having gone', 'her doing the splits was the funniest thing I have ever seen' and not 'she doing the splits'. The word *gerund* is now used, especially in American English, as a synonym for *present participle*: that is not the case in British English, when it refers specifically to the construction I have just illustrated.

Hyphenation Opinions differ on the hyphenating of words, as will become apparent if one reads a selection of newspapers and magazines and notes how they do it. From my point of view, in writing, hyphens should be used in compound adjectives, such as 'half-witted bore' or 'richly-endowed foundation'. There are different rules for compound nouns. One would write 'a forty-nine-year-old man' and 'a forty-nine-year-old'. It is hard to lay down rules with nouns, even when the first component in a compound noun has the role of an adjective (so it is *butter knife*, not *butter-knife*), but better to treat each case on its merits. And, in any case, many nouns that began as compounds have fused to become one word – *doormat, lapdog, tallboy, treehouse* and so on. When reading newspapers, magazines and websites, one often notes that these publications have their own respective house styles, as they are entitled to do, and hyphenation, like capitalisation, is one feature that will vary from one to another.

Interjections These are single words or short phrases that express a strong emotion, usually surprise: and they are usually followed by an **exclamation mark**, a punctuation device that should otherwise be sparingly used in order to avoid exhausting the reader. Obvious examples are 'Damn! I've forgotten my wallet', 'Ouch! I've stubbed my toe' and 'Good grief! It's Carruthers'. Some interjections are quizzical by nature and these require a question mark, as in 'Oh really?' or 'Surely not?' They do not normally occur in formal writing outside novels and short stories.

Nominatives These are the form of the noun when it is the subject of the sentence, and is one form of a pronoun. We correctly say 'I ran for a bus' or 'she telephoned her mother', not 'me ran' or 'her telephoned'. Therefore these pronouns are not used as the object of the sentence, except inarticulately – one does not say 'he gave it to I' or 'she saw he'. It has for centuries been normal and accepted in speech to say 'it's me' rather than the theatrical 'it is I', though one should still probably write it. In English, the verb *to be* always takes the nominative case of the pronoun – one says 'for it was he' not 'for it is him'.

Nouns   These are names, either proper names (John, Mary, Essex County Cricket Club, Australia) that are usually distinguished by an initial capital letter; names of animals (dog, cat, rhinoceros, albatross); species and classes (quadruped, bird, reptile, human being); plants, fruits and vegetables (daffodils, roses, bananas, carrots); or inanimate objects (chair, carpet, window, road). They can be qualified by an adjective ('the comfortable chair', 'the broken window') and are usually the subject of a verb ('the chair stood by the wall', 'the window was repaired'. Apart from proper names they have no gender, though idiomatically a ship was always referred to as 'she', as were some cars and other vehicles early in the motor age: but the habit appears largely to have died out.

Nouns of multitude   When dealing with nouns that represent a number of people – a corporation, an institution and so on – it is common to see them with both plural and singular verbs, though there are certain idiomatic uses that require specifically one or the other, especially if one is obviously singular or plural in name. Therefore one would say 'the Grenadier Guards *are* a fine body of men' but 'the Brigade of Guards *is* a fine body of men', because the respective idioms note, in the first example, the plurality of 'Guards', and in the second example the singularity of 'Brigade'. However, one notices during cricket commentary that it is always 'England *are* taking the field', though an Australian tends to say 'England *is* taking the field'. Otherwise, it is just as common to hear that 'the BBC *are* biased against the Conservative Party' as it is to hear that 'the BBC *is* biased against the Conservative Party'; or 'Tesco's isn't a bad shop' and 'Tesco's aren't a bad shop'.

The key consideration is to remain consistent, and not to shift between singular and plural in one piece of writing.

Paragraphs These are passages of writing usually comprising several sentences. The logic of when to end a paragraph is when the specific point the writer is making within it has been fully developed, and it is time to move on to a different point in a different paragraph. Because the close of a paragraph comes at the end of the sentence it will finish with a full stop or a question mark, or in an exceptional circumstance with an exclamation mark. In good style paragraphs are not over-long, any more than sentences are, or they become tedious and hard to understand. The rules are different with dialogue, in which each new speaker is accorded a new paragraph.

Parentheses There are various forms of these in prose writing, and they come within a sentence in order to make a subsidiary point. In this example the parentheses are interchangeable: 'Mary lost her earring on the beach (her husband was always telling her to be more careful with her valuables) and, despite searching for hours, she couldn't find it.' That sentence could as easily be written: 'Mary lost her earring on the beach – her husband was always telling her to be more careful with her valuables – and, despite searching for hours, she couldn't find it.' The choice depends on the taste and style of the writer. If one form of parenthesis has just been used, it may suit to use the other. Another common form of parenthesis appears later in the sentence, the phrase 'despite searching for hours' that is included between commas. Commas are a better idea for that parenthesis because the information is directly rather than indirectly relevant to the overall import of the sentence. The other form of parenthesis commonly used is square brackets, usually deployed to make an editorial comment. Thus one might write 'he said

"I never done [sic] it"', in which the writer reporting the statement indicates that the grammatical error is not his own; or it is useful in a situation where the writer needs to explain something relevant, and smartly: 'John told Mary [Susan's sister] that the bus would be along soon.' See also **dashes**.

Prepositions A preposition is a word that describes the relation of a noun to another part of the sentence, usually a verb either real or imagined. Prepositional phrases can either be simple ('go with the flow' or 'pass on the other side', in which *with* and *on* are the prepositions) or relatively complicated ('the woman to whom I spoke was sitting under a tree on a bench') in which *to*, *under* and *on* are all prepositions. Others include *of*, *by*, *from*, *over*, *among* and *for*. The old prejudice, beloved of Victorian schoolmasters, that a preposition could not appear at the end of a sentence – thus banning phrases such as 'Who is he talking to?' in favour of 'To whom is he talking?' – is now well and truly dead, more so than the Latin language, an imitation of whose rules brought it about. Not only was it always a far less grave offence than the split infinitive (which existed for much the same reason, though in stylistic terms with more justification), but it really wasn't an offence at all. Churchill memorably joked that 'this is the sort of English up with which I will not put', and he had a point. If it sounds contrived or forced to avoid placing the preposition at the end of a sentence, then don't.

Pronouns These little words take the place of a noun, to avoid repeating it. In that last sentence, 'it' was used to save the inelegance of my repeating *a noun*. There are personal pronouns such as *I*, *you* (singular and plural), *he*, *she*, *one*, *we* and *they*. *It* is the impersonal pronoun used for things that have no gender – 'the door was open, and the table was next to it'. Each of the personal pronouns (apart from *you* and *one*) has a different accusative form – *me, him, her, us, them* – and all, and the impersonal *it*, have possessives – *mine, yours* (singular and plural), *his, hers, one's, its, ours, theirs*. They also have adjectives that some regard as pronouns – *my, your* (singular and plural), *his, her, its, our* and *their*. *One's* technically exists but one would idiomatically, in that context, always say or write 'mine' or 'someone's'. It is natural to say 'that book is mine' and not 'that book is one's'. It is important not to confuse *its* with *it's*, which is merely a contraction of *it is*. There are also the relative personal pronouns *who* and its accusative form *whom*, and the impersonal pronoun *which*: so we have 'who laughs last laughs longest', 'to whom it may concern' and 'the house, which I saw in the distance'. They can also act as interrogatives: 'Who do you think you are?', 'Whom were you calling?' or 'Which is it to be?'

Relative pronouns refer specifically to something or someone in a preceding clause in a sentence, and are *that, which, who* and, when the object of a verb, *whom*. *What* is expressly not one, though it regularly appears in demotic speech, as in 'the bloke what I knew was a real bastard' or 'the door what I went through was blue'. It should in the first case be *whom* (though that is highly unlikely in colloquial speech, so it would more probably be *who*) and in the second should be *that*. This would change to *which* if it were in a subordinate clause, as in 'the door, which I went through, was blue', the implication of the statement being that he might not have gone through the door. In the original statement it implies a choice of door, and he went through the blue one. In the first example, to put 'who(m) I knew' into a separate parenthetic clause would emphasise that the speaker knew the unpleasant man to whom he refers; without the parenthetic clause it implies that there was another man, referred to by his interlocutor, who was not in fact a bastard. Technically, it is not incorrect to use *that* to refer to a person – as in 'the woman that runs the shop is always charming' – but this is an increasingly archaic usage, and *who* is now accepted as usual.

Punctuation To give an impression of punctuation while speaking – whether by intonation or by precise pauses – is hugely helpful to one's listeners or interlocutors, as it helps them to take in accurately what is being said and, thus, to fulfil the speaker's presumed aim of communicating with others. In writing, which can be studied over and over again in the pursuit of the true meaning, it is essential to punctuate correctly if the writer wishes to be considered as clear and intelligible. For individual examples *see* **apostrophes, colons, commas, dashes, exclamation marks, full stops, hyphenation, paragraphs, parentheses, question marks, quotation marks, semicolons** *and* **sentences.**

Question marks Despite its usually being obvious when a question is a question – though not always when it is a rhetorical question, which is one that expects no answer ('How stupid do you think I am?' is a notable, if dangerous, example) – in written English a question must be completed by a question mark. Therefore if, for example, one writes 'Does anyone today remember Smith's writings?' the sentence has to be ended thus.

Quotation marks The obvious use for these – which according to preference may be single or double – is to signify a direct quotation. Sometimes, as I am about to show, a quotation has another quotation within it. Therefore if the writer is using single quotation marks, he or she should double them when using another quotation within them: 'He told his friend: "You have never even tried to get on with your wife, so it is not surprising she has run off with another man."' If you are quoting a complete sentence beginning with a capital letter, the quotation mark must come after the full stop; and if you are quoting within a quotation, remember to put the overall quotation mark after the one ending the internal quotation, as in the last example, even if it means putting what appears to be three marks in a row. *See also* **reported speech**.

Reported speech Quite simply, this is the means of relating, usually in written English but sometimes in speech, something someone else has said, without putting it directly in **quotation marks**. In speech the speaker will need, as well as the obligatory 'he said' or 'she said', to use the third person singular or plural. The other key consideration is the logical one that because someone is reporting something that was said in the past, one uses the past tense. Thus an example of reported speech is: 'When I stopped the accused as he walked away from the scene of the burglary, he said that I had stopped the wrong man and that the real culprit was still in the building.' What the man who was stopped would have said was: 'You've stopped the wrong man. The real culprit's still in the building.' If the speech being reported was already referring to the past – if, for example, one was reporting the statement 'I told him that if he didn't close the gate all his livestock would escape', then the main verb goes into the pluperfect: 'She said that she had told him that if he didn't close the gate all his livestock would escape.' The current demotic version of this form, repeatedly using the expression *like* ('so she was like, I told him that if he didn't close the gate'), takes little or no account of tense or of quotation marks, and should be avoided unless one wishes to convey an impression of inarticulacy.

Semicolons In a written sentence such as 'he hated certain vegetables; for example, onions, turnips and leeks' the punctuation is correct, but were the phrase 'for example' not used, the semicolon would need to be replaced by a colon. Semicolons may also follow a colon in a construction such as the one below, acting as a link between clauses that are in sense and relevance closely related to each other, and used instead of a conjunction: 'There were a number of reasons why Smith was unsuitable: he was idle; he was stupid; and he was dishonest.' It is not in most contexts interchangeable with a comma. *See* **commas**.

Sentences These are among the basic components of any attempt to convey meaning, the orderly arrangement of words in a sequence to represent an idea, an observation or an instruction. They need a subject, a verb and an object. In 'I have written this book', 'I' is the subject, the verb is 'to write' and 'this book' is the object. Sentences should be as short as possible, as an aid to comprehension, although if all sentences are short the overall style can appear staccato or robotic. However, many have additional clauses that make them longer and sometimes more complicated – as with this sentence – and in such sentences good punctuation is vital if the meaning is to be clear. There is a prejudice that sentences cannot begin with a conjunction such as *and* or *but*. It is precisely that. Sentences can take various forms, some of them far more complicated than 'the cat sat on the mat'. For example, the main subject and main clause can come after another clause – whose subject it must be to avoid the hanging participle: 'Being rather drunk, he resolved he would call a taxi to pick him up rather than try to walk home.' One of the main causes of an incorrect sentence is the absence of a main verb, when somebody makes a sentence out of what should be a clause better preceded by a colon, semicolon or comma, as in: 'The thugs beat up the old man. An ugly business.' It would have been grammatically correct had the second sentence been a clause introduced by a colon. However, this mistake is not confined solely to tabloid journalists.

George Eliot, who has a fair claim to be the greatest novelist in the English language, perpetrated this in Chapter XVIII of *Middlemarch*:

> It was clear that Lydgate, by not dispensing drugs, intended to cast imputations on his equals, and also to obscure the limit between his own rank as a general practitioner and that of the physicians, who, in the interest of the profession, felt bound to maintain its various grades. Especially against a man who had not been to either of the English universities and enjoyed the absence of anatomical and bedside study there, but came with a libellous pretension to experience in Edinburgh and Paris, where observation might be abundant indeed, but hardly sound.

That second sentence, despite its length and complexity, contains no main verb, and should be preceded by a semicolon; or it could have been rectified by the addition of the verb *to be* as the main verb, by saying, for example, 'This was especially so against a man'.

Subjunctives In normal speech the verbs we use are in the *indicative* mood: but in formal English until relatively recently (the last century or so) certain verbs were always used in the *subjunctive* mood, which had some different inflections – the ending of some verb forms – and used different auxiliary forms. The verbs that required this mood were, as in the classical languages, verbs of desire, command, will and suggestion. It may also be used in conditional sentences, after the words *if*, *whether* or *though*. The subjunctive remains in intensive care, having become a barrier to effective communication because (thanks to the nature of language teaching in our schools) it is so little understood now, whereas it used to offer distinctions in meaning. Although I have ribbed the Americans throughout this book for the damage they (or rather the people in Britain who choose to imitate them) do to our supposedly common language, they must be commended on continuing to preserve the subtlety of the subjunctive, and the precise state of affairs it indicates. In Britain now hardly anyone uses it in speech, and it is scarcely more often seen in formal writing.

The easiest way to depict it is to give some examples, which are most obvious in the third person present tense, because it loses the normal '-s' verb ending. So instead of saying 'I suggest she puts on her coat before going outside' one would correctly say 'I suggest she put on her coat'. Similarly: 'I desire that he stay for dinner' rather than 'that he stays for dinner', 'we insist she leave her luggage here' and 'I order that he come before this court'. Some such usages now seem consciously archaic, but they are technically correct. However, the inclination among most contemporary speakers of British English would be to use an auxiliary verb, probably but not inevitably **conditional**, in each of the examples above: 'she should put on her coat', 'he should stay for dinner' but, after a verb of command, 'he must come before this court'. When *if* is used, the subjunctive works as follows in the active voice, with the subjunctive mood of the verb *to be*: 'If he were to come, I should go', or 'if she were to get the job they would be far better off'. The mood may correctly also follow *whether* – 'the bus is leaving at ten o'clock, whether they be there or not', or 'whether she be awake or asleep, we are watching television'. In sentences with *if*, ultra-purists would simply use the subjunctive of each verb without a subjunctive auxiliary – 'if he come' or 'if she get', but these are now archaic. The mood may also occur in sentences without the conditional auxiliaries that contain nouns of desire, will or suggestion, as in 'he gave an order that the man go to prison', or 'she expressed a desire that he be free to do as he wish', or 'my decision is that she take the jewellery and leave', or 'they were adamant that no one know of their intentions'.

In the passive in all persons the auxiliary becomes *be* instead of *is* or *are*, and this is a form in which the subjunctive in British English still turns up without appearing too consciously pedantic: 'I order that you be taken to prison', for example, or 'I suggest they be put on leave until business picks up', or 'I ask that he be allowed to stay a little longer'. It persists in certain idioms, notably after the word *lest*, meaning 'in case', in phrases such as 'lest it be forgotten, Mary won a medal in that race' and 'lest they be careless, they need to be reminded that the vase is worth £10,000'. And there are other idiomatic survivals in phrases such as 'let them be', 'so be it' and 'God save the King!' Other than in such usages the subjunctive in spoken English appears to have gone. There is nothing wrong in using it in written English, but if you do and it has the ring of archaism about it then it probably is archaic, and thus an impediment to effective communication.

For the avoidance of doubt, it may be used in reported speech – 'he suggested the door be left open' – and in the past tense – 'Mary recommended that John see the Eiffel Tower when he went to Paris'. And in some subjunctive clauses greater economy of expression may be achieved by inverting the word order of the verb *to be*, thus eliminating *if* – as in 'were he to do that I should be extremely cross' instead of 'if he were to do that I should be extremely cross'. This is one of the other survivals of the subjunctive in contemporary usages. Another is in the stock phrase 'if I were you': despite years of trying, I have never yet heard 'if I was you'. One also hears it in subordinate clauses introduced by *though*, as in 'she is a good pianist, though were she to play in public it would be a disaster'. The subjunctive is out of favour with progressives because of the alleged implication that one has to have had an elite education in order to understand it. This is not so: it simply requires intellectual curiosity and the ability to read a book or use an internet search engine.

Verbs Verbs are what primary school teachers – in the era when it was still not considered elitist, exclusive or divisive to educate children and young people about points of grammar and parts of speech – called 'doing' words. *To read, to write, to buy, to sell, to say* and *to think* are just a few of thousands of examples. Verbs can be transitive, intransitive or both. The first category includes verbs that describe something happening to something else, that something else being the object. Examples of this are in sentences such as 'John carried the box', 'Mary dug the hole' or 'they flagged down the bus'. None of those statements would make much sense without the objects. An intransitive verb is one that requires no object, as in 'John slept for hours', 'Mary coughed' and 'the ship sank'. Verbs that can be both transitive and intransitive – they can function with or without an object – include those such as *sing* and *understand*: 'she sang beautifully' or 'she sang a song beautifully', and 'he understood well' or 'he understood Greek well'.

Verbs also have voices, the active and the passive. The *active* is the voice in which something or someone performs an act towards something or someone else, the *passive* describes how that act is performed by someone or something. In its simplest form the active is, for example, 'John called Mary', and the passive is 'Mary was called by John'. Stylists prefer the active because it is more direct. If the passive could be avoided without contorting the prose or altering the sense – and usually it can – then it would be better to do so. Several writers about the English language – Orwell was among them – have noted a political aspect to the use of the passive, as it can disguise responsibility and accountability. On a basic level, consider the difference between 'I have decided to stop your allowance' and 'it has been decided that your allowance will be stopped'. Such avoidance of responsibility goes all the way up to the dictatorship's 'it has been decided that you will be executed'. Most statements in the passive voice are far less grave in their meaning, but the principle is the same. Passive constructions are also verbose.

Verbs have moods: in English they are the *subjunctive* and *indicative* (classical Greek also had something called the *optative*, which did not make the journey into English). The indicative is all that touches the consciousness of most speakers of British English today, though as I point out in my separate entry on the **subjunctive**, the Americans are very good at the other mood, and full praise to them for it. It adds a degree of subtlety to the language that other tongues take for granted and pride themselves upon (especially the French) but that we seem to find dispensable. *See also* **conditionals**.

Finally, verbs have tenses. Most English speakers instinctively understand how the different tenses of a verb convey meaning about time. Thus the *present* tense describes events happening now – though there is a form of *historic present* that describes things that exist now but were created in the past, justified by the effect these works have on us now, as in 'Dickens tries to convey to us the misery of the London poor in the 1830s' or 'Constable is showing us the beauty of the rural landscape'. There is also a *continuous present* – 'he is looking for a book' – and indeed continuous versions of most tenses – 'she was cooking the dinner when he came home' or 'if you arrive at six I shall be making cocktails'. The *past or imperfect* tense is straightforward – 'I walked to work while it rained' – and the *perfect* tense is another way of describing a completed action in the past. Were one to say 'I have walked to work while it rained' it would be an observation about a particular occasion in the past when the speaker had endured such a martyrdom, with the suggestion that it might happen again in the future; the use of the past tense carries no such inference, but simply refers to a single completed action from which no other conclusion can be drawn. Consider, too, the difference between 'we were married for twenty years' (the past tense) and 'we have been married for twenty years' (the perfect tense). In the first, the speaker is either widowed or divorced; in the second, the conjugal state continues.

Shall and *will*, the auxiliary verbs of the future tense, have a distinction of meaning and therefore in how persons use them. This also has ramifications for **conditional** tenses and for variants of the perfect tense, such as the *future perfect* and the *pluperfect* – 'He had had no luck in finding his dog.' The former includes usages such as 'I shall have read that book by tomorrow' or 'you will have finished that job by Tuesday'. Both are observations: 'I will have read that book' is by contrast an expression of resolve and determination; 'you shall have finished that job' is an order, implying consequences if the job is unfinished.

Verbs, strong Put simply, these are verbs almost always of Germanic origin that form their past tenses by the alteration of a vowel rather than the addition of the suffix *-ed* or *-t*. In some cases the change is even more radical than that. Therefore we have *bought* and not 'buyed', *drove* and not 'drived', but also *gave* and not 'gived', *made* and not 'maked', *rode* and not 'rided', *sought* and not 'seeked', *strove* and not 'strived', *thought* and not 'thinked', *trod* and not 'treaded'. Past participles may sometimes give further trouble, with the imperfect *trod* becoming the perfect *trodden*, *rode* becoming *ridden*, and *strove* becoming *striven*. Sadly for those learning the language, these forms are not consistent: in America the past tense of the verb *to dive* is *dove*, but in England it is *dived*. Although *give* becomes *gave* and *given*, *live* becomes *lived* in both the imperfect and perfect tenses. Also, time has eroded some of the old usages. Although some of us were brought up to believe that the past tense of *thrive* was *throve*, and the past participle was *thriven*, the form *thrived* now occurs in numerous cases and appears to be embedding itself in British English. Something similar has happened to the verb *shrive* – meaning to present oneself to a priest to make confession – though it is hardly in everyday use in Britain, a continuing casualty of the Reformation: *shrived* is now apparently acceptable in place of *shrove* and *shriven*, though we are yet to have Shrived Tuesday imposed upon us. *Wrought* as the past tense of *to work* (as in work to make something specific happen, such as to create a piece of metalwork) survives now mainly in the term 'wrought iron', or in idiomatic phrases such as 'the animals wrought havoc when they were let loose' or 'the hurricane wrought extensive damage'.

Acknowledgements

I am grateful in the first instance to my publisher, Nigel Wilcockson, for asking me to undertake this third revenge raid (after *Strictly English* and *Simply English*), on those who assault our language, and for his typically unstinting support throughout the project. I am also grateful to Laurie Ip Fung Chun, who meticulously oversaw the production process, Mary Chamberlain, who copy-edited the book with exceptional precision, and not least to Caroline Pretty, whose proofreading was of the highest standard and who saved me from some utter horrors. Various family, friends and colleagues provided ideas and suggestions about what to include, notably my wife, Diana, who from her copious reading brought a number of excrescences to my attention, and provided the constant support without which this, and indeed all of my other books, would never have been created. Shannon Mullen, as a fluent American speaker, provided me with regular advice on how English on the other side of the Atlantic differs from that in Britain. Alex and Hermione Burghart also had some crucial input, as did Emily Gray, David McDonough, John Adamson and the late Michael Tanner. I suppose above all I am grateful to the defective education system, whether state or private, of the British Isles, which despite the supposed achievement of universal literacy still routinely turns out students some of whom, through no fault of their own, have a poorer grasp of English than decently-educated people who speak it as a second or third language. But for that dismal failure, books such as this would not need to exist.